WOMEN AND FILM

Women & Literature

New Series   Volume 4

Edited by Janet Todd

Previously published as a quarterly, the new series of *Women & Literature* will appear in this format. Each volume will focus on a specific theme in literary or artistic criticism. Standing orders for the series are invited.

WOMEN AND FILM

Women & Literature
New Series   Volume 4

Edited by Janet Todd

HOLMES & MEIER
New York   London

Published in the United States of America 1988 by

Holmes & Meier Publishers, Inc.
30 Irving Place
New York, NY 10003

Copyright © 1988 by Holmes & Meier Publishers, Inc.
All rights reserved

Book design by Dale Cotton

This book has been printed on acid-free paper.

Library of Congress Cataloging-in-Publication Data

Women and film / edited by Janet Todd.
    p. cm.—(Women & literature; new ser., v. 4)
  Bibliography: p.
  Includes index.
  ISBN 0-8419-0936-9 (alk. paper)
  ISBN 0-8419-0937-7 (pbk.: alk. paper)
  1. Women in motion pictures. 2. Women in the motion picture
industry. 3. Feminism and motion pictures. I. Todd, Janet M.,
1942– . II. Series.
PN481.W65 new ser., vol. 4
[PN1995.9.W6]
809'.89287 s—dc 19
[791.43'09'09352   87-28834

Manufactured in the United States of America

Contents

PART
I

FEMINIST FILM THEORY

The Problem of
Women in Film

1

Introduction

JAMES LYNN
University of Southampton

Ideology, as Althusser has argued in his rereading of Marx, is less the palpably false representation of a manifestly true state of affairs than the true state of affairs itself. This is ideology, nor are we out of it; it belongs to the air that we breathe. From a critical and theoretical point of view, it may very well be the case that the representational systems (sociopolitical discourses, images, moral and religious beliefs, and myths) that we call ideology are but distorted or inverted accounts of the real relations in which people live. Yet these fictitious orders are the ones in terms of which people (families, groups, classes, societies, nations) both experience and understand their relationships to those real relations. Ideology, we might say, is an operative or material reality, a largely unreflected condition of being and acting in the everyday world, as opposed to being a collection of voluntarily held and consciously accessible "ideas." Individual historical subjects neither

3

choose nor inaugurate ideologies, but rather they are chosen by them. We enter into and are embraced by them in the same way that we enter unconsciously and are folded into language itself. Long before we become self-conscious critics of—or willing colluders in—ideologies, we are their oblivious practitioners and involuntary sources of production and reproduction. The feeling of mingled indignation and triumph that accompanies the recognition of ideology derives less perhaps from its explicit substance than from our sudden perception of its general shape or form: its trick of remaining invisible while, so to speak, brazenly staring us in the face. The most potent ideologies of our culture are always "already there," seemingly without origin or end, and our reflective awareness of them appears condemned to take the form of retrospection.

As an unconsciously lived relation as distinct from an object of conscious reflection, ideologies lurk on the blind side of being, their place unmarked. Ideology does not represent itself as such; it always appears as something else: invariably as a truth so fundamental and intrinsic that to question it would be to risk flying in the face of "nature," "logic," or "Reason" itself. Because of this, the critical analysis of ideology calls for the education of eye and ear in matters of "how" rather than "what," in the particular strategies and techniques of ideological self-effacement; the often extraordinarily intricate ways in which it contrives to circulate unnoticed on the everyday surface of things.

This camouflaging process is necessarily flawed and incomplete. Although ideological constructions depend for their effectiveness on their success in tricking themselves out with the appearance of naturalness and disinterestedness, they cannot actually be natural and disinterested without defeating their purpose. However obliquely, and by whatever arts of indirection, ideology is committed to a certain show of presence. The sign of this presence is less the barefaced falsehood, visible for all to see and to challenge, than a kind of tell-tale omission or discursive hiatus. As that which can neither fully declare nor completely disavow itself, ideology is inscribed upon cultural representations in the appropriately subliminal form of microscopic logical rupturings, random discordances, and strategic silences. It is to be found in those aspects of images and discourses that display the lowest degree of intentionality or rational deliberation; those that are therefore offered as the most self-evident and uncontentious.

The critique of ideology is thus a painstaking "brushing against the grain," a conscious reconstruction of its hypnotic "truth effects," rather than any attempt to restore a defaced higher "Truth." There is no inviolate realm of absolute certainty waiting to be rediscovered above or behind ideology, for ideology is not so much the malign adversary of eternal truth as the historical-material practice by which ideas such as truth's eternity are first produced and distributed.

Of all the ideologies to which the flesh of humankind is heir, the manifold discourses, practices, and representations that feminism has grouped together under the name of "patriarchy" possess a degree of pervasiveness, implicitness, and historical-cultural resilience that situates them in a class apart from all others. Indeed, it is arguably misleading even to envisage such representations as particularized ideological forms, because patriarchy appears to be not so much one type of ideology among others, however privileged or special, but the "ideology" of ideology itself: a repression that precisely cuts across and precedes all the others, a silencing and exclusion by gender that is always already in force before other ideologies have begun their work. For women, as they probe their own past along a steadily increasing number of disciplinary fronts, patriarchy has come to look less and less like a circumscribable variable of Western history, or, for that matter, of any other history, and more and more like its enduring foundation. Much, if not the bulk, of modern feminist theory, in particular the work of the last decade, has been concerned with the consequences and implications of this archaeological recognition for contemporary feminist practice.

The feminist perception of patriarchy has found powerful, if ambiguous, theoretical support in the psychoanalytic writings of Jacques Lacan, whose omnipresence in the current debate is one of its most striking features. In Lacan's work, patriarchy is divested of all contingency and becomes coextensive with human culture. Arbitrary though it may be in point of origin, the psychic edict that prescribes the status of woman as the inferior other is, in effect, nonreversible. What psychoanalysis provides, according to Lacan, is not an absolute or metaphysical definition of the "feminine," but a description of how such definitions are enacted within the symbolic order. Indeed, by taking the phallic order at its literal word, psychoanalysis exposes the fraudulence at the heart of its economy. Its "feminine" is a phantom: nothing more than the requisite, and nothing less than the symptom, of its own equally prescribed delusion of self-sufficiency. This, however, is how things are, and the way they are likely to remain. For the symbolic order inaugurated by the Oedipal drama is not comparable to a contract on which the individual subject, whether male or female, retains an option. The unconscious, in Lacan's famous words, "is structured like a language," and the individual can neither personally endorse nor voluntarily terminate that which, for better or worse, is the precondition of her dissenting speech and the ground of her refractory self-definitions. Woman has no history outside of the infinitely repeated narrative of her absence from history, no language other than her silence, no being or essence other than as "she who takes on nothing whatsoever of her fate" (Lacan).

Feminists who have embraced Lacan's critique of patriarchy have thereby committed themselves to a fundamentally tragic account of sexual difference that often seems to go well beyond anything required by the second wave of feminism as a caveat to the optimism and sexual-political voluntarism of the first. According to Lacan, woman's exclusion is not just a historical cultural practice but a transhistorical inscription analogous to Christianity's original sin. Redemption is possible, though barely imaginable, for Lacan's representation of the feminine through the dissolution of the very category of the feminine leaves woman knowing herself only as an absolute lack. Taking the phallic organization of sexuality to heart implies, for Lacanian feminists, a recognition of the necessarily self-defeating character of oppositional practices based upon definitions of "true" or essential femininity. The essence of woman is a question mark; the "feminine" a name for that which never was and is not yet, a concept without legitimation in the symbolic order within which it is nonetheless compelled to articulate itself.

"Man created woman—but out of what? Out of a rib of his God, of his 'ideal.' . . ." Regardless of its often very helpful frankness, there is always, of necessity, a deeper layer of unsurrendered narcissism in the phallic self-critique. Nietzsche's aphorism, which can hardly be said to exhaust his discourse on the feminine, is a relatively elementary case in point. It really goes without question for Nietzsche that woman is created in the image of man. His real concern, as the self-appointed gravedigger of nineteenth-century liberal humanism, is with the shoddy character of the materials used, with man's failure, in other words, to write meatier and more adventurous parts for women in a culture prophetically construed as lying under the threat of death by boredom. In the altogether more self-conscious case of Lacan, on the other hand, the moment of unrelinquished phallocentrism is to be found in the superb generosity with which the arbitrariness of the relation he describes is conceded, in a clever fudging of the answer to the question of the ground or necessity of the supposedly necessary interdependence of symbolization and the privileging of the phallus in the structuring of the subject. Or, to put it another way: in a world that is split along the lines he describes, Lacan's own gender identity compels him to mystify the origin of patriarchal domination. Regardless of the degree of scrupulousness he has brought to bear, sexual difference can only be defined coercively where the defining party is already one of the terms of the difference to be described.

"Tragic" feminism has acknowledged Lacan's implication in the phallocentrism he describes, yet it emphatically opposes the attempts of his renegade pupils and associates to fashion "feminine" discourses, uncontaminated by patriarchal assumptions. However manifestly phallocentric, the Lacanian scenario is nevertheless the stuff of history. Woman's resistance to the symbolic order can only be organized upon the clearest possible understanding of herself as its principal "effect." Modern French feminism, on the other hand, is articulated upon a refusal of the tragic vision. Its method is philosophical, its target the binary mode of thought that it identifies as the enabling act of patriarchal domination from Plato to Freud, and its project the siting of the feminine within a discursive practice that is jubilantly beyond, or sublimely indifferent to, the *differences* necessitated by male instrumental thinking. The post-Lacanian feminist secession is a paradoxical combination of breathtaking critical subtlety and prefeminist naiveté. Its programmatic refusal to "name" the feminine has been repeatedly undercut by essentialist definitions that fully accord with many of the creakiest and most down-at-heel male romantic preconceptions. Confronted with its own deconstruction of history as the eternal recurrence of the same patriarchal logic, this feminism that isn't one has attempted to locate the feminine, of which it is nonetheless compelled to speak, in a place beyond the symbolic order and its tyranny of differences, and in so doing has inadvertently underwritten precisely that order. Patriarchy has always been more than happy to accommodate the feminine within the mute "outside" of nature, the nonrational, mysticism, and infinity, to name but a few of the places where the constraint of distinction is deemed to have been positively transcended.

Although the projection of patriarchy as the ideology of ideologies certainly implies that crucially important aspects of women's oppression have remained more or less unchanged since the dawn of the ages, it seems both mistaken and—more significantly perhaps for a movement that is nothing if not political—tactically immobilizing to overlook the historically changing character of the patriarchal meditation on the feminine. French feminism's repeated recurrence to exactly the kind of metaphysical definitions of woman it was most concerned to avoid, its replaying of many of patriarchy's most resourceful variations on the theme of "das ewig Weibliche" (the eternal feminine), is directly related to its confrontation of difference at the level of language and logic rather than history. In the same way the *aporias* of what I have called the tragic vision can be traced to a reading of psychoanalysis that is culturally and politically a good deal more disabling than its proponents are prepared to allow. Neither "tragic" feminism nor French utopian feminism can simply be disregarded. In problematizing the question of feminine subjectivity, each has drawn attention to the fatal moment of gender-purblindness in the egalitarian rhetoric of the past and to the self-deluding aspect of modern feminist assimilationism. Yet both utopian feminism and its adversary collapse history into patriarchy, and hence both are unable to deal with the question of historical determinacy. If patriarchy's interpellation of women hasn't changed since Homer, how did they ever come to get the vote? What exactly is it that distinguishes the lives of women today from the lives of women before the Ark? Maybe it would be difficult to prove that women's achievement of formal democratic rights convulsed the Oedipal triangle, but is it really any easier to prove that it didn't? And doesn't the existence of a theoretical practice called feminism at least go some of the way toward answering the second question? Radical feminism's essentialist lapses seem ultimately to be bound up with its failure to reflect the historicity of the feminist intervention itself.

If the concept of the feminine resists definition, this is because the "feminine" is neither a total lack nor a mystical plenitude, but a historically changing constellation of moments. In the particular discursive practices within which it is mediated, patriarchy is likewise not a kind of metaphysical content that remains forever untouched by its many particular forms, for these forms are always at the same time the vehicles of specific historical meanings. To ignore this is to surrender to the ideology of ideology, to ratify the unitary appearance or convergent effect of discourses that are not only autonomous of one another but also historically mutable: open upon the future, that is to say, and thus never at any point closed or finished. It is precisely because it tends to address itself to historically specific configurations of patriarchal supremacy that what might broadly be termed historical feminism has also, inevitably, revealed—in studies of law, education, culture, custom, fashion and, above all perhaps, aesthetic representation—patriarchy's incurable contingency: its history as a chronic dependence upon particular instrumentalities.

Historical feminism recognizes the abiding aspect of patriarchy, but what it also perceives is that its work is never done. What is the testimony of the documents, legalities, and representations of the past if not the story of strategic and logistical efforts required to shore up the future against the real or imagined threat of the present? Where essentialism discovers (or better rediscovers) woman as eternally the same, historical feminism is the narrative of feminist and proto-feminist activities, aspirations, and desires, of overt and concealed rebellions, of undercurrents and eruptions, progress and regression: a shifting history of female subjectivity under patriarchy that has inscribed and continues to inscribe itself upon the forms of the social-psychological rhetoric deployed to contain, mollify, and silence it.

Finally, and perhaps most importantly, historical feminism draws attention to the origin not so very long ago of modern feminism in the explicit politicization of patriarchal domination, as well as to the coincidence of that confrontation with a so-called "crisis of masculinity." It coincides with Western patriarchy's own troubled awakening, in the second part of the twentieth century, to the insolvency of its traditional ideologies. Historical feminism surveys the aetiology of that bankruptcy from the vantage point of the present, throwing into stark relief the historical instability of patriarchy at all the levels of its institutionalization. If there is a lesson to be learned from feminism's collective and nowadays also international project, it is perhaps that patriarchy and its ideologies are in the first and last instances operative. That is to say that within the inherited circumstances of this particular moment, these institutions and ideologies of patriarchy represent what it takes to make women continue to feel, to internalize, and to enact the idea of their difference from and inferiority to men. These operations require constant revision and retuning. For a whole host of reasons, not the least of which is the formation of a specifically feminine self-awareness, patriarchy's "idea" has become more and more difficult to enforce. This is not to say that it is likely to give up trying to do so. Male culture may have lost its older, quasi-religious faith in its prerogatives, but it is still prepared to defend them, and, as even the most casual glance at the history of the twentieth-century press and media will show, it is rarely stuck for new constructions. It is not its devotion to the demystification of these constructions that constitutes the political importance of historicism within the women's movement as a whole; it is rather its preservation of futurity, its untragic, nonhypostatic perception of patriarchy as a name for what men have been allowed to get away with by women that is important.

Within aesthetic culture, whose history over the past two hundred years furnishes so many instances of the mutability of the apparently same, it would be difficult to overestimate the importance of cinema in the twentieth century as an agent of symbolic patriarchal reinforcement. As the contributions to the present volume show, women have from its beginnings acted, written, and in rare instances directed for the cinema. Yet the unmanipulated body, the unventriloquized voice, and the resonance of the un-self-censored text remain marginal phenomena of film history. They are only sporadic defiances of the odds far greater than those facing woman writers or painters. It is perhaps no accident that much of the most provocative and original feminist political and theoretical analysis of the last decade has been produced by women working in the relatively new disciplines of film and media studies. As the most socially mass-oriented, dynamic, and technically inventive producer of patriarchal scenarios of femininity in the first half of the twentieth century, cinema, and preeminently Hollywood cinema, confronted the new feminism of the sixties and seventies with an established repertoire of images, stereotypes, and myths. The meanings of these images were more often than not scandalous, but their hallucinative efficacy could hardly be disputed. As long as there existed no exploration of the precise techniques and rules by which such meanings were produced and received, feminist resistance remained in danger of getting stuck in mere critical gesticulations.

The average cinematic construction of the feminine is an effect of male-orchestrated signs, codes, and conventions that have established themselves in the perception of both male and female audiences as normal. That is to say, they neither draw nor are seen to draw attention to themselves as particular constructions, but on the contrary they are silently accepted as more or less inseparable from the idea of cinematic representation as such. The task of these constructions is then in turn construed as the authentic reproduction of the real world. Such has been the naturalizing force of "classic" cinematic realism's subliminal text on femininity that the rare film that breaks the rules and actually takes the cinematic construction of woman as its theme or content runs the risk of appearing totally inscrutable. The ideological supremacy of the realistic convention rests in its power to control the reception and consumption of works that run counter to its aesthetic. The fate of *Pandora's Box* (1928–29), G. W. Pabst's silent screen adaptation of Frank Wedekind's Lulu plays, is a particularly striking case in point. Only now, in fact, some fifty years after it was made is Pabst's remarkable film beginning to be viewed as the finely calculated defamiliarization or estrangement of the devices of American cinematic realism that it is. It shows up the fetishistic imaging of the feminine that cinema was in the process of normalizing through the institution of the star. Far from being seen and understood as the figure of a filmic thesis on the cinematic representation of woman, Louise Brooks's rendering of Lulu was everywhere dismissed by the critics as mere technical incompetence. Pabst's profoundly dialectical critique of a visual code that under the hegemony of Hollywood was to remain virtually uncontested for the next three decades was swiftly made to illustrate the supreme folly of trying to translate an emphatically verbal dramatic text into a sequence of wordless images.

Obviously we must take account of the historical psychosocial determinants behind misrecognitions of this kind. Like Wedekind's plays at the turn of the century, Pabst's celluloid contemporization of the Lulu material no doubt triggered the very unconscious mechanisms of repression and paranoia whose structures it was rendering intelligible. Yet in its quality of exception to the rule, the example of *Pandora's Box* seems almost pedantically to elucidate the primacy of form in the generation and consolidation of ideological meanings in the cinema. Its subject is less the image than the image-making process, the "reality" of woman as a mechanical construction. In the film for the (male) audience, Lulu is no more than the embodiment of dreams and desires, for whose confusions, contradictions, and impossibilities she, whoever "she" really is, must nonetheless bear all the blame. Psychologically complex, nuanced, and unsparing though it may be, however, it is not so much Pabst's representation of woman as the victim of male desires, anxieties, and sexual doublethink that has conserved *Pandora's Box* for the present. It is instead his cool visual identification of the male psyche with the cinematic image itself that speaks to us. It is for this reason that Louise Brooks's Lulu is so undeniably "false" in terms of the codes of cinematic realism that had reached their maturity by the end of the twenties. *Pandora's Box* exposes the patriarchal character of those codes by turning them into content, just as Frank Wedekind had earlier thematized the *dramatic* construction of femininity by sabotaging the decorum of naturalistic illusionism. Unspoken though it may be, Pabst's fidelity to Wedekind is intense and acute. Considered in relation to Wedekind's plays, his own art is the embodied recognition of how Wedekind could only problematize the representation of woman by simultaneously problematizing representation itself. Pabst's interests as filmmaker coincided exactly with Wedekind's as dramatist.

Pandora's Box remains something of a unique, one-off cinematic achievement, just as Wedekind's plays were never to be emulated either in German or world theater. Although the switch to sound immediately after its release doubtless had a hand in the international box office failure of Pabst's film and in its virtual disappearance for

over thirty years, the enormous success barely one year later of Von
Sternberg's altogether more compromising woman study, *The Blue
Angel* (1930), and its long reign as the all-time classic of its period and
genre looks nowadays like a statement of the precise degree of devia-
tion from the norms of screen femininity that audiences and producers
of the period were prepared to countenance. If Lola-Lola/Dietrich was
to prove eminently translatable from Berlin to Hollywood, there could
be no question of Louise Brooks returning to America as Lulu. For
where Lola-Lola was no more than a certain narrative "type," Lulu was
the embodied unreality of woman in the cinema, a threat to the entire
edifice of its sexual economy. The auratic or star image of femininity
jointly deconstructed by Pabst and Brooks in Germany as early as 1928
went on to serve Hollywood and its client industries (press, publicity,
fashion) faithfully until the demise of the dream factory at the end of
the fifties. It is therefore scarcely surprising that the discovery of
Pandora's Box had to wait for the passing of the era whose beginnings
it had anticipated. Given the unchallenged hegemony of Hollywood
and the underdeveloped condition of film theory in general and of
feminist film theory in particular throughout the "golden" years, it was
a work that necessarily remained invisible until the trance was lifted.

But what of the trance itself . . . ? Three articles of this book deal
with aspects of Hollywood female stardom. Their common theme,
within a wide divergence of methods and approaches, is the star image
as a discourse on femininity in the epiphanic mode. Together they
trace the evolution of that discourse and its vocabulary from the
thirties to the present.

In "Dietrich, Empress of Signs," Michael Wood beholds in his subject nothing less than "a figure for the destiny of woman." This sounds
epiphanic enough perhaps, but it refers to something other than what
Von Sternberg may be assumed to have had in mind when he created
Marlene Dietrich. For as Wood sees it, Dietrich's exemplariness was
truly heroic. She is the supreme ironist. Deep in the dark age of
feminism, she was an actress who persistently contrived to image a
certain mocking private immunity to the particular myth of femininity
that became her specialization. Wood's reading is intricate and his
quest difficult, for he refuses any explanation of the Dietrich effect
based on the notion of extradiegetic interference: both the embodiment of the myth and the suggestion of distance from it are aspects of
the same performance, equally essential ingredients of Dietrich's dis-
quieting screen persona. The Dietrich character is always in the world,
but never entirely of it. There is, for Wood, "always a gap in a Dietrich
scenario: the space between the often maudlin plot and the privacy of

the untroubled face." In the now lost epoch of the cinema when the face in close-up (Gish's, Garbo's, Dietrich's) was the "privileged field of meaning and beauty," Dietrich's look eluded the categories within which Von Sternberg tried to confine it. The detached sadism, the mocking insolence of the flawlessly arched brows are less the prescribed features of the thinking man's vamp than the armory of a "survivor of men's attentions." The key film, the consummation of her project, is *The Scarlet Empress* of 1934, in which Dietrich as Catherine of Russia appears, in the famous bell-ringing sequence, for once to soar entirely free from Von Sternberg's contaminating obsessions and exultantly to proclaim this face's sovereign independence of the known constructions of woman and possibly its freedom from the constraints of sexual identity altogether.

Refashioned by Wood, Dietrich's screen image becomes the sign of a utopian hope for women. It is a freedom resting on a kind of frame-by-frame passive resistance by Dietrich to the manner in which she knows the camera wishes her to appear. A freedom resting on this face's refusal, that is to say, to respond to the male gaze in a "civilized" way.

All stars are the celluloid incarnations of ideas and ideals of transcendent female perfection. No star could be allowed to be seen without the soft-focus halo that was both the cause and effect of her incomparability or matchlessness. Yet each star is also a particular myth, and, as Richard Dyer demonstrates in his "Monroe and Sexuality," such myths have a mortal history. Stars are important to us because they act out aspects of life that matter to us, and though we may tend to think of the things that matter to us as immutable and enduring, they are nonetheless only ever encountered in a culturally and historically specific context. The fifties hardly invented sexuality as a talking pint, but it was a period characterized by a particular, widely disseminated, and intensely popularized discourse on sexuality. Monroe's image, and Monroe herself to the extent that she identified herself with it, both expressed and were in turn overwhelmingly determined by that discourse. The components of the Monroe screen persona, which Dyer enumerates with consummate scrupulousness—innocence, sexual desirability, naturalness, dumbness, blondness, vulnerability, even the way her body was molded by the camera—are, he argues, exact visual analogues of the philosophy of desublimated sexism pioneered and promoted by *Playboy* magazine and its fellow-travelers from the early fifties onward. *Playboy's* scoop of the *Golden Dreams* nude shot as its very first centerfold effectively sealed the fate of Monroe's image. Henceforth she was to lend herself exclusively to the embodiment of emancipated maledom's uncensored dreams of easy, unthreatening, casual and, above all, guiltless heterosexual relationships. Dyer acknowledges Monroe's later attempts to speak and perform against the grain of her image, but he insists that these attempts are in substance no more than a poignant confirmation of just how overwhelmingly she was constructed in terms of sexuality: In press interviews and some of her more problematic films, such as *Bus Stop,* Monroe sometimes conveyed an awareness that she was being represented as a pure sex object, an effect which was, however, always pathetically undercut by her continuing self-objectification as the generic dumb blond playmate. Yet if feminists of the seventies and eighties have begun to reflect more sympathetically on Marilyn Monroe, it is, Dyer suggests, due less to any earlier failure to recognize her as a rebel in disguise than to their own now historical insight into the scale of the odds against her. Perhaps what made Monroe such a negative role model for female audiences of her time and provoked the scornful dismissals of her that were almost *de rigueur* during the first wave of contemporary feminism was the very social and cultural currency for women of the discourse she articulated: "She can be taken now as a talisman of what we are rejecting, of the price people had to pay for living in the regime of sexual discourse of the fifties."

Barbara Seidman's stern critique of Jane Fonda in "The Lady Doth Protest Too Much, Methinks: Jane Fonda, Feminism, and Hollywood" takes issue with one of the most recent metamorphoses of the star image. Like those of no other actress of her generation, the fortunes of Jane Fonda mirror all the complexity and contradictoriness of the feminist decades and their impact upon Hollywood. If Monroe's tragedy now seems sadly symbolic of an age of rampant male chauvinism, Jane Fonda's progressive dilution of her feminism during the eighties seems to Seidman to be provocatively thin on historical inevitability, given her very real control of her screen image. Her personal success as a feminist star and media presence does not, so far, represent any truly tangible gains for feminism as a movement. Seidman concedes that Fonda deserves the respect of American feminists for her struggle to give women fuller and fairer dramatic representations on the screen, yet she sees her increasingly offering herself for emulation as a personal entrepreneurial success at a time when feminism as a still-growing movement could truly profit from a little stimulation from within the apparatus itself. For all the enormous power she now wields—and she is arguably the first woman in Hollywood to achieve such power in this degree—Fonda has not only signally failed to set about creating a platform for women in Hollywood, but she has also repeatedly mortgaged her feminism to the commercial logic of her stardom. To the "bankable stereotypes" she has advocated as Hollywood heroines of the eighties corresponds a string of tough, resilient, and spuriously self-sufficient middle-class women, women who manage to make their way in the world without inflicting any noticeable damage on the male order surrounding them. Similarly, the activist rhetoric of the *Work-Out* books is more than somewhat offset by the accompanying photographs of a body that, even though it is well launched into its forties, still manages to pack an impressive amount of pretty conventional sex appeal.

Clearly there is much for which the lady can be called to account. . . . One wonders, however, just how much it lies in Fonda's personal power to construct herself in terms of the feminist militancy that Seidman appears to have in mind. Is her career perhaps not the clearest demonstration to date of the mutual exclusiveness of Hollywood female stardom and a truly feminist cinema? Don't the thoughts, desires, aspirations, and dreams of today's feminists always already exceed the limit of Hollywood's expressive capacity because it is a patriarchally overdetermined institution? Jane Fonda's self-rationalizations and backslidings perhaps need to be seen as structurally, as well as individually, determined. She represents the extent of what it is currently possible for a star to say without ceasing to be marketable as a star. Were she to go the way we want her to, she would no longer be recognizable as Jane Fonda. But were she to become no longer recognizable as Jane Fonda, it is difficult to see what, if any, support she could continue to give to the women's movement. The case of Fonda crystallizes something of the ambiguousness of feminism's relations to the star image *per se:* on the one hand, feminists can certainly find a use for it; on the other hand, it may just as readily end up by using them.

Melissa Sue Kort's historical survey of the still largely underestimated role of women screenwriters in the classic Hollywood period may serve to take some of the heat off its female stars. In her "Shadows of the Substance," Kort weaves an exemplary tale of female success, power, and influence in the unglamorous though highly lucrative business of writing for the voracious screens of the thirties. Gritty, hard-working, and toughly professional, many of these women became forces to be reckoned with in the studios to which they were contracted, and they were often regarded, like many other screenwriters of the pre-auteurist era, as more vital to the success of a picture than the director. The material lifestyles and fulfilled careers of these women contrasted sharply with the often degradingly stereotyped lives of the women depicted in their scripts, and it is difficult to conclude that they were not also bought with them. No pattern of identifiably feminist concern may be observed in the screenplays of these women writers. As well-rewarded experts on the woman's picture or the "female angle," they appear to have worked just as hard as men to fashion precisely those images of women that feminist critics nowadays view with such distaste. Renegades to their sex, cynical collaborators . . . ? Kort sees such judgments as anachronistic. To make them tell, we would need to be able to inflict "fifty years' work of consciousness-raising on products originally intended to last only as long as dreams do."

The question of the nature of the historical distance between modern feminist consciousness and the consciousness of the thirties and forties is taken up in contrasting ways by Judith Mayne in "The Female Audience and the Feminist Critic" and by Debra Fried in her virtuoso close reading of Cukor's The Women. Judith Mayne's essay combines a critical introduction to modern feminist film theory with an exploration of specific ways in which it cancels more traditional interpretive models, notably the familiar "Images of Women" model with its emphasis on woman the misrepresented. Following Laura Mulvey's now-classic essay on feminist film criticism, "Visual Pleasure and the Narrative Cinema," Mayne argues that far from being misrepresented in Hollywood films, women are simply not represented there at all. What is represented in these films—as the overwhelming norm—is a male heterosexual construction of female subjectivity, with which female audiences are then invited to identify themselves. The formal procedures and visual ideology of this solicitation need to be carefully investigated and understood. If women identify themselves with the screen, they do so as alienated spectators, taking a point of view that is essentially that of man. Taking as her example the imaging of American womanhood in the feature, newsreel, and documentary films of World War II, Judith Mayne attempts to show how such self-alienating identifications are induced. With a large slice of the industrial male workforce away at war, women entered the official American economy with a vengeance during the war years, and they were encouraged by the media of the day to see themselves as integral to the national war effort. In many of the movies of the time, we see the notion of the home, woman's traditional place, being extended to include the workplace, conflating the roles of mother/wife and worker for the sake of America. Women who lived through this period recall the enthusiasm with which they greeted the massively promoted new doctrine of their indispensability in the public domain, and Mayne looks at recent documentaries in which they record their subsequent disappointment and dismay upon seeing themselves swiftly thrust back into traditional familial roles as men came flooding back into industry with the cessation of hostilities. Mayne's point is not that wartime female film audiences were particularly gullible or naive, but that because they did not at that time perceive the male viewpoint of cinema, they were also unable to register the similarities between the new images and the old. What strikes us about Rosie the Riveter and her wartime sisters today is the way they seem to image a temporary displacement: we see their visual construction as women whose "real" place continues to be the home in the narrower, prewar sense. Modern feminist film criticism changes our way of looking at films by showing us precisely why we can do nothing to change the way they were seen in the past.

In typical Hollywood screen narratives, the bearer of the male look is usually a male character in the film. We tend to see the latter as standing in for or representing the look of the male spectator. The constant presence on the screen of men looking at women, or of men being looked at by women who are being looked at by them, the whole complex dialectic of spectatorship, tends on the other hand to obscure the origin of everyone's looks and of looking itself in the eye of the camera. The inclusion of the male look in the frame may be normal in film narrative, but it is not indispensable. As Debra Fried shows in "The Men in *The Women*" the camera can if need be actually make a point of drawing all the functions of the male gaze into itself.

Cukor's *The Women* (1939) proclaims itself as a film in which no men appear. As Fried sees it, however, this apparent absence is actually a kind of omnipresence. Precisely by clearing the set of men, *The Women* becomes a representation of the unseen: the film is, so to speak, saturated with the absence of men behind the camera. Read against the grain of its many visual gimmicks, *The Women* betrays itself as a full dress rehearsal of Hollywood's traditional discourse on women. The would-be exception simply proves the rule. So comprehensively do the women represented in *The Women* offer themselves as creatures incapable of life outside the male look that the real existence of an offscreen world of men can hardly be disputed. *The Women*, according to Fried, measures the extent and formal ramifications of male control over the representation of women in classical Hollywood cinema. With the fiction of the absent male, Hollywood flashily demonstrates just how nonchalantly it could afford to turn the demystification of its own practices into a sensational visual pleasure, confident that the real trick would remain invisible on the screen.

The male-centered look is an always-unseen or implicit dimension of the screen image that we are still in the process of exploring. Lucy Fischer and Anca Vlasopolos take the discussion a stage further in their studies of two somewhat neglected genres, the actress movie and the woman's picture.

Films about movie actresses are, according to Lucy Fischer, always in some sense meditations by Hollywood on itself as an institution. Because stars tend to be viewed by men as metaphors for women, the star in such films is always both the particular woman whose story is being narrated and the archetype or quintessence of her gender. In "*Sunset Boulevard*: Fading Stars" Fischer looks at perhaps the most famous, and possibly also most tasteless, example of the genre. Drawing upon Simone de Beauvoir's *The Second Sex* and *The Coming of Age*, she shows how in *Sunset Boulevard* director Billy Wilder's obsessive presentation of Norma Desmond as a blasphemy of womanhood activates a set of images—*femme fatale*, lascivious crone, vampire—that point to a male cultural dread of the "otherness" of woman, and particularly the otherness of the older woman. Read against the grain of the plainly sadistic manner in which she is figured, Norma Desmond (played by the "faded" Gloria Swanson) serves as a reminder that not the least of patriarchy's privileges is its control of discourses of ageing. Men are allowed to grow older more slowly than women. The diva of *Sunset Boulevard* is pathetically suspended in time by her internalization of a discourse that forbids maturation on pain of un-death. Through Fischer we see her as the abandoned bride of a Dracula whose home is Hollywood itself.

Anca Vlasopolos's analysis of *Kramer vs. Kramer* (1979) in "The 'Woman's Film' Genre and One Modern Transmutation" offers further evidence that it is more often than not the unorthodox or aberrant variants of a particular genre that most clearly demonstrate its conventional parameters. According to Vlasopolos, *Kramer vs. Kramer* does not so much supersede the woman's film genre as simply reverse its customary terms. Its problematization of masculinity is merely apparent, a superficial effect of the inversion device. In *Kramer vs. Kramer*, Dustin Hoffman is already in training for the explicit sex role reversal of *Tootsie* (1982). Imagine him as a woman, and you have a story that follows the classic formula of the thirties and forties: If she has been spared punishment by death and wasting disease for her transgressions, the rehabilitation of the woman at the end of the woman's picture is always conditional upon her willingness to re-feminize, to concede the emptiness and futility of her worldly longing for personal autonomy, financial independence, professional fulfillment and the like by resuming her place within the organic order of marriage, home, and the family. In *Kramer vs. Kramer,* we see Ted (Dustin Hoffman) progressively abandoning his male identity in order to become a "good mother" to his small son. There is in *Kramer vs. Kramer* no implied revision of traditional ideas of masculinity in the light of the modern feminist critique, nor any significant attempt to define a new role for an old genre. As Vlasopolos sees it, Robert Benton's movie amounts to no more than a statement of what women cannot afford to be without forfeiting their ability to bring up and care for children . . . namely men.

In "Woman as Genre," the last of the Hollywood-oriented contributions presented here, Robert Phillip Kolker argues that the representation of women in American cinema is so totally conventionalized and stereotyped as to constitute what he terms a "transgeneric" genre. The mode in which woman is narratively figured is as predictable in form and content as such "official" genres as the western or the horror movie, and this mode remains constant both across genre boundaries and within the individual genre. Looking back on the last fifteen years or so of Hollywood film production, Kolker sees little positive disruption of codes that are as old as cinema itself. Certainly the early seventies saw the emergence of able female filmmakers prepared to question them and the oppression they inscribed, yet, once in Hollywood, they seem to have been unable to sustain their initial radical momentum, as the example of Claudia Weill clearly shows.

There are, however, one or two ambiguous crumbs of comfort in Kolker's presentation. A certain revisionism is discernible in the work of some of the leading male directors of the last decade. However weakly—often enough as the random deposit of crises of masculinity or of a more generalized misanthropy—the films of directors such as Altman, Scorsese, and Kubrick have begun to reveal some of the stresses in the dominant ideology. In disparate thematic contexts and at different levels of awareness, their recent work acknowledges something of the historic complicity of their medium in the symbolic annihilation of woman.

The cinematic construction of the feminine is mediated by an historically resilient and effortlessly adaptable system of signs that is likely to remain operative for as long as it is necessary to describe our culture as patriarchal. The identification of the formal moment of patriarchal legerdemain in narrative cinema supports the development of new signifying practices by clarifying the inheritance with which they are attempting to break. The creation of a feminist cinema cannot simply be a matter of substituting positive or "correct" for negative or "incor-

rect" representations. Women did not invent the representational systems that they have always been obliged to use for their own self-
expression, and their relation to them is thus necessarily problematic.
If traditional narrative cinema is premised on the symbolic effacement
of female subjectivity, feminist filmmakers might appear to be con-
strained to reject it out of hand. Will not a feminist cinema that does
not incorporate a consciousness of the ideologically invested character
of its medium run the risk of reproducing the very modes of looking it
most needs to avoid?

According to Susan Léger in "Marguerite Duras's Cinematic
Spaces," the films of Duras are a kind of continuing meditation on the
question of a cinema for women. As a director, Duras sees herself as
working in the "primitive zones" of cinema. Disclaiming all knowledge
of the customary procedures of filmmaking, she sets out to rediscover
cinema for herself. Her move away from novel writing to film is
interpreted as a continuation of writing by other means, and Leger
presents an exhaustive interpretation of the cultural, filmic, and interior spaces of her film work as a whole. Duras's space is, for Leger, the
space of the present: a classically sparse statement of the cultural,
formal, and subjective positionings from which a feminist film culture
must necessarily begin. Bafflingly "other" in its austere renunciation
of all the familiar sociocultural references and cinematic languages,
Duras's cinema is the representation of the mysterious other side of the
conventional patriarchal epiphanies: a figuration of woman as she
whom the camera can neither see nor grasp; a subject whose being we
have to piece together from information the screen refuses to divulge.
"Remaining in the 'primitive zones' of a cinema whose history and
parameters are masculine, Duras has succeeded in approaching a
redefinition of this territory, moving us ever closer to a feminine
cinematic language and a truly feminist cinema."

The elimination or subversion of established cinematic strategies by
Duras and other younger directors such as Helke Sander and Ulrike
Ottinger has inevitably influenced the responses of contemporary feminist film critics to feminist filmmakers who have chosen to work
within the traditional realistic conventions. If the task of a feminist
cinema is to use the resources of cinema visually to interrogate the
very idea of the "feminine" as patriarchy has constructed it, then a
conventionally narrating director such as Margarethe von Trotta inevitably stands accused of operating in a mode in which the category
"woman" is unproblematically assumed. In "Discourses of Terrorism,
Feminism, and the Family in von Trotta's *Marianne and Juliane*," E.
Ann Kaplan takes the weight of this criticism but goes on to show in a

detailed analysis of von Trotta's most successful film to date how the director's intentions as a feminist are frequently at odds with the essentialist position imposed upon her by her commitment to conventional narrative form. Von Trotta does far more with realist strategies than any of the supposedly feminist films made in Hollywood over the past decade and a half, manifesting a clear awareness of the ways in which public, political, and sexual discourses have shaped her heroine's way of seeing. Because she is unable to express her own exploratory position within realist devices, however, *Marianne and Juliane* leaves itself open to contradictory readings as either progressive or reactionary.

2

The Female Audience
and the
Feminist Critic

JUDITH MAYNE
Ohio State University

An important component of feminist film criticism, like most film theory and criticism of the last decade, has been an examination of the classical cinema. Although a term like "the classical cinema" is by no means unproblematic, it is not too much of a generalization to assert that there exists a cinematic institution that defines the way films are produced and the way we are asked to respond to them. Central to that institution are realist narrative conventions that generally conclude at a real or an imaginary altar; and their production has been determined by and large by the American film industry.

Two methodologies have defined the feminist critique of the classical cinema, methodologies corresponding to two major stages of feminist film criticism. First, there is the analysis of "images of women," which usually points out the pernicious representations of women and their lack of correspondence to women's lives in the real world. Distorted images of women appear on screen as if to assert and maintain the role of film as a powerful means of social conditioning. Take *Mildred Pierce* (1945), for example, one of the most frequently discussed films in feminist film criticism. From the perspective of "images of women," the film is structured by the classic dichotomous representation of woman as either good or bad, virginal or vampish. If this weren't enough, the film tops off its dichotomization with a reminder to women that they belong in the home rather in the world of business. The message corresponds to that addressed to women workers after World War II. Writing of Mildred Pierce's role as a career woman and wife/mother, June Sochen notes that "Mildred Pierce had to be destroyed to eliminate any troublesome thoughts held by working mothers. Rosie the Riveter and Mildred Pierce had to go home again."[1]

A second feminist approach might be called the "reading against the grain" of the classical cinema. Here the assumption is that the classical cinema consists of images that are not so much "accurate" or "distorted" as they are components in a system. Thus notions of the film image as a kind of social imperative are, from this point of view, less important than is an understanding of the film's contradictions, of the lapses in what might appear to be a coherently structured whole. To read the classical cinema against the grain is a deconstructive enterprise. Hence, *Mildred Pierce* may well function as a slick piece of propaganda concerning postwar female experience and expectations. But even while this film appears to impose a rigid ideological framework on that experience, it can be seen to undermine the very message that it presumes to convey. For example, *Mildred Pierce* concludes with a curious image of Mildred and her first husband, reunited, walking away from the police station where the murder investigation has taken place. Order is restored; Mildred is on her way home again. But in the foreground of the image, there is a disturbance in this vision of order: two cleaning women are down on their knees, scrubbing the floor. They remind us, perhaps, that Mildred is back where she belongs, but they remind us as well that women's work is a constant, whether in the home or in the official public sphere of business.[2]

These two stages of feminist film criticism can be understood chronologically. If the early stage was concerned with the absence of real female experience from the screen, the later stage would consider how that "absence" might be better understood as repression and displacement. The difference between these two approaches is theoretical as

Mildred Pierce, Warner Brothers Inc.
Courtesy of Museum of Modern Art/Film Stills Archive

well as historical. Between the "images of women" approach and the
"reading against the grain" approach, there is an opposition that has
had reverberations throughout feminist theory and criticism. To speak
of "images of women" suggests that the male presence behind the
camera (and in the editing room, the production office, and so on)
creates the world in its own image, and the very word "male" is
presumed to denote an identity wholly of a piece with patriarchy itself.
A "reading against the grain" of the classical cinema does not assume
that patriarchy is either so monolithic or so coherent as to be able to
produce images that serve no other ends but its own. Theoretically
then, the difference between these two approaches concerns above all
different conceptions of ideology. "Images of women" suggests a relatively simple manipulative system of social control, while "reading
against the grain" suggests a system full of contradictions, gaps, and
slips of the tongue.

There are obvious parallels to be noted between feminist film criticism and feminist literary criticism. In a review of three works of feminist literary criticism, one critic notes a movement over the last decade from "naive but conciliatory assertions of loving sisterhood," to the placement of "womanhood and the patriarchal enemy in rigid opposition," to a "revision, which recognizes the age-old potency inherent in the myth of femininity and attempts to make use of the past."[3] If recent developments in both feminist literary and film criticism focus on the contradictions in patriarchy's ideals and on the process of revision, the emergence of a feminist critique of the classical cinema speaks nonetheless to a specific and somewhat peculiar set of circumstances. As feminist film critics, we do not have Jane Austens or Virginia Woolfs or George Sands to remind us of what an enormous investment women have made, historically and theoretically, in writing. This is not to subsume these women authors under the male canon, but rather to stress that the feminist film critic encounters a gap between the institution and its alternatives that is considerably wider than is the case with literature.

Certainly, there have been instances of women involved in the production of the classical cinema. But as directors (Dorothy Arzner, Ida Lupino, Claudia Weill) they are the exceptions that prove the rule; as screenwriters they have been rendered virtually invisible. And what of the female star? Some feminist critics have written off female presence onscreen as just one more instance of male fantasy. Others have resorted to the notion of a "positive role model" to define what a few actresses have accomplished (usually actresses of the 1930s and 1940s such as Katharine Hepburn, Bette Davis, Rosalind Russell, and so on). More often, however, the quest for a positive female role model suggests what Hollywood refuses to deliver. The "images of women" approach often simply reverses the images of patriarchy without considering the problematic relation of the viewer to the original image.

Bluntly put, then, the classical cinema seems to be so identified with patriarchal values at their simplest and most transparent that the implications of a feminist reading against the grain are at once more precarious and more strategically important than in many of the fields where such readings have been theorized. And so we might conclude that if patriarchy in Hollywood is full of contradictions, then patriarchal ideals rest on shaky ground indeed.

If feminist criticism seeks to demystify the classical cinema, a reading against the grain encourages us to assume that the cinema does not "reflect" as much as it signifies, and that narrative is a complex and multileveled system. Such a reading bears the clear imprint of deconstructive modes of criticism. In film studies, some of the most influential deconstructive readings have come from the French journal *Cahiers du Cinéma*. In the late 1960s and early 1970s, the editors of *Cahiers*, taking their cue from Louis Althusser, began "symptomatic readings" of the classical Hollywood cinema, the best-known of which is their analysis of John Ford's *Young Mr. Lincoln* (1939).[4] Here is how the editors describe the ambiguous status of some classical films, in which the contradictions of dominant ideology are made apparent:

> There are films which seem at first sight to belong firmly within the ideology and to be completely under its sway, but which turn out to be so only in an ambiguous manner. . . . If one reads the film obliquely, looking for symptoms; if one looks beyond its apparent formal coherence, one can see that it is riddled with cracks: it is splitting under an internal tension which is simply not there in an ideologically innocuous film. . . . This is the case in many Hollywood films for example, which while being completely integrated in the system and the ideology end up by partially dismantling the system from within.[5]

The relevance of such a model of reading to feminist criticism should be obvious enough. If an early moment of feminist film criticism demonstrates the relevance of sexual politics to the cinema, another moment goes on to demonstrate the fragile bases upon which much of that ideology has been erected. Consider the point made by Gertrud Koch, for instance, à propos of Howard Hawks's film *Rio Bravo* (1959). The character portrayed by Angie Dickinson in this film corresponds to the image of woman as nothing more than the object of spectacle, a stereotype of sexual seduction. But a more persistent and diffuse representation of the female is to be found in a character not portrayed by a woman, but by a man: this is the character portrayed by Walter Brennan, who nurtures the other men, cooks their meals, and tends to their everyday needs. He performs women's work. But in this particular example of the classical cinema, it is not possible to represent male-female relations in terms of a possible dependence of the male on female labor. And so the labor remains—like one of those persistent "cracks" of which the *Cahiers'* editors speak—while the visual representation of woman is erased.[6]

Much has been made of how, in the resolutions of classical film narrative, the male-female couple is restored so as to function simultaneously as a principle of sexual, social, and narrative coherence. I mentioned the disturbance of that order in the final image of *Mildred Pierce*. A similar disturbance takes place in Howard Hawks's *The Big Sleep* (1946). It is well known that the plot of Hawks's film is quite convoluted and confusing. If there is a single discovery in the film's complex web of blackmails and murders, it is the following: Vivian (Lauren Bacall) was determined to protect her sister Carmen. This fact is revealed to us and to Marlowe (Humphrey Bogart) at the same moment; and at the same moment as well, Vivian declares her love for Marlowe. Of the two confessions, Vivian's protection of her sister and her love for Marlowe, surely the solidification of the romance is the more important. From the vantage point of images of women in *The Big Sleep*, we have a classical hierarchy where the relationship between the two women is made secondary to the declaration of love between a woman and a man.

Yet there is a strain beneath the surface of this declaration. One wonders why the relationship between Carmen and her sister, which is of such strategic importance for solving the riddles of the film, has been so impossible to represent. Rarely are the two sisters seen in the same frame; and in one of those few instances, Carmen is, appropriately, unconscious. The inability to represent the relationship between Carmen and Vivian suggests another perspective on the formula of male-female romance as it is presented in the film. The declaration of love between Vivian and Marlowe may assume a hierarchy of relationships, but it is a hierarchy that is neither as confident nor as firmly established as it might at first appear. For Vivian's protection of her sister is literally unspeakable until Marlowe has taken his rightful place in their relationship. With few exceptions, any representation of the two women together is virtually censored. To read *The Big Sleep* in this way reveals that male-female romance is full of uncertainties. For this relationship between a man and a woman not only requires a hierarchical suppression of the relationship between the two sisters; the male-female romance is also threatened by the possible revelation of a relationship between two women; and thus it is more appropriately described as fragile than as hegemonic.[7]

A feminist reading against the grain reveals the repressed contents of classical narrative—female labor in Koch's example from *Rio Bravo*, relations between women in *The Big Sleep*. One could go on and on with examples of this sort, revealing again and again those kinds of cracks in the seams of dominant ideology. There is an undeniable if somewhat curious pleasure involved in such analysis: you can still like the classical cinema without turning it into a "bad object." But it is necessary to question the extent to which such readings as these inform the consumption of films. One of the major advantages of a reading against the grain of the classical cinema is that it allows us to analyze films from the standpoint of the viewer. Indeed, one of the major drawbacks of the "images of women" approach has been that the viewer seems to exist as nothing more than the miniature "mass public," eagerly and unthinkingly consuming the ideology that is being screened.

The fundamental question, it seems to me, is how and why women like and enjoy the very films from which—if recent analyses are correct—our absence seems to be a precondition. Now we may know that women have always gone to the movies. But if a feminist reading against the grain does not take into account the ways in which female audiences have been constructed in the course of film history, then we risk developing a kind of tunnel vision that never sees much beyond the livingrooms of contemporary feminist critics watching 1930s and 1940s movies on television.

However obvious it may be, it is worth recalling that "feminist" and "female" are not the same thing, and if feminist critics can undermine the ideology of the classical cinema, this hardly means that women viewers throughout film history have resisted the ideology of film spectacle simply by virtue of being female. In what has become by now a classic essay of feminist film theory, "Visual Pleasure and Narrative Cinema," Laura Mulvey designates the male as bearer of the look, the female as object of the look in a hierarchical system of spectacle.[8] The implications in this essay for men and women spectators are straightforward enough: if women identify with the screen, they do so as alienated viewers, adopting a point of view that is primarily that of men. I prefer Ruby Rich's designation of the female viewer as the "ultimate dialectician":

> . . . Brecht once described the exile as the ultimate dialectician in that the exile lives the tensions of two different cultures. That's precisely the sense in which the woman spectator is an equally inevitable dialectician. . . . As a woman going into the movie theater, you are faced with a context that is coded wholly for your invisibility, and yet, obviously, you are sitting there and bringing along a certain coding from life outside the theater. How does one enter into the experience of the film given that kind of structure? . . . the cinematic codes have structured our absence to such an extent that the only choice allowed to us is to identify either with Marilyn Monroe or with the man behind me hitting the back of my seat with his knees.[9]

Essential as a counterpart to reading films against the grain is a consideration of how such readings might illuminate the nature of film viewing. Read through a grid composed of notions like "woman as spectacle," or a "hierarchy of looks," which make the female viewer an alienated spectator, the notion of a "female audience" becomes every bit as mystifying and problematic as that of the "mass audience." On the one hand, it could be noted that this female viewer, so essential to marketing strategies, is a pure construct, an exhibitor's fantasy. On the other hand, this female viewer might be seen as essential only to the degree to which she reflects that hierarchical system. This brings to mind what Sylvia Bovenschen calls a "complicated process of trans-ference": "The woman could either betray her sex and identify with the masculine point of view, or, in a state of accepted passivity, she could be masochistic/narcissistic and identify with the object of the masculine representation."[10] In either case, the position assigned the woman viewer is one of absolute passivity.

Most of what we know about female audiences comes from reports of exhibitors, managers, and producers; occasionally from critics; rarely from viewers themselves. There is a certain kind of audience research, of course, that polls audiences to determine what factors influence their film selections and preferences. Analysis of the con-struction of the female film audience, however, involves a much more complex process than a survey of actual viewers to verify whether individual scenes were indeed read and interpreted in certain ways. Analysis of the film audience is hardly a simple reporting of "I like this movie because . . ."

If the analyses of *The Big Sleep* and *Mildred Pierce,* both mid-1940s films, are excellent examples of what a feminist reading against the grain of the classical cinema might demonstrate, they suggest as well how feminist film criticism might engage itself most productively with the question of female audiences. The experience of World War II gave to both women and to movies a special place in American culture. The most striking symptom of the demands of the war economy was the participation of women in the war industries. If advertising was the principal means by which images were created to sustain and con-textualize women's war work, the movies were never far behind. Both advertising and the cinema are image systems and myth-making in-stitutions, and that the two forms share important characteristics, both substantive and historical, has been argued persuasively by a number of critics.[11] This analogy between cinema and advertising is useful in a consideration of the female film audience, because the ways in which women viewers were addressed during the war years suggest devices and strategies similar to those of advertising.

June Sochen mentions Rosie the Riveter in relation to *Mildred Pierce,* and if there is any single image that sums up the relationship between women and work during World War II it is surely Rosie,

Mildred Pierce, Warner Brothers Inc.
Courtesy of Museum of Modern Art/Film Stills Archive

depicted in Norman Rockwell's famous illustration on the cover of the *Saturday Evening Post* 29 May 1943, as she takes a lunch break with lunchpail in hand and riveting gun on her lap. Her rugged physique and self-sufficient air create a portrait of an emancipated woman. Yet the wartime image of the working woman still focused by and large on her traditional place in the home. Advertising created an image of working women that suggested they had never worked outside the home before, and that in any case, they were really only working for the sake of their men. One could of course criticize these images of women as blatant distortions of the real situations of women workers. Such a critique of these images of women is certainly valid. But the image of woman created during the war years relies on a myth that is anything but simple and to which a reading against the grain has particular applicability. Historian Leila Rupp points out that Rosie the Riveter is an "exotic creature," who seems somehow out of place in the public sphere of men's work. Thus the potentially jarring quality of the image of a working woman is softened by the appeal to women's traditional roles as wives and mothers.[12]

Contained within the image of Rosie the Riveter, then, are conflicting definitions of female identity: woman as independent worker, as wife or mother. These conflicting definitions might also be described in terms of the private and the public: the realm of the home, of personal relations on the one hand; the realm of work, business, and official history on the other. Perhaps during any war, the relationship between the private and the public is bound to be problematic, particularly when idealized notions of the private sphere as an autonomous refuge suddenly must accommodate the demands of war. Specific to 1940s America in this respect is the fact that the institutions of consumerism, and of advertising in particular, were already firmly in place. Never before had there been such minute orchestrations of the possible harmonious interchanges between the two spheres—the battlefront and the homefront, the world of men and the world of women. Yet these interchanges were often more indicative of conflict than of harmony, for the home could be regarded simultaneously as a recuperative refuge and as a battlefront. Put another way, American culture was straining under the tension of different ideals of private and public existence. Emblematic of that strain was the image of the wartime woman worker. Her participation in the war industries suggested an integration of the private and the public, but she is constantly being addressed (particularly through advertising) as if she were a pure creature of domesticity.

American films of the 1940s reflect that strain between a vision of private and public life as separate and autonomous realms and a vision of an integration between the two spheres. Indeed, a prevalent characteristic of many 1940s films is a profound ambivalence toward the realms of private and public life. Many of the films popular during the war were built around war themes. More important, they were often dramas that connected the official public sphere, the war effort, with the home and the family. *Since You Went Away* (1944) immediately comes to mind. The film depicts how a family of women adjusts to the war when the husband/father leaves for service. The process traced is precisely one of socialization, of women adapting their domestic roles to the demands of war. In the famous words of producer David Selznick, *Since You Went Away* portrays an "unconquerable fortress"—the American home.

If films themselves examined possible relationships between the private and the public, the very experience of moviegoing was also a symbolic mediation of the private and the public. From the very earliest years of motion picture history, when the movie house functioned as a space where immigrant audiences not only became acculturated to the ideals of American society but also acted out their own complex relationships between work and the family, between leisure and consumerist society, moviegoing has always been a kind of symbolic mediation between the realms of private and public life.[13] The movie theater is a public space where cultural ideals are celebrated and where individuals are invited to indulge their private fantasies on screen. During World War II, this function of moviegoing was adapted specifically to the demands of war.

We know that film attendance peaked during the war. Some theater managers commented on the increasing number of unescorted females who were attending motion pictures.[14] Newsreels were shown with virtually all feature films, and a strategy first developed in Detroit to attract the attendance of women is an interesting case in point of the way women viewers were addressed and spoken to. Noting that women were less inclined than men to be interested in newsreels, exhibitors put together a one-hour program, focusing whenever possible on footage of areas where Michigan soldiers had been sent. Advertisements were put in the newspapers, offering free admission to the mothers and wives of soldiers, who were asked to send in the names of the relatives in question. The program proved to be a smashing success, leading to an extended run and similar programs in other cities. The drawing card was the possibility of identifying loved ones. On opening day, one woman recognized her son's plane in a newsreel from its number and nickname. The plane was landing in Egypt. And when she returned home that day, there was a letter from him confirming what she had just seen at the movie theater.[15] One can hardly imagine a more striking mediation of the personal and the political: newsreel journalism became a narrative of family life. And it comes perhaps as no surprise that, as *Variety* reported, "it is believed numerous identifications are erroneous and it does not detract from the mounting interest. Houses have reported that different families have asked for film snips of the same soldier, both insisting he is their son."[16]

That women tended to show less interest than men in the newsreels is one of those "facts" of film history that merits closer consideration. One wonders just how such lack of interest was noted. Perhaps women viewers tended to arrive at the movie theater after the newsreels, only in time for the feature; or perhaps these "unescorted females" chatted among themselves during the newsreels. Or women's lack of interest in the newsreels might have been assumed rather than documented. Perhaps exhibitors projected onto female spectators their own discontent with the unpopularity of newsreels. Now even though these kinds of questions cannot be answered definitively, they encourage us to speculate on the significance of this recruitment of women viewers.

Tender Comrade, R.K.O. Pictures
Courtesy of Museum of Modern Art/Film Stills Archive

The scene that took place in a Detroit movie theater—the woman's recognition of her son's plane—is worthy of many a stirring moment in the feature films that might have accompanied the newsreels. In Edward Dmytryk's *Tender Comrade* (1943), for instance, several women who work at the same war plant move into a house together while their husbands are overseas. Newspaper headlines and radio reports of the war—analogous to the newsreels in Detroit—are presented initially from the women's point of view as irritating intrusions on their relationships with their loved ones. The film traces the socialization of these women to the demands of war, and in the process they begin to respond quite differently to the news, now eager for clues as to the whereabouts of their husbands or sons. The personal motivation has not changed, but it has widened considerably in scope.

Thus it was assumed that whether onscreen or in the movie theater, women can only respond when personal relations are at stake. Such a form of address to women viewers is entirely in keeping with the way women were spoken to during the war as wives and mothers of soldiers. And at the same time, this personalization of history speaks precisely to the very nature of the filmgoing experience as a symbolic mediation of private and public existence. To speak of a female audience, then, is less suggestive of a male-centered industry colonizing women viewers than it is an assurance that the function of moving pictures remains intact. In other words, the recruitment of women viewers suggests the rule rather than the exception in relation to the classical cinema. Attracting women to the newsreels was a way of connecting newsreels more forcefully with the narratives of life, love, and war that followed them on screen.

While there are many reasons why feminists have taken a particular interest in the analysis and critique of motion pictures, the appeal of the cinema in relation to private and public life suggests a strategic point of intersection between feminist criticism and the cinema. For the relationship between the personal and the political, the home and the workplace, the private and the public, has been of central interest in feminist theory. If feminism stresses the importance of the personal, it stresses also the tenuous and often false boundaries that separate the two realms. The special attention paid to women viewers in the example of wartime film exhibition suggests some tension between the two realms. That the women viewers perceived by exhibitors needed to be recruited to the newsreels in the first place is a symptom of the precarious balance between the spheres of private and public life that characterized American culture during the war. Moviegoing may not have resolved the tensions, but it certainly offered powerful images that elicited, simultaneously, the active engagement of the audience and, if not their passivity, then at least their identification with the universe represented on film.

The visibility of women viewers during the war years is a vantage point from which to evaluate the recruitment of women viewers in the course of film history. Specifically, the example of the 1940s speaks to how feminist critics and female spectators respond to the classical cinema in our own time. It is surely no accident that most readings against the grain of classical films have been directed toward films of the 1930s and 1940s. One can argue, of course, and quite justifiably, that this was when the classical cinema was at its best, or at least at its peak. But I suspect that a certain nostalgia defines our critical choices, not just for an era so beautifully denoted on celluloid, but for a certain status of the moviegoing experience. Many Americans went to the movies in the 1940s, regularly and eagerly; and the movie theater seemed then to have a genuine social function. Contemporary statistics suggest that most Americans in our time rarely go to the movies, perhaps only two or three times per year. And if shopping mall cinemas have a social function, it is one so overdetermined by consumerism as to be dystopian. The trend, particularly with the development of television, has been toward image-consumption as an individual or a family affair. To be drawn to movies of the 1940s and to how female audiences responded to them is then a kind of wish for the moviegoing experience to be something of what it used to be.

However different the experience of moviegoing in the 1940s and today, there is at least one common denominator between these two periods of film exhibition, and that is the appeal to the female viewer. Since the mid-1970s, there has been a great deal of discussion about the new so-called "women's films," and about Hollywood's versions of female emancipation. The earlier classical cinema may have been at its peak in the 1940s, but the contemporary classical cinema shapes both our expectations of film and the critical vantage point we adopt toward films of the past. When we look at movies and audiences of earlier times, there are fascinating contradictions that emerge. We might ask if similar contradictions are to be found in contemporary films.

Yet to read films like *Julia* (1977), *The Turning Point* (1977), *Kramer vs. Kramer* (1979), and many others against the grain seems to bring the two approaches of feminist film criticism that I have described closer together. *The Turning Point* appears to depict sympathetically a female friendship but in order to do so it relies on a tiresome dichotomy between love and work; *Kramer vs. Kramer* can only portray father-son love by vilifying the mother. When we read

Hollywood films of the 1940s against the grain, there is a process of genuine discovery at work, a sense in which the apparent innocence and transparence of the film image is revealed to be something else altogether. With the contemporary cinema, however, something has changed. It seems curiously inappropriate to propose a reading of these films against the grain, since so often this conforms quite closely to the spirit in which the films have been produced, exhibited, and received. A dominant trait of the contemporary American cinema is its seemingly overt recognition of diversity. Modern films seem to promise something for everyone: *Ordinary People* can appeal to feminists for its portrayal of nonmacho men and to defenders of the family for its awesome respect for the sanctity of the parent-child relationship. Julia Lesage has written in this context of "structured ambiguity" in contemporary films: "Any of us may like a film because it has a 'good portrait' of x or y but that sympathetic element (i.e., sympathetic to us) has been structured into the film to allow for a certain amount of criticism."[17]

And so as feminist critics we are often in the position of condemning the "structured ambiguity" as a facile cover-up for patriarchal assumptions. I have no basic quarrel with the view that in *Ordinary People* (1980), for instance, the men discover emotions and feelings and conveniently get rid of the mother at the same time. (Or, as the man in the Jules Feiffer cartoon put it, the film shows us that men have a lot to learn from the women's movement. Plus, he says, we get back at those lousy broads.) Arguments and counterarguments about what is potentially progressive or reactionary about individual films can go on indefinitely. I think that feminist criticism gets much more to the heart of the matter when we deal with and embrace the ambiguity for which such differing arguments are a symptom, rather than declare films to be really progressive or reactionary, tentatively feminist or sexist to the core. Robin Wood has advanced the notion of the "incoherent text," which might be seen as an alternative to "structured ambiguity." Writing of films like *Looking for Mr. Goodbar* (1977) and *Cruising* (1980), Wood writes:

> the only way in which the incoherence of these movies (the result, every time, of a blockage of thought) could be resolved would be through the adoption of a radical attitude . . . in *Goodbar,* a commitment to feminism, in *Cruising,* to Gay Liberation . . . There is still no possibility of this within the Hollywood context: the radical alternative remains taboo. Yet the films' incoherence—the proof that the issues and conflicts they dra-

matize can no longer even *appear* to be resolvable within the system, within the dominant ideology—testifies eloquently to the logical necessity for radicalism.[18]

The testimonies to the necessity of radicalism of which Wood speaks point back to Ruby Rich's designation of the woman viewer as the "ultimate dialectician." If we are caught between Marilyn Monroe and the man sitting behind us hitting the back of our seats with his knees, that dialectic affirms the complex nature of identification and recognition in film viewing.

A feminist critique of identification and recognition stands to profit not only from an examination of moviegoing itself, but also of moviegoing as metaphor, many examples of which are to be found in contemporary novels, films, and television programs. One such example occurs in a contemporary novel, and it is indicative of what that complicated process of identification entails for feminist critics. The scene in question calls upon our experience as film viewers, and it takes us back to the same time frame as my World War II newsreel anecdote in the Detroit movie theater. This is a novel that is marked by some of the same ambiguities that we see in contemporary films, ambiguities that are perhaps all the more striking for the considerable skill with which author John Irving shapes them. I am referring to *The World According to Garp*. Feminism is associated with many things in Irving's novel, not the least of which is mutilation, from the self-mutilation of the Ellen Jamesians to Hope Standish's mutilation of her rapist. It is relatively easy to dismantle the ideology of the novel, and to dismiss its endless variations on the themes of adolescent male fantasies. But it is something else again to understand the connections between that ideology and the considerable eagerness with which I, and most readers I know, consumed the story.[19] Such an ambiguity of response is much more complicated, I think, than a simple formula like "good art, bad politics" might suggest.

The opening scene of *The World According to Garp* (1982) depicts the first of many acts of mutilation: it is Boston, 1942, and Jenny Fields slices open the arm of a soldier who had made advances to her in a movie theater.

In the movie theater she had to move three times, but each time the soldier moved closer to her until she was sitting against the musty wall, her view of the newsreel almost blocked by some silly colonnade, and she resolved she would not get up and move again. The soldier moved once more and sat beside her.[20]

As readers we are situated here like spectators at the movies, jarred by yet another spectacle in the audience. And we are situated with Jenny Fields as well, for whom the newsreel on screen and the persistent soldier next to her have become considerably more than a dialectical experience. There may be nothing particularly ambiguous about Jenny Fields turning a knife onto the man for whom a movie theater and a pass in the dark go hand in hand. But we are asked to place ourselves in what is surely an ambiguous place: a movie theater where the real spectacle occurs offscreen, a spectator's seat representing both aggression and passivity.

The ambiguity of texts like *The World According to Garp* and *Ordinary People* shapes the vantage point of contemporary critics of the classical cinema. That vantage point is shaped as well by the growth of an independent women's cinema, which since the early 1970s has challenged the classical cinema both in terms of its images of women and its audiences.[21] Connie Fields's 1981 film *Rosie the Riveter* is one of the finest examples of the new women's documentary, and it is immediately relevant to our discussion of women viewers, newsreels, and World War II America. The film shows us archival material—newsreels, advertising, women's magazines—illustrating how women were encouraged to enter the war industries when the economy demanded it and then to retreat quickly from the factories at the war's end. Alternating with these documents concerning the manipulation of women workers are interviews with a number of women, themselves former "Rosies," who describe their personal experiences during the war and after. They speak directly to the camera, and therefore, directly to the audience. The women's testimonies serve as critiques of the images of women presented in the vintage World War II archives.

The structure of *Rosie the Riveter,* the alternation between interviews and archival footage, evokes an ongoing debate in feminist filmmaking and criticism. This debate concerns the desirability of a cinema that attempts to set the record straight, to speak the truth about female experience, without critical examination of the very forms through which "truths" are spoken. The intimate and direct conversations with the camera and the audience characteristic of *Rosie the Riveter* have been a particular focus of this debate, as have the conversations in women's documentaries such as *Janie's Janie, Union Maids,* and *Growing Up Female.*

It is possible to see *Rosie the Riveter* as a critique of the "images of women" approach to criticism. The alternating structure of the film relies on an overly simple opposition between patriarchal images of women, which lie, and feminist images of women, which tell the truth.

Yet from another point of view, that of the construction of the female audience, *Rosie the Riveter* explores not so much the "truth" of women's real lived experience as the possibility of an active, critical engagement with images and texts of the past. For the women in *Rosie the Riveter* were themselves part of that female audience spoken to during World War II, and their participation in this film amounts to a revision, not just of images of women, but of the very relationship of women to those images in the first place.

In the movement from "images of women" to "reading against the grain" in feminist film criticism, the key issue that emerged is one of audience, of female spectatorship. Analysis of female spectatorship requires us to engage with both the appeal and the complicity of ambiguity in films like *Ordinary People;* to walk out of the theater with Jenny Fields and to leave *Garp* behind and stay to watch the rest of the show. Such an analysis is located in a hypothetical space between the feminist critique of women's alienation from the screen and film exhibitors' perceptions of the audience, and it entails a mapping out of the complicated intersections between critic and viewer, between feminist and female, and between resistance and investment.

Notes

1. June Sochen, *"Mildred Pierce* and Women in Film," *American Quarterly* 30, 1 (Spring 1978): 13.

2. For discussions of the conclusion of *Mildred Pierce,* see Joyce Nelson, *"Mildred Pierce* Reconsidered," *Film Reader* 2 (1977): 70; Pam Cook, "Duplicity in *Mildred Pierce,"* in *Women in Film Noir,* ed. E. Ann Kaplan (London: British Film Institute, 1978): 81; and Janet Walker, "Feminist Critical Practice: Female Discourse in *Mildred Pierce,"* *Film Reader* 5 (1982): 171.

3. Julie Stone Peters, "She's No Angel," *Village Voice Literary Supplement* 10 (September 1982): 19.

4. See "John Ford's *Young Mr. Lincoln,"* *Screen* 13, no. 3 (Autumn 1972).

5. Jean-Louis Comolli and Jean Narboni, "Cinema/Ideology/Criticism," *Screen Reader,* vol. 1 (London: British Film Institute, 1980).

6. Gertrud Koch, "Female Sensuality and its Love-Hatred of Cinema," an unpublished translation and condensation of "was ist und wozu brauchen wir eine feministische filmkritik," *Frauen und Film* 11 (1977): 7.

7. Raymond Bellour analyzes this scene in detail in "The Obvious and the Code," *Screen* 15 (1974): 7–17. For a further discussion of *The Big Sleep* in relationship to the problem of woman and spectacle in feminist film criticism, see my "The Limits of Spectacle," *Wide Angle* 6, 3 (1984): 4–15.

8. Laura Mulvey, "Visual Pleasure and Narrative Cinema," *Screen* 16 (1975): 6–18.

9. Ruby Rich, in Michelle Citron et al., "Women and Film: A Discussion of Feminist Aesthetics," *New German Critique* 13 (1978): 87.

10. Sylvia Bovenschen, "Is There a Feminine Aesthetic?" *New German Critique* 10 (1977): 127.

11. See, for example, Charles Eckert, "The Carole Lombard in Macy's Window," *Quarterly Review of Film Studies* 3 (1978): 1–22; and Stuart and Elizabeth Ewen, *Channels of Desire* (New York: McGraw-Hill, 1982).

12. Leila J. Rupp, *Mobilizing Women for War; German and American Propaganda,* 1939–1945 (Princeton: Princeton University Press, 1978), 151.

13. For further discussion of the function of moviegoing vis-à-vis early immigrant film audiences, see my "Immigrants and Spectators," *Wide Angle* 5, 2 (1982): 32–41.

14. A Pittsburgh theater manager recommended that exhibitors change movie posters, and "Make 'em more glamorous for the nowadays unescorted femmes." This item was reported in *Variety,* 11 March 1942, 1.

15. The program is described in *Variety,* 31 March 1943, 1.

16. Ibid.

17. Julia Lesage, in Michelle Citron et al., "Women and Film: A Discussion of Feminist Aesthetics," *New German Critique* 13 (1978): 94.

18. Robin Wood, "The Incoherent Text: Narrative in the 70's," *Movie* 27–28 (1980–81): 42.

19. Marilyn French discusses these issues in "The 'Garp' Phenomenon," *Ms.* September 1982, 14–16.

20. John Irving, *The World According to Garp* (New York: Pocket Books, 1976), 1.

21. See Claire Johnston, "Women's Cinema as Counter-Cinema," in *Notes on Women's Cinema* (London: British Film Institute, 1975), 24–31.

PART
II

WOMEN AS IMAGE

┌─────────────┐
│   │
│   3   │
│   │
│   │
│   │
│   │
└─────────────┘

The Men in *The Women*

DEBRA FRIED
Cornell University

A Hollywood film that assembled a large and predominantly female cast often provided an occasion for a studio to display its stable of actresses. Chatty, crowded comedies such as RKO's *Stage Door* (1937) and MGM's *The Women* (1939) were not so much star vehicles as studio vehicles. Metro-Goldwyn-Mayer itself is the draw in *The Women;* what feeds the box office is not Norma Shearer or Joan Crawford or Rosalind Russell but the sheer might of one studio to exhibit at once all this star material before its cameras. In films like these, the camera displays women as studio resources. When Ginger Rogers and Katharine Hepburn meet as sparring roommates in *Stage Door* and each is awarded a glowering and glamorous close-up, we can feel RKO counting its nickels as it offers up for our admiration the two rising talents on its lot, in roles that comment on the alleged offscreen quarrel between them. The same self-celebratory hawking of expen-

43

sive wares motivates the satirical opening titles of *The Women*. Each star is shown in a close-up, subtitled with her name and the character she plays, which dissolves to a shot of an animal indicative of her screen character (Rosalind Russell's face is succeeded by a cat, Joan Fontaine's by a lamb, and so on). This witty billing sequence tells us not only that we are in for broad caricature, but that MGM commands such a wide range of stars that it can deliver a whole menagerie of female types.

The more women such a movie can boast and the more virtuoso their ensemble playing, the more we are reminded of the patriarchal studio system that codifies the status of star actresses as prize commodities who must be seen to be sold. Where then does that place *The Women*, the most shrill and brittle of star showcases, one vicious catfight from start to finish, with barely a break for Norma Shearer's famous tears, and, most significantly, a film with an all-female cast? Compared to *The Women, Stage Door* offers a placid and flattering picture of women. The aspiring actresses work together, for all their teasing, and the fastpaced overlapping banter at the Footlights Club is harmless fun compared to the manic invective that grows increasingly venomous as *The Women* moves from beauty salon to fashion show to Reno ranch. Gregory La Cava's camera reinforces the shift in *Stage Door* from rivalry to sympathy, and the rapid cutting from one girl to the next as each gets off a wisecrack (as in the scene of Hepburn's entrance) later becomes a fluid pan from face to tearful face as the girls are moved by Hepburn's opening night performance. Director George Cukor's visual style in *The Women* is as unrelenting as the script's insults; our one respite from the backbiting is the patent studio promotion of a Technicolor fashion parade. A withering portrait of rich wives and parasitic salesgirls wrecking each other's marriages in the service of exhibiting the stars in the thrall of the MGM lion, *The Women*, as a film with no men in it, might be adduced as particularly acid proof that, in Claire Johnston's terms, on the Hollywood screen "the image of woman becomes merely the trace of the exclusion and repression of Woman," because "within a sexist ideology and a male-dominated cinema, woman is presented as what she represents for man."[1] A contemporary poster for the film pictures stars Shearer, Crawford, Russell, Paulette Goddard, and Mary Boland, and printed above them is the triple promise that these are "WOMEN . . . With One Prayer in Their Hearts . . . 'GIMME'/WOMEN . . . With One Word on Their Lips . . . 'MEOW' / WOMEN . . . With One Thought on Their Minds . . . 'MEN' ": again a preponderance of women attests to the preeminence of men.[2]

The Women, Metro-Goldwyn-Mayer Pictures
Courtesy of Museum of Modern Art/Film Stills Archive

To speak of *The Women* as a film with no men in it, then, constitutes a deception, a contradiction in terms. In so far as it is a major studio film released in 1939, there are men in it in the sense that there are men behind it and men controlling the cinematic medium and mode of production. That women both speak and write all the dialogue (Anita Loos and Jane Murfin's screenplay adapted Clare Boothe's 1936 Broadway success) only strengthens this point. The absence of men from *The Women* serves to underscore the "fetishization of women" propagated by Hollywood movies and the star system.[3] *The Women* purports to offer a privileged peek at women's exclusive clubs and their attendant rites and initiation ceremonies. To judge from this film, women's shared life without men is entirely a backstage or off-camera life, the preparatory and therefore unglamorous life of the fitting room, beauty

salon, and ladies' lounge. We see women continually getting ready to
be seen. In these places women see everything that goes into the
making of a film-perfect image, which means that they see images of
each other that are far from film-perfect. And it is just these images—
women in mudbaths, tousled after bouts of catfighting, trying on
clothes—that this film finds so photogenic. But the film's claim to
show how women behave when men are not around is belied by its
status as a Hollywood production. Yet to say only that is to do an
injustice to the particular interest of this film. It is easy enough to
claim that Hollywood films underscore the repression of women, but
The Women manages as well to suggest a model for how that repression, and its representation, works. Its all-female cast grants *The
Women* the fascination of the limiting case, a status it shares with films
like Robert Montgomery's experiment in subjective technique, *Lady
in the Lake* (1941). By confining his camera so exclusively to point-of-
view shots that his narrator-detective (Montgomery himself, both directing and starring) appeared onscreen only when he looked into a
mirror, Montgomery ended up demonstrating with unintentional and
often comic clarity how false it is that the subjective camera must
foster identification between the audience and the character whose
point of view the camera shows them. By clearing the set of men, *The
Women* can explore how the camera behaves in an all-female world
and how that behavior is shaped by an offscreen world that is not all
female (the world inhabited by the absent husbands mentioned in the
film, the wider world of the sound stage and of the movie's audience).
Like *Lady in the Lake*, *The Women* hinges on the gimmick of a critical
absence. Montgomery's film lacks the image of its star, who is also its
director, because the camera is standing in for him; *The Women*, I
wish to argue, lacks the image of men for much the same reason.

The Invisible Man

It is an instructive exercise to buy the gimmick, to allow ourselves to
forget for a moment that men are behind the camera, and to limit our
knowledge of what men are to what *The Women* shows us. Such an
exercise must also delimit our knowledge of what a film is. The
absence of men in *The Women* redefines film as a medium: within the
enclosed world of this movie, film becomes a medium that will not
record men. Conversely, men become defined as creatures who cannot
show up on film. Men seep through into the elite female world of this
film by indirection, leaving traces of their presence. Men can make
telephones ring and (we must presume) provide the unheard part of

telephone conversations; their remarks are quoted, their opinions predicted, their arrivals awaited. But they are present only in what they have left behind them: clothes, gift bottles of perfume, notes, children, lonely wives, and photographs—not ones they appear in but ones they have taken, because, like the film itself, the snapshots shown in this film refuse to record men. The world of *The Women* may be littered with clues to the presence of men, but throughout men cannot be heard and they cannot be seen. The note that the unfaithful but repentant husband writes to his wife Mary Haines (Norma Shearer) just before she leaves him pleads, "What can I say?" and within the confines of *The Women,* the answer is, precisely nothing.

Even the final fadeout over the requisite happy ending stalwartly upholds the rule of male invisibility. *The Women* is over at the moment when, for the story to be able to continue, a man would have to appear onscreen. In the final shot of the wronged wife reclaiming her husband, Norma Shearer's outstretched arms and yearning expression anticipate an embrace of what the film will not embrace, and her choice enforces the film's closure.[4] That this reunion is where the film must end is suggested not only by the conventions of Hollywood narrative but also within the film by the observation of the gossiping manicurist (Dennie Moore) that "anybody's life would be a plot if it had an exciting finish" and by the consolation offered by Mrs. Morehead (Lucille Watson) to her betrayed daughter that "it's being together at the *end* that really counts." Reconciliation with the strayed husband at the end may be what really counts for Mary Haines, but not for the movie about her, or for the camera that records it. The fadeout just before the man shows up to meet his wife's triumphant welcome seems impolitely to undercut the tearful triumph of Shearer's performance. The excitement of this finish is playfully censored. It's an odd coyness, as if the embrace of husband and wife were not a proper subject for the movies. We may be reminded of other comic endings in which the production code necessitated that the couple's reunion, however sanctified, be censored, as in the final will-they-won't-they minutes of screwball comedies (Cary Grant moves offscreen to Irene Dunne's bed as a fadeout ends *My Favorite Wife* [1940], for instance). But this film is subject to its own production code. *The Women* ends when the man earns the right to appear in the select universe the film records, but just as he is to appear, the film declares that it has nothing to say about him.

It cannot be simply that good, faithful men would make for dull dialogue among the women who discuss them (as in the bland lines given to the Joan Fontaine character), and therefore must bring an end to a film devoted to women as foulmouthed tattlers and cheats. The censorship of that final embrace deprives us of the sight of a man about whom we have heard in the preceding 134 minutes many, many words. Women in this film discuss little but men—their attention is focused occasionally on the charms but chiefly on the philanderings and follies of those creatures who, as far as the visible world of *The Women* is concerned, simply do not exist. But in a movie saying is not believing. Characters much talked of but never appearing in a movie are consigned to an existence more nebulous and doubtful than those discussed but remaining absent in a stage play. It is hard to believe that men inhabit the world of *The Women* because the men blabbed about, berated, stolen, and swapped have no stars to portray them. We can readily imagine how much more vivid our sense of the Haines marriage would be if the two-timing husband were, for instance, Fredric March, or Tyrone Power, or Robert Montgomery, to name three of Shearer's co-stars in other MGM vehicles. The identification of character with star is one of the chief features differentiating film from theater. Citing Panofsky, Stanley Cavell notes in *The World Viewed* (p. 27) that a film character must be "incarnated" in a star to be a character at all. Offstage characters in a play take on a credibility and power we do not as readily grant to offscreen characters. Even women's news of men purported to be in the next room, responses to them in telephone conversations, or approving rehearsals of their remarks ("My boyfriend says I got legs like Jeanette MacDonald's"; "Little Johnnie said the cutest thing the other day. He said da-da") cannot fully convince us that men exist, since we never see them.

But all this is nonsense, of course; men must exist. If they did not, why would these women be spending their days in Park Avenue salons, fashion showrooms, fitting rooms, or, for that matter, on a dude ranch in Reno? The film's most memorable sequences are probably those in the multidepartmental Sidney's, a beauty salon as big as a sound stage. In the opening sequence, the camera travels to show us crowds of society women subjected to every imaginable treatment, from mudpacks to manicures, hairdressing to hair removing. These women appear to spend the day preparing themselves to be seen by men (though the film opens with the joke of a matron entering the salon to get dolled up for her coddled Peke). The film's references to itself as a studio product begin to gather in this sequence: as Cavell observes, "The opening elaboration of the beauty establishment in *The Women* is an allegory of Hollywood studio film-making."[5] It is in this context that we can begin to see that if men are present, they must be outside this film in a different way from the way an offscreen character is outside a film. In the world of film, when an actress dresses for men she is also, or primarily, dressing for the camera. It is the camera's eye and requirements that judge what Norma Shearer should wear for any scene of the film, however much she may solicit her mother's advice about what gown to choose for the evening or however much her daughter may ask to help her. Never quite allowing us to forget that this film is a gathering of stars on the MGM lot, *The Women* includes men as it includes—without ever showing—the camera, the eye before which these women preen. Allowing the camera to show would of course be a flagrant violation of the canons of Hollywood continuity editing. This film plays a game whereby allowing men to show would be a comparable violation of its visual code.

If men are never in the film, it must be because they are taking the picture. Men are behind the camera in the sense that they are in control of it, and for this reason they cannot appear on film at the same time. Film refuses to record men because they are all the time choosing that it shall not record them; because they control the camera, the continuance of their absence from the picture pervasively attests to their presence as its recorders. In an early scene, Mary Haines, as yet undeceived about her fool's paradise of a marriage and packing for a trip with her husband back to their honeymoon retreat, shares with her daughter Little Mary (Virginia Weidler) some snapshots taken on her honeymoon. "Where's daddy in this one?" daughter asks. "He's taking the picture," mother explains. "Oh, I see his shadow . . . look . . . there in the snow!"[6] This little dialogue about a photograph points to the duplicity in the film that contains it. In refusing to acknowledge visually the presence of men while at the same time including men as the obsessive subject of the women's discourse and the spur to their actions, *The Women* suggests simultaneously that men are fictive, shadowy, marginal, and also that men are all-powerful, hovering, central, and never shown by the camera because they are behind the camera, absent precisely because they are so supremely present. (In this context, it is worth remembering that actress Norma Shearer's offscreen husband was until his death in 1936 the powerful MGM producer Irving Thalberg; as the film's top-billed star, Shearer's relation to the men behind the scenes is a particularly charged one.) In this film's world of women, men are as insubstantial as ghosts who cannot show up on film, and as substantial and necessary to the film as a director is. If we look closely enough at *The Women,* will we see the man's shadow?

A glimpse at another film may help to bring out that shadow. Early in *The Women* we do see what a man looks like from a sketch (an

advertisement?) of a man's head on the back of a magazine read by one
of the guests at Shearer's luncheon. Only the camera and the viewer
see it; the woman reading the magazine merely happens to hold it up
to us as she flips the pages and chats. The brief glance the camera
makes at this sketch acknowledges the presence of the overseeing
man who cannot stand before the camera, much as does Hitchcock's
celebrated cameo in *Lifeboat* (1943). Because its sole locale was a
lifeboat adrift in the sea with a diminishing cast of survivors, the
director of this film had the problem of how to make his usual cameo
appearance—the signature of his presence that declares "Directed by
Hitchcock"—without breaking the strictures of the single set. Hitchcock's solution was ingenious: as one of the shipwrecked characters
discovers an old newspaper left on the boat, the camera picks up an ad
printed in the newspaper for weight-reducing pills, featuring a sketch
of a full-bellied Hitchcock as the "before" and a slimmer Hitchcock to
illustrate the results "after." As in *The Women,* in *Lifeboat* the print
medium is used to acknowledge what the film medium otherwise
could not—to show the man in charge of the film, the one standing
behind the camera and possessing the authority to think of recording
this trace of himself in a self-contained film world that otherwise could
not represent him. According to the convention of the cameo appearance, it is the most prestigious figure or star who gets the smallest
part, who is onscreen for the smallest fraction of time, and, in these
instances, in the most mediated way (as though it were a more honor-
ific gesture for a film to record an already-recorded image of someone
than to ask him to show up in person before the camera). Hitchcock's
cameo appearance in *Lifeboat* suggests another way that the invisibility of men in *The Women* should not be taken as indication of their
powerlessness or insignificance in the world the film constructs or in
the offscreen world in which the film is produced, photographed, and
promoted. It may rather be that men are absent from this film in the
way a god is absent from ours—to encourage supplications that he may
show us his mysterious and awesome presence, by revealing from time
to time just enough of himself to chastise disbelief in his existence.

Home Movies

The otherwise-invisible man makes his cameo appearance in *The
Women*—the man's shadow can be spotted in the photograph—at
moments when the film looks at its own shadow, that is, at other
movies contained within it. My discussion will focus on two main
concerns: on scenes of women as moviemakers, with particular atten-

tion to the relations between the home movie-within-the-movie and the Technicolor fashion show, and on what such scenes suggest about the kinds of sexual control attributed to voice and appearance, or in terms of moviemaking, to soundtrack and picture. To notice the evidence left in this film of the man behind the camera is to sweeten its bitter portrayal of women by revealing that portrayal as constructed, not simply reproduced or mirrored, by the film. As photographs taken by women solely to display themselves appealingly to men, the home movies, as well as the fashion show analogous to them, declare movies as a distorting male-controlled medium, and reassure the female viewer that the distortions we perceive in the behavior of women in film attest not to the true, offscreen nature of women but to the desires of the male spectator. That reassurance is, however, qualified by the film's fictions about the desires of the female spectator.

The first time we see Norma Shearer she has just finished a race on horseback with her daughter, in which she has reined back to let the child win. To make that winning complete and real, they decide to record it on film "for Daddy," so as the daughter rides up triumphantly as though having just crossed the finish line, her mother captures it all on her handy portable movie camera. A movie character handling a movie camera is readily interpreted as in some sense a surrogate for the movie director, or at least as possessing in some form the image-making power that makes possible the film we are now seeing. But when this character is a woman taking a picture to certify an event for a man who never shows up in the film (and in this case a staged or restaged event repeated just so the camera can record it for the absent male), the identification between the onscreen filmmaker and the offscreen one becomes vexed. As Cavell points out (p. 126), whenever a camera is shown in a film "one can feel that there is always a camera left out of the picture: the one working now." The woman with the camera reminds us of the man with the camera recording this specious image of woman as image maker. And surely Daddy will know that this little home movie is a fake, a reproduction, and not a record of the event as it occurred, since how could the daughter be shown winning a race with Mommy (even a fixed race) when it must be Mommy behind the camera? Taken in the context of the beauty salon sequence that precedes it, the scene suggests that a woman uses a movie camera as she does cosmetics or nail polish or any other device to alter her image: she uses it to impress or fool a man.

That in the woman's hands the movie camera becomes a device by which she may stage her image for the unseen male viewer is made more explicit in the other home movie in *The Women*. Again a collaboration of two generations of women, this is the movie we see of Mary Haines and her mother on a vacation in Bermuda. Each has taken some shaky footage of the other and together they screen the results for the benefit of Little Mary. The home movie is disarmingly unpolished: silly clips of Shearer lounging on the beach and mugging for the camera while pretending to resent its prying, grandmother falling off a bicycle, Shearer fishing, it seems just the sort of compilation made with no other motive than the tourists' wish to authenticate their travels, to claim, simply, we were here. But this home movie is a fake. The vacation to Bermuda was taken not, as the two women halfpretend for each other's sake, to cure grandmother's throat (in this talky film a woman's most vital and vicious organ), but to give the straying husband a chance to get tired of his mistress. Like the faked horse race, the home movie is all a show, staged for Daddy, to win Daddy's love, to remind Daddy that Mommy exists and cares by showing him evidence of her absence. Whether a film taken of her when she has absented herself to Bermuda, or, in the first, briefer, instance, in a film taken by her in which her absence from the picture attests to her presence behind the camera, the movies a woman shoots have ultimately another, hidden audience and author.

A dialogue between mother and daughter after the home movie is over makes clear how much it is directed toward the absent male viewer: "Don't take the pictures out yet, mother, I'm going to run them for Daddy." "I ran them for Daddy last night." "Bet Daddy wished he was there when he saw you catch that fish!" "I bet he did!" The fish that mother catches in the vacation one-reeler is dead, as Little Mary spots immediately. Like the fishing scene, the entire home movie is a staged performance, not a series of candid shots but a baited hook to bring the man home. This points not only to its clever simulation of a real home movie, its look of amateur photography skillfully faked by the professionals who photographed and directed *The Women,* but also to the home movie's failure to catch the man it was designed to reel in. (The tired metaphor of women going fishing for men is a favorite one in the film: Olga the loose-tongued manicurist calls Crystal Allen "the girl who's hooked Mr. Haines"; commenting on Crystal's sob story, invented as she purrs over the telephone to her lover, a salesgirl cracks, "Holy mackerel, what a line!"—a lie is a fishing line by which a girl hooks her man.) Catching a dead fish seems as good an emblem as any for the Shearer character's attempts to save her marriage: the very first fish she caught after her husband taught her how on their honeymoon was stuffed and displayed, as dead as the one she pretends to catch in the Bermuda movie. That the home movie only displaces

The Women, Metro-Goldwyn-Mayer Pictures
Courtesy of Museum of Modern Art/Film Stills Archive

but does not solve the problem of how to get your man to look at you is suggested by Shearer's joke about the vacation shot that shows her weeping: "What were you crying about, mother?" "Something I love very, very much,"—the shot in the home movie opens up to reveal Shearer weeping over Bermuda onions. If this home movie is the wife's lure to reclaim her straying husband—what happened "last night," we may assume, was both a showing of the movie and an attempt at sexual reconciliation—it curiously portrays women as fakers, catching dead fish, weeping counterfeit tears, vacationing for feigned reasons. (Perhaps what made the Haineses' marriage go sour was not that the husband cheated with a shop girl but that the wife regularly communicated with him via home movies.) Like the home movies in Cukor's *Adam's Rib* (1949), these remind us of the high artifice of movie acting; stars performing in Cukor's inset home movies behave as people who are not actors do when confronted by the demands of a camera aimed at them—they become hyperconscious of their own movements as filmed and betray in everything they do in front of the camera their awareness of its intrusions. This only serves to remind us of the camera in front of which the film's actors are performing in seeming ignorance of its presence. But in this film without men, such a reminder is more duplicitous than the comparable sequence in *Adam's Rib* or in the old honeymoon pictures the estranged couple screen for themselves in *Rebecca* (1940).[7] In *The Women's* home movies, authored by women for the film's invisible husbands, we can begin to see man's shadow in the photograph, but that shadow is simultaneously revealed and concealed.

By showing us women who feel uncomfortable or start to show off playfully when a camera is aimed at them, the home movie reminds us that the women we see enacting *The Women* are themselves being filmed. They strike that curious attitude in which the camera places those subjects who are unable to conceal that they are aware of its demands. "Once I feel myself observed by the lens, everything changes," as Roland Barthes writes; "I constitute myself in the process of 'posing,' I instantaneously make another body for myself, I transform myself in advance into an image."[8] Posing for the camera is like going to a beauty salon: it demands (in Shearer's words as she enters Sidney's) "a thorough overhauling." The home movie equates its amateurish posturing with the professional acting of the studio film that contains it—it equates both as posing. It thus asks whether all female behavior is posing, and if so, for what or whom? And it thereby intimates that the women in this unflattering movie behave the way they do because, whether offscreen or behind the camera or in the movie theater, men are watching. Showing women behaving as if there is a camera around, the home movie confesses that there are men around. By acknowledging that *The Women* is a Hollywood movie, the home movie it contains frees us to recognize that in this malicious portrait of women, we have been seeing merely a male fiction of how women act when men are not looking. But at the same time, the home movie is a screen behind which men can conceal themselves. The inset film's charmingly self-conscious playing to the camera—again, a camera held by a woman but ultimately controlled by the man for whom the picture is being taken and will be projected—validates the fiction that the studio movie we are watching indeed records the way women behave when men are not looking. Such obvious camera-conscious acting makes the performing of this film's stars appear by contrast entirely natural, not acting at all. In this way the movie-within-the-movie denies its own confessions. The power of the home movie is that it prompts reflection on why women need images and how they use them, and thus it makes problematic what the opening sequence takes for granted: the female instinct for self-adornment. That such adornment is directed at men is something we hear only later; the gag about the matron doing herself over for her lap dog ("Muddy's getting all booful for her precious little girlie") hints that women invent a male audience for their painting and prinking merely to excuse their vanity, that women preen so that their mirrors, not their men, will give them a good report. The sequence of the home movie and the exchange between Shearer and her mother that follows it is central to a feminist reading of *The Women* in its address to the question of women's image-making.

The film's hectic pacing marks out this slower sequence for considered attention. The gentle teasing among grandmother, mother, and daughter is a break from the brisk insult-swapping of the broader scenes dominated by Russell and Crawford. With the movie projector silenced and the daughter coaxed off to her lessons, a hush falls on the film against which we are to measure the resonance of the dialogue that follows. The camera pulls in close as Shearer begins to dismantle the portable movie screen on which the home movie was shown. Going behind the screen while her mother stands before it and facing it, Shearer pulls down the screen from the back until she is revealed behind it, with her mother facing her from the other side of the dismantled screen. The effect is at once like the lifting of a veil and the creation of a mirror. For the moments before Shearer lifts the bottom support of the screen to fold it vertically with its stand, the two women are framed by the L of the screen, one on each side, and it is as though each were looking in a mirror and seeing the other. On one level it is not surprising that in looking in a mirror Mary Haines should see her mother, in light of the earlier scene in which her mother suggests the therapeutic trip to Bermuda and in which we learn that, like mother, like daughter, both had husbands who were unfaithful. The knowing mother extends this family likeness to all the opposite sex with the comforting counsel, "This is not a new story. It comes to most wives." Both mother and daughter have lived through the same story, the same movie plot, the one in which being together at the end is all that really counts. Even when Mary patently lies to her mother while facing her through the mirroring space unveiled by the dismantled movie screen, insisting twice that she is "divinely happy," that her troubles with her husband are over, her lie follows her mother's advice to do nothing while the wandering husband returns to the fold of his own accord. Having made a movie, using some obviously false props, about a trip taken on a false pretext, these two wronged women know something about the powers available to them through the manipulation of images, and about the limits of that power.

One of this film's fictions is that there is an intimate link between changing one's image and changing one's mate, that they are versions of each other. According to Shearer's mother when she first advises her daughter to keep still about Stephen's mistress, men's infidelity results from their incapacity to renew and reshape their own images, to change what they see in their mirror (I quote from the slightly fuller version of this speech in Clare Boothe's play):

> Time comes when every man's got to feel something new—when he's got to feel young again, just because he's growing old. Women are just the same. But when *we* get that way we change our hair dresser. Or get a new cook. Or redecorate the house from stem to stern. But a man can't do over his office, or fire his secretary. Not even change the style of his hair. And the urge usually hits him just when he's beginning to lose his hair. No, dear, a man has only one escape from his old self: to see a different self— in the mirror of some woman's eyes.[9]

Philandering is turned into a failure of representation, an inability to find other, more mediated modes of change. Men have no mirror but women's eyes, no shield of artifice between themselves and mortality. Rather than depending on men's eyes to be their mirror, women can manipulate their looks and their surroundings (rather as a set designer shapes a film's mise-en-scène) in order to refurbish their own images. In this sense it is only right that men, unable to mold new images of themselves, should be denied the image-shaping power granted to women appearing before a Hollywood camera, and so men remain invisible.

The face-to-face meeting of mother and daughter through a framed space occupied moments before by a movie screen intimates as well, however, that when women confront each other, even in an intimate and private moment when much is at stake, they are separated from each other by something that this shot tempts us to label a movie screen. Watching Shearer dismantle the screen from behind should remind us of how flat and one-dimensional the filmic image is—what is a movie, what is this movie, but flickering shadows projected on a flimsy and collapsible surface? That moment of demystification of the movies rather makes us grant anew to *The Women* as it proceeds a truth and a three-dimensionality: the magician's demonstration that he has nothing up his sleeves is designed to make us believe his tricks.

Lady in the Look

The flashiest of these tricks follows, when this intimate exchange between mother and daughter is interrupted by a message for Mary Haines to meet one of her friends at a fashion show, and we dissolve to a smart Park Avenue salon, and to Technicolor. The color footage is patently an insert, with a pace, a look, and a cinematographer different from those of the black-and-white sections. Director Cukor confesses that the sequence was included per orders from the front office: "they just wanted us to put in a fashion show."[10] Spliced in and standing out even in this episodic movie, the sequence is nevertheless of a piece with the film that contains it in the way it reveals the workings of the front office.

The Technicolor fashion show is, in effect, another movie-within-the-movie, another sequence of women watching women in such a way that the unseen male watcher is connoted. A commentator announces the fashion show with the promise that the models will parade before the prospective buyers "in a manner which will demonstrate the fashions of the day in *action*" so that "You will see yourselves as you actually go through the motions of your daily occupations, amusements and sports and you will be able to study the flow of the new line as it reacts to the flow of the body." This sounds like an early awe-struck advertisement for motion pictures, promising the screen's special thrill of seeing ourselves in motion, as if before a perfect mirror in which to judge our dress and appearance. The fashion show holds up to women a curious mirror. Like the home movies in being silent, in featuring an all-female cast and an all-female onscreen audience, and in having as its unspoken and unspeaking audience the men it appears to exclude, the fashion show is as telling a reflection on the relation between women and men as are the home movies and the studio movie that contains them.

The way the sequence is shot and edited sharpens that reflection. Both the home movies and the fashion parade represent rich women in what this film deems their daily amusements and occupations. The fashion models parade on and off, in their exaggerated Adrian clothes, through stylized sets and stylized motions of outings at the zoo, at the theater, on a picnic, at the beach, and so forth. In its flow of look-alike beauties gliding along to musical accompaniment and in its fluid shift from scene to scene through wittily masked cuts, the fashion show looks more like some of Busby Berkeley's elaborate production numbers than like anything even the swankiest fashion salon could provide (a cut to caged monkeys to begin the zoo section of the fashion parade conjures up a similar transition in the "Petting in the Park" number from *Gold Diggers of 1933*). While the fashion show eschews the trademark shots of Berkeley's spectacles—there are none of Berkeley's erotic tracking shots here, none of his extreme overhead angles—it shares one significant editing practice of the Berkeley numbers from the thirties: the onscreen audience is not reestablished by reaction shots after the production number has commenced. Once the fashion show starts, the camera tracks in so that the frame is filled with the models arranging themselves in tableaux and then moving on as a new set of models enters. Without cuts back to the faces of the women in the audience, or even shots that include a row of their heads to place them as the audience to the show, we easily lose the sense of this as a staged spectacle for onscreen female viewers. By not inserting reaction shots of Shearer and her friends as they watch and judge what they will buy, the sequence purports to place us in their seats for a while, as if we were watching from their point of view. The poster for the film encourages this reading with its excited fanfare: "BEAUTY PAGEANT DICTATES FASHIONS OF 1940! Hollywood's most glamorous lovelies in a stunning display of famous Adrian's style creations for the coming year . . . All in TECHNICOLOR!" The camera places the 1939 audience in a front-row seat at a swanky fashion salon as if they too could purchase these expensive styles. It is entirely appropriate to the promotional campaign's encouragement of the audience's social aspirations that Crawford is shown cashing in her "meal ticket" by ordering the most expensive of the Adrian gowns featured in the fashion parade.

Here the camera's absorption into the staged spectacle is the opposite of its strategic withdrawal at the beginning of the home movie sequence. There the first thing we see is a scene from the film-within-the-film of Shearer cavorting around a palm tree, shown fullscreen so that for a few moments we believe the action of the film has moved to Bermuda, until the shot tracks back to reveal that the Bermuda scene is being projected on a smaller screen within ours and is being enjoyed by three women in their own darkened living room. In contrast to this scene's clever revelation of a female onscreen audience (though we know that if the camera continued to track back it would reveal the offscreen male audience), the Berkeleyan fluidity of the fashion show insists on male spectators behind the female salon customers. Without a man in the story or onscreen to serve as "bearer of the look of the spectator," in Laura Mulvey's terms in "Visual Pleasure and Narrative Cinema," there is no means of neutralizing the tendency for "woman as spectacle" to "freeze the flow of actions in moments of erotic contemplation."[11] Called in the advertising poster a "beauty pageant," the fashion sequence conceals its staging for the male viewer by masquerading as a spectacle staged for the onscreen female viewer and her offscreen counterpart, eager to eye the fashions of 1940.

The fashion pageant disrupts or delays the narrative and slackens the pace of *The Women*. Its slender link to the movie's characters and story hardly conceals that it is primarily a showcase for MGM's trend-setting costume department, as well as for its advanced Technicolor process—and, like the film as a whole, a showcase for the female pulchritude under studio contract. While the visual shock of the Technicolor footage brings film technology to the audience's attention in a way that might seem to break the primary law requiring Hollywood editing to efface itself, the film has calculated the gains from that transgression. The shock is muted: the promotional campaign prepared the audience for the shift to color, and in its interpolation of a color sequence in a black-and-white film, *The Women* followed a convention that was in 1939 already over a decade old. While it was not a common technique (chiefly because of its expense), color footage had been inserted in other films for spectacular effects, conflagrations, climactic musical numbers, or fantasy worlds, as in probably the best-known instance, also from 1939, of a Technicolor Oz, doubly dazzling in contrast to a sepia Kansas.[12] In *The Women,* however, the color footage represents not a different sort of world from that treated in the rest of the film, but a concentrated version of the same world. Technicolor strengthens the show's forging of a link between the women in this film and those watching it. It reminds us to what degree the look of women can be dictated by the look of movies. Women's fashions during Hollywood's classic era were often shaped by the strictures of the black-and-white film. What was considered alluring adornment was in large part what was worn in movies, and what was worn in movies was what would look best when photographed in black and white; as Anne Hollander has documented: "As the sense of luxury began more and more to depend on the confections of the movie imagination, color drained out of elegance, and was replaced by the whole black-and-white spectrum. . . . These visions were built on the newly powerful sensuality of colorless texture in motion, in which American dreams were being acted out."[13] Women dressed as though they were being seen in the chastened achromatic world of black-and-white film; high fashion was what could be recognized and favored by the glossiness of black-and-white photography. As film technology advanced, so did clothing styles: the most desirable and alluring fashion is that which mimes the up-to-date fashions in film photography. *The Women*'s Technicolor fashion show displays the latest in female adornment and in film technology. (Even "Jungle Red," the film's nail polish of choice—the "newest color," as Olga touts it—sounds like a shade on the gaudily stylized Technicolor spectrum.)

The Women most debunks its fiction of showing how women look and act when men are not watching in the scene that purports exclusively to show women watching women. A movie that pretends to show how women are shows that they are as the movies have made them. Female self-display is directed to an invisible camera technologically designed to favor what movies propagate as aesthetically most pleasing. The fashion show then declares what *The Women* itself is, a pageant of movie stars, enacting daily female "occupations, amusements and sports" as fanciful as those mimed in the fashion parade: gossiping at the beauty parlor, bickering at a luncheon, snooping in a department store, bitching on a Reno divorce ranch. And of course MGM's Adrian, the creator of the costumes worn in *The Women*, has designed appropriate styles for each of these activities as well.

The fashion pageant challenges the premise that in dominant cinema we ever see how women look through female eyes, without the filter of the male lens. Such staples of continuity editing as the point-of-view shot become open to scrutiny. It is not only in the fashion sequence that the man's gaze intervenes between woman's gaze and woman as spectacle. In perhaps the film's most interesting point-of-view shots, women's sightings of other women are explicitly filtered through the eyes of an absent man. These shots open the scene in which Rosalind Russell and Phyllis Povah make an expedition to the perfume counter at Black's department store to see if they can spot Crystal Allen and give her a piece of their minds (though defending the wronged wife is clearly of less interest to them than defending their moneyed clique from the incursions of shop girls). Since they have never seen Crystal, in order to find her they must inspect every likely candidate through the eyes of a temptable man. The right girl will be the one who looks most like the kind of girl Stephen Haines would fall for. Skulking around the perfume department, the two snoops first spot a girl with her back to them who has (as the stage directions say) a "beautiful figure." Edith pipes to Sylvia, "Gorgeous torso, dear! Maybe that's little Crystal!" But when the girl turns around and shows her plain face to the two snoops (and the camera), they reject her as a candidate ("From the neck *up*, I'd say no"), rather as a man might who was checking her over for his own interests. Sylvia then spies an attractive blonde behind the counter and decides she's their girl: "How about Baby?" Sylvia gestures and in response the camera shows the blonde as Edith spots her and agrees, "Why, of course! It *couldn't be anyone else!*" When they learn her name is Pat, not Crystal, they can only wonder, "Well—I don't know why he overlooked *her!*" That puzzle is solved when, again in response to Sylvia's pointing, Edith lets out a whistle as "the camera moves quickly along the line of the girl's gaze to a close-up of Crystal" (in the screenplay's directions). A lingering close-up then displays Joan Crawford as the male spectator sees her—glittering, glamorous, a star. The most important thing about Crystal Allen, this shot intimates, is not that she is, as Sylvia and Edith see her, a golddigging tramp, but that she is Joan Crawford. To find their prey, Sylvia and Edith must put themselves in a man's place; they must turn women into spectacles the way a man would. Our first shot of Crawford, then, is from Russell and Povah's point-of-view, but they have consigned their point-of-view to the man, or temporarily borrowed it from him. This is not to say, of course, that the shot of Crawford from their point-of-view implies that they find her desirous or alluring as a man would—they make it plain that they find her a contemptible mansnatcher—but that they must mark her out as the proper object of their contempt by first seeing her as she must look in the eyes of a desiring man. We, and the camera, first look at Crawford as these two women look at her in the act of imagining the way a man would look at her.

On some level this is always the way women appear to women in dominant cinema. What is striking about this scene from *The Women* is the boldness with which it dramatizes the defeminization of the female spectator through the hegemony of the male gaze in the rhetoric of Hollywood editing, a control so pervasive that to follow the film from shot to shot, the female spectator must "identify with 'masculine' modes of address."[14] An extended analysis of *The Women* shot by shot, paying more complete attention to framing and editing than is possible here, might well reveal how consistently the onscreen dominance of women is undercut by the camera's language, or how uneasily the translation is made from the inframe woman's gaze to the offscreen male gaze. Another way to speak of the pilfering of the women's point-of-view shots is as a kind of photographic gaucherie, a cinematic slip of the tongue, a mistranslation, or an expression incomprehensible because it is unidiomatic, as if the camera were not quite speaking in its native dialect. And in some sense it is not, for the classic language of continuity editing depends on there being two (male-defined) sexes, as it depends on the man being behind the camera and at the editing bench.

The Strong, Silent Type

We have been discussing how the man's invisibility is compromised by his command of the woman's gaze through the shooting and editing of this movie and of the filmic spectacles within it. The man is inaudible as well as invisible in *The Women,* however, and we need to turn briefly to the question of what his silence says and how he may make himself heard. If everything the camera sees proves to be staged for the unseen male viewer, is the same true for what the microphone hears? Does the soundtrack from which the male voice has been banned in fact announce his prerogative over all speech? For to discuss women as primarily shapers of images seems to go against the grain of our primary experience of this film. The film's busy soundtrack insists that women do not deal in images half as vigorously or viciously as they deal in words. They visit beauty salons less to change how they look than to chat about it and each other, and the movie squeezes its share of laughs from the various beautifying tortures that prevent speech. When the blast of the hair dryers makes it impossible to be heard without screaming, the process of adornment turns women into shrill monsters; the requisite joke about the facial is here, too: scolded by the salon attendant for gossiping, Edith Potter (Phyllis Povah) retorts: "Listen, relaxing is part of my facial," and gets slapped in return with, "Then you should relax completely, Mrs. Potter, from the chin up." The beauty salon sequence upsets the balance of image and speech: if women must labor to be beautiful, they cannot talk at the same time. For woman, the soundtrack and the picture are not in synchronization. The joke about what repulsive eyesores women appear in the process of making themselves gorgeous milks the same laughs as the gag about how they pretend to be devoted friends while sniping and slandering behind each other's backs. These combine in the scene of Olga buffing Mary Haines's nails while babbling the most damaging things about the Haines marriage. Hypocrisy or infidelity becomes defined in this film as a mismatch of speech and action. Mantrap Crawford, while lying glibly on the phone to Stephen Haines, bandies words with another wisecracking salesgirl, so that the man on the other end of the line gets only half of what is going on, the soundtrack without the action that betrays the skewed relationship between Crawford's seductive lines to him and her sassy retorts to her friend.[15] As the beauty salon sequence suggested that women put on one look for women and a different look for men, Crawford's telephone act reveals that they likewise adopt one voice for women and another for men.

Again it is a useful exercise to buy the gimmick, to work out the implications of this film's game, that a movie soundtrack will not pick up men's voices. To play this game, *The Women* requires some special equipment. Mechanical contrivances for transmitting and recording the voice—radio, telephone, dictograph, and the movie soundtrack itself—seem to be the only ways men can hear women or women men. We never hear a man's voice in this film any more than we see his face, but the imminence of men's voices somewhere just beyond our earshot is more often suggested than is the imminence of their physical presence. There are frequent telephone conversations in *The Women*, including the tender and the malicious varieties, both between women and men and between women and women. From the start the telephone takes on an emblematic resonance. At first it seems to be the instrument for female gossip, as Sylvia Fowler rushes to a phone to pass on the latest to Edith Potter (though Olga the manicurist seems to operate as a central switchboard for the dirt on the Haines marriage). But the telephone is primarily used as a way for women to speak to men, and men to women: it underscores the separation of their worlds.[16] In the memorable scene of Joan Crawford (now married to Stephen Haines) soaking in a bubblebath while awaiting a call on her private line from her new lover, the secret telephone clues Rosalind Russell in to the extramarital liaison: she gloats: "You put that phone in to talk to a *man!*" Where there is a phone, there must be a man. Similarly, whenever Norma Shearer is called to the telephone, it is sure to be her cheating husband on the line, and we are sure to witness another of her feats of wifely stoicism in an intimate close-up the star shares only with the telephone receiver.

In a film with an all-female cast, in which a phone implies a man somewhere offscreen, there is an obvious equation between the telephone and the cinema's relay of voices (from microphone to soundtrack to sound head on the projector and to loudspeakers in the theater). In any movie the telephone is a "surrogate for the microphone," as Charles Affron calls it, an object that "concentrates the performer's presence in a voice." The telephone conversation emblematizes the fact that the screen actor speaks in the presence of two audiences; in telephone scenes, as Affron says, "voice is simultaneously directed to the single, private ear of the receiver and to the collective, public ear of the audience."[17] As the instrument of amplified intimacies, the telephone subordinates the spreading of female gossip to the wider broadcasting of woman's secrets of which the film itself is guilty. At the same time, it reminds us that those secrets are invented just to be recorded and replayed; they are the idlest tattle.

It seems appropriate, considering the invisibility of men in this film and their reliance on mechanical transmitters to make themselves heard by women, that the Countess de Lave (Mary Boland) should choose a radio star for her latest husband, or that Sylvia Fowler, who first passes on the tattle that starts the plot, should find that her husband gets evidence for divorcing her by recording her voice: "Did I know he had dictographs hidden all over the place? Did I know I'd given him complete grounds for incompatibility . . . all recorded on discs . . . in the *most awful sounding language?*" She might be talking about the garrulous soundtrack of *The Women*. Its unrelenting acoustic onslaught of chat, gossip, counsel, complaint, sweettalk, cracks, bicker, and gab make it easy to understand why talkies may contain a moment of nostalgia for the silent era. As Panofsky suggested, this nostalgia may be embodied or identified with particular actors or characters, as in the silent Harpo of the Marx brothers talkies.[18] Panofsky's reading of Harpo's silence recasts a line from the stage version of *The Women* as a comment on the movie version. In a late scene from the play, the now divorced Mary Haines explains why she has not remarried: she saw plenty of men, she says, but "They never leave you at your own front door without a wrestling match." Miriam Aarons corroborates this with the crack, "It beats me how in a taxi, the nicest guy turns into Harpo Marx." The character who retained the silence of early films into the era of the talkies, a relic of a time when films were in their infancy and their gestures were broader, the mute masher Harpo Marx becomes the figure for the undiscriminating and inarticulate desire of all men. Miriam's line reduces male sexuality to the slapstick mauling of a clown, but also, in the context of the all-female film, into the wordlessness bestowed on men by a technological recalcitrance. Maleness itself becomes identified with the forsaken era of the silent film. In this context we can reread the pleading note Stephen Haines leaves his wife before she takes off for Reno. Projected nearly fullscreen, like most inset shots of notes, letters, and telegrams in films of this period but also like a dialogue title in a silent movie, the note explicitly comments on the man's speechlessness. "What can I say?" voices silently the man's frustration at being excluded from this film's female world of speech conjoined to image. It is as though men must resort to the title cards of the silent film, having failed to progress into the age of talkies, stranded Harpos all. Accordingly, the male gaze is most explicitly catered and alluded to in the fashion parade, the film's only sustained segment featuring woman's images pure of talk.

We can now look again at the film's ending, the restoration of Mary Haines to her husband and at the demarcation of the limits of the film's ability to exclude him. The film must end when the man would appear—not only would his appearance break this film's "women only" rule, but more important, the film has been working for 134 minutes to make conditions right for his arrival. And his arrival allows us to see where we have progressed without him. Conventions of Hollywood plotting might seem to account sufficiently for the man returning when he does: he has reformed and realized the error of his ways and is justly rewarded with the restored affections of the faithful wife who loves him. But the Shearer character has reformed, too—the wife Stephen Haines embraces offscreen under the fadeout is not the wife he left behind, not the sweet girl we met on horseback at the beginning of the movie. For another way to view the ending of *The Women* is to say that it has been delayed until the Norma Shearer character acknowledges that she is in a movie, or rather, that the way to bring her man back is to look and act as though she were. That is not the way she puts it, of course: her battle cry as she takes off for the last round-up at the Casino Roof is, "I've had two years to grow claws, mother . . . *Jungle red!*" She calls for what is to be her armor in the fight, her "new evening gown," a glittering outfit, which, though not as garish as Crawford's sequinned affair in this scene, is the most gaudy of Shearer costumes in the film, and she now has the language to match. She has at last learned to be as crystalline and hard as the competition, which is to say, at last as consciously adorned for the camera's eye. Her silvery costume is a nod to the black-and-white medium that alone can record its allure. And she now talks so as to be picked up by those hidden dictographs, represented in the last sequence by gossip columnist Dolly de Puyster (impeccably cast with Hedda Hopper), who is instrumental to Mary's plan to break up Crystal's marriage. Thus armed and educated, Shearer commands the camera's complete attention as it follows her in a long forward tracking shot as she goes to meet her man. It is as though her concessions to the film medium conjure up the lost man at whom this spectacle is directed. If we can now answer with greater confidence the wise child's question—"Where's Daddy in this one?"—it may be because we can know with greater certainty where Mommy is in this one: dressed in a shimmering gown, brandishing a cutting tongue as sharp as her nails, she can be nowhere but in front of a movie camera.

Notes

1. "Myths of Women in the Cinema," in *Women and the Cinema: A Critical Anthology*, ed. Karyn Kay and Gerald Peary (New York: E. P. Dutton, 1977), 411, 410.

2. This poster is reproduced in Leslie Halliwell, *The Filmgoer's Companion*, 6th ed. (New York: Avon Books, 1978), 781.

Those who have seen the film are more likely to recall a few choice vignettes or juicy bitching bouts than to retain the episodic and improbable story, which goes something like this: From the chatty new manicurist at Sidney's beauty salon, Mrs. Sylvia Fowler (Rosalind Russell) learns that Stephen Haines, husband of her friend Mary, is cheating on his wife with a perfume salesgirl, Crystal Allen (Joan Crawford). Relishing this piece of choice dirt, Sylvia passes it along to Edith Potter (Phyllis Povah), and thence to other guests they meet later that morning at a luncheon given by the sweet-tempered and as yet unsuspecting Mary Haines (Norma Shearer). Sylvia maliciously drops a hint that Mary should try Sylvia's new manicurist and that divine new shade of "Jungle Red." Mary does and hears the bad news from the irrepressible Olga (Dennie Moore). Mary's mother, Mrs. Morehead (Lucille Watson), gets the scoop from the same source, and, advising her daughter from experience that the best tactic is to wait it out, takes her on a brief vacation to Bermuda.

On her return, Mary lives with the bitter knowledge until she accidentally has a run-in with Crystal Allen, now clearly her husband's kept woman, buying the latest fashions at a Park Avenue salon. When this run-in, much embellished, is printed in the scandal sheets, Mary and her husband have a showdown (reported to us blow-by-blow as the Haineses' maid tells it to the cook). Mary sues for divorce and—after breaking the painful news to her young daughter, Little Mary (Virginia Weidler)—hops the train for Reno, along with her gentle friend Peggy Day (Joan Fontaine), whose marital troubles prove to be merely monetary and short-lived. On the train she meets a wistful veteran of "l'amour" and three divorces, the Countess de Lave (Mary Boland), and a sassy chorus girl, Miriam Aarons (Paulette Goddard). All await their divorces at the same Reno ranch, presided over by Lucy (Marjorie Main). There they are soon joined by Sylvia Fowler, whose husband, too, it seems, has been playing around, and, as Sylvia then discovers, with Miriam Aarons. Sylvia and Miriam skirmish, Mary Haines gets her divorce, and her husband marries the salesgirl.

Two years pass before Mary, still unattached, learns by indirect means that Crystal has a lover (the countess's latest husband) and that Stephen, although unaware of this, is tiring of her. On a sudden impulse, putting to good use the doublecrossing ploys she's seen other women turn against her, Mary throws the evidence in Crystal's face while all are gathered at the Casino Roof. The result is, as she planned, the immediate return of her wayward husband, into whose arms Mary is about to rush as the picture fades out.

3. The star system governed the production of a studio's A pictures. As George Cukor put it in an interview, "Certain novels or plays or properties were acquired for a certain star. There was the next Shearer picture or the next Crawford picture, or the next Garson picture," as cited in Carlos Clarens, *Cukor* (London: Secker and Warburg, 1976), 149. Directors and cameramen would be selected who could most ably capture the special charms of certain star actresses: "Remarkable directors have existed solely to examine the same women over and over again through films," as Stanley Cavell notes in *The World Viewed*, enlarged edition (Cambridge, Mass.: Harvard University Press, 1979), 48.

4. Citing *The Women* as a perfect instance of the way in which even those films that focus on the trials of a female character "aim at reasserting the dominant position of men," Melissa Sue Kort points to the film's ending: "Norma Shearer welcomes with open arms the wayward husband finally returning to the fold. She reaches directly to the camera; the audience becomes that husband, becomes that man reappearing to take his rightful place on the throne" in " 'Spectacular Spinelessness': The Men in Dorothy Arzner's Films," in *Men By Women*, ed. Janet Todd, *Women and Literature* (New York and London: Holmes & Meier Publishers, 1981), 2:190. While my argument follows Kort's in seeing the film's malelessness as compromised by its ending and its man-crazy dialogue, I cannot agree that for these reasons "one barely notices that a man never appears on the screen" (190).

5. Stanley Cavell, *Pursuits of Happiness: The Hollywood Comedy of Remarriage* (Cambridge, Mass.: Harvard University Press, 1981), 221.

6. I have recalled the film's dialogue with the help of the screenplay by Anita Loos and Jane Murfin in *Twenty Best Film Plays*, ed. John Gassner and Dudley Nichols (New York: Crown, 1943). This screenplay does not match at all points the dialogue spoken in the film.

7. For a reading of the home movie in *Adam's Rib*, see Cavell, *Pursuits of Happiness*, 204–14.

8. *Camera Lucida: Reflections on Photography* (New York: Hill and Wang, 1981), 10.

9. *The Women* (New York: Random House, 1937).

10. Gavin Lambert, *On Cukor* (New York: G. P. Putnam's Sons, 1972), 137.

11. *Screen*, 16, 3 (Autumn 1975). Reprinted in Kay and Peary, *Women and the Cinema*, 420, 419.

12. For a list of color sequences in black-and-white films, see Halliwell, 159–60. In this context it is worth recalling that George Cukor turned to *The Women* after he was divested of the directorship of one of the first all-color efforts, *Gone with the Wind* (Clarens, 48). An exchange on the train to Reno between a little girl and her mother sounds like an in-joke on this shift in Cukor's career: "Mummy, where is Daddy?" "He's gone with the wind—*the big*

white Zombie!" If so, it seems appropriate that *The Women* refers in a sidelong way to its director via the question of where an absent father is.

13. *Seeing Through Clothes* (1978; rpt. New York: Avon Books, 1980), 343–44.

14. Annette Kuhn, *Women's Pictures: Feminism and Cinema* (London: Routledge and Kegan Paul, 1982), 64.

15. The salesgirl compliments Crawford on her stunning telephone performance, much as Maggie the cook applauds Jean the eavesdropping maid ("Quite an actress, ain't you?") on her reenactment of the offscreen showdown between their employers, Mr. and Mrs. Haines. A split or delay between vision and hearing separates upstairs from downstairs, rich society wives from gold-digging salesgirls, as well as men from women.

Without detailing *The Women's* presentation of social classes, I will merely note in this context that while the film claims that at least some forms of female desire are a product of economic need (Shearer's husband is Crawford's "meal ticket"), the demonstration that women of all classes can behave like bitches (as in the department store scene where salesgirl Crawford meets the insults of society wives Russell and Povah tit for tat) blurs the distinction between social classes in favor of the classless category Woman.

16. Films whose setting or world is restricted or closed in some way seem to require many telephones. To take a familiar example, the action of *His Girl Friday* (1940) is almost wholly confined to the pressroom (as in the stage version), awash with telephones as the only means of reaching to an area outside the film's setting. (An interesting study would be a comparison of Rosalind Russell's telephone conversations in *The Women* and in *His Girl Friday*.) While the mise-en-scène of *The Women* is more varied (even if the beauty salon, the fitting room, and the night club lounge all turn out to be analogous versions of the Hollywood sound stage), its exclusion of men operates as does *His Girl Friday's* restriction to a single room.

17. *Cinema and Sentiment* (Chicago: University of Chicago Press, 1982), 114, 113.

18. Erwin Panofsky, "Style and Medium in the Motion Pictures," in Daniel Talbot, ed., *Film* (1959; rpt. Berkeley and Los Angeles: University of California Press, 1966), 21.

4

Monroe and Sexuality

RICHARD DYER
University of Warwick

The denial of the body is delusion. No woman transcends her body.
—Joseph C. Rheingold

Men want women pink, helpless and do a lot of deep breathing.
—Jayne Mansfield

Stars matter to us because they act out aspects of life that matter to us; and performers get to be stars when what they act out matters to enough people prepared to pay to see it. You can understand this "what matters" in universal terms, and there is a sense in which stars must touch on things that are deep and constant features of human existence. However, such features never exist in the pure form that their universality often implies. They always exist in a culturally and historically specific context; and, even if the feature is universal, it won't necessarily be held to matter much in its specific context.

Sexuality is just such a feature. It would be absurd to deny that in all human societies sexual intercourse takes place. However, what that intercourse means and how much it matters alters from culture to culture, and within the history of each culture. The argument in this essay is that, in the USA of the fifties, there were quite specific ideas of what sexuality meant, and that it was held to matter a very great deal; and because Marilyn Monroe acted out those specific ideas, she was charismatic, a center of attraction, who seemed to embody what was taken to be a central feature of human existence at that time.

In stressing the importance of sexuality in Marilyn Monroe's image, it might seem that I am just another commentator doing to Monroe what was done to her throughout her life, treating her solely in terms of sex. Perhaps that is a danger, but I hope that I am not just reproducing this attitude toward Monroe but also trying to understand it and historicize it. Monroe may have been a wit, a subtle and profound actress, an intelligent and serious woman. I have no desire to dispute these qualities and it is important to recognize and recover them against the grain of her image. But my purpose is to understand the grain itself, and there can be no question that this is overwhelmingly and relentlessly constructed in terms of sexuality. Monroe's sexuality is a message that ran all the way from what the media made of her in pin-ups and movies to how her image became a reference point for sexuality in the coinage of everyday speech.

She started her career as a pin-up girl, and one can find no type of image more singlemindedly sexual than that. Pin-ups constituted a constant and vital aspect of her image right up to her death, and the pin-up style also indelibly marked other aspects of her image, such as her public appearances and promotions for her films. The roles she was given, the way she was filmed, and the reviews she got do little to counteract this emphasis.

She plays, from the beginning, "the girl," defined solely by age, gender, and appealingness. In two films, she does not even have a name, *Scudda Hoo! Scudda Hay!* (1948) and *Love Happy* (1950), and in three other films, her character has no biography beyond being "the blonde," *Dangerous Years* (1948), *The Fireball* (1950), and *Right Cross* (1950). Even when any information about her character is supplied, it serves to reinforce the basic anonymity of the role. For instance, when her character has a job, it is a job that, while it may be genuinely useful, like that of a secretary, is traditionally (or cinematically) thought of as being a job where the woman is on show, there for the pleasure of men. These jobs in Monroe's early films are chorus girl in *Ladies of the Chorus* (1948) and *Ticket to Tomahawk* (1950); actress in *All About Eve* (1950) (the film emphasizes that the character has no talent); or secretary in *Home Town Story* (1951), *As Young As You Feel* (1951), and *Monkey Business* (1952). There is very little advance on these roles in her later career. She has no name in *The Seven Year Itch* (1955); even in the credits she is just "the Girl." She is a chorus girl in *Gentlemen Prefer Blondes* (1953), *There's No Business Like Show Business* (1954), *The Prince and the Showgirl* (1957), and *Let's Make Love* (1960), and she is a solo artiste of no great talent in *River of No Return* (1954), *Bus Stop* (1956), and *Some Like It Hot* (1959). She is a model (hardly an extension of the role repertoire) in *How to Marry a Millionaire* (1953) and *The Seven Year Itch* (1955), and a prostitute in *O. Henry's Full House* (1952). Thus even in her prestige roles, *Bus Stop* and *The Prince and the Showgirl*, the social status of the person she plays remains the same. The tendency to treat her as nothing more than her gender reaches its peak with *The Misfits* (1961), where, instead of being the "girl" from the early films, she now becomes the "woman," or perhaps just "Woman"—Roslyn has no biography, she is just "a divorcee"; the symbolic structure of the film relates her to nature, the antithesis of culture, career, society, history.

There is no question that Monroe did a lot with these roles, but it is nearly always against the grain of the way they were written, and the way they were filmed too. She is constantly knitted into the fabric of the film through point-of-view shots located in male characters—even in the later films, and virtually always in the earlier ones, she is set up an an object of the male sexual gaze. Frequently too she is placed within the frame of the camera in such a way as to stand out in silhouette, a side-on tits and arse positioning found equally in the early *Monkey Business* and *As Young As You Feel* and the prestige production, *The Prince and the Showgirl*.

It is not surprising that Monroe became virtually a household word for sex. What is equally clear is that sex was seen as perhaps the most important thing in fifties America. Certain publishing events suggest this—the two Kinsey reports (on men in 1948; on women in 1953), the first issues of *Confidential* in 1951 and *Playboy* in 1953, both to gain very rapidly in circulation; best-selling novels such as *From Here to Eternity* (1951), *A House Is Not a Home* (1953), *Not As a Stranger* (1955), *Peyton Place* (1956), *Strangers When We Meet* (1953), *A Summer Place* (1958), *The Chapman Report* (1960), *Return to Peyton Place* (1961), not to mention the thrillers of Mickey Spillane.

This seems to be one of the high points of the trend that Michel Foucault has discussed in his *The History of Sexuality* as having emerged in the seventeenth century. Sexuality is designated as that aspect of human existence where we may learn the truth about our-selves. This often takes the form of digging below the surface, on the assumption that what is below the surface must necessarily be more true and also be what causes the surface to take the form it does. This is equally the model of the psychoanalytic inquiry into the uncon-scious (peel back the Ego to the truth of the Id), of the best-selling novel formula of "taking the lid off the suburbs" (*Peyton Place* "tears down brick, stucco, and tar-paper to give intimate revealing glimpses of the inhabitants within," said the *Sunday Dispatch*) or of the endless raking over the past of a star, like Monroe, to find the truth about her personality. And the below-surface that they all tended to come up with in the fifties was sex.

Probably the most lucid interpretation of the fifties discourses on sexuality remains Betty Friedan's *The Feminine Mystique,* first pub-lished in 1963 and clearly a major influence on everything written about the fifties since. Friedan suggests that sexuality in the fifties became constructed as the "answer" to any of the dissatisfactions or distresses that might have been voiced by women as a result of living under "the feminine mystique," or what Friedan also calls "the prob-lem that has no name." Time and again in interviewing women, she found that they would "give me an explicitly sexual answer to a question that was not sexual at all."[1] She argues that women in America "are putting into the sexual search all their frustrated needs for self-realisation."[2] Similarly, in her survey of some films of the fifties, *On the Verge of Revolt,* Brandon French notes how these films "reveal how sex and love were often misused to obscure or resolve deeper sources of female (and male) dissatisfaction."[3] If, in Foucault's account, sexuality is seen as a source of knowledge about human existence, Friedan and French show how that knowledge is also offered as the solution to the problems of human existence. All three argue that sexuality, both as knowledge and solution, is also the means by which men and women are designated a place in society and are kept in their place.

In line with these wider trends in society, sexuality was becoming increasingly important in films. One of the cinema's strategies in the face of the rise of increasingly privatized forms of leisure (not only television, but also reading, do-it-yourself, home-based sports, enter-taining at home, and so on) was to provide the kind of fare that was not deemed suitable for home consumption—hence the fall of the family film and the rise of "adult" cinema. Though the huge increase in widely available pornography did not come until later, even mainstream cinema at this time became gradually more "daring" and "explicit" in its treatment of sex. Taboos were broken, not only in underground cinema but in big Hollywood productions too. Monroe was herself a taboo breaker, from riding the scandal of the nude *Golden Dreams* calendar to showing her nipples in her last photo session with Bert Stern and doing a nude bathing scene in the unfinished film, *Something's Gotta Give,* which was unheard of for a major motion picture star.

Monroe was (and is) relentlessly seen in terms of sexuality and she appeared in a period when the question of sexuality was experienced as intensified in the cinema, in popular culture, and in general intellectual life, as well as in everyday life. Monroe's image spoke and articulated the particular ways that sexuality was thought and felt about in the period. These ways of thought and feeling can be organized around two discourses—that of the "playboy," crystallized by *Playboy* magazine but by no means confined to it; and that of the "question" of female sexuality itself, which at the clinical level revolved around notions of the vaginal orgasm, but in popular culture centered more upon the particular mysterious or mystifying nature of female sexual response. These two discourses draw into them many others; they are united by the notion of "desirability" as the female sexual role that meets the needs of the playboy discourse. Monroe embodies and to a degree authenticates these discourses, but there is also a sense in which she begins to act out the drama of the difficulty of embodying them.

1953 was the first year in which Monroe was voted top female box office star by American film distributors. She was a center of attraction, in films, promotions, and publicity. The first three films in which she had starring roles were released (*Niagara, Gentlemen Prefer Blondes,* and *How to Marry a Millionaire*); she appeared on the cover of *Look* magazine; she walked off the set of *The Girl in Pink Tights;* and, in 1954, she married Joe DiMaggio in January and visited the troops in Korea in February. 1953 was a year in which the most directly sexual of stars was also the star of the moment, and it was also a year of extraordinarily compelling significance in the history of American sexuality. In August, the Kinsey report on women was published with the most massive press reception ever accorded a scientific treatise.[4] In December, the first issue of *Playboy* appeared. The very publication of a sex report on women, with an attendant publicity far in excess of that surrounding the male report in 1948, focused the "question" of female sexuality, even if the way in which this question continued to

Gentlemen Prefer Blondes, Twentieth Century-Fox Productions
Courtesy of Museum of Modern Art/Film Stills Archive

be set up was actually at considerable variance to Kinsey's findings. I'll
come back to this and to the relation between Monroe and the question
of female sexuality. The *Playboy* connection is more direct.

Monroe was on the cover of the first edition of *Playboy* and inside
her *Golden Dreams* nude calendar photo was the magazine's first
centerfold. When Molly Haskell observes that Monroe was "the living
embodiment of an image of woman immortalised in *Esquire* and
Playboy,"[5] this is no mere suggestive link between Monroe and
Playboy—the two are identified with each other from that first cover
and centerfold.[6] Both articulate a discourse of sexuality, though the
nature of their contributions differ. *Playboy* elaborates the discourse
through its developing house style, in copy and photography, and,
eventually, in its "philosophy." As a star, Monroe legitimates and au-

thenticates this discourse, not just by being in the magazine, although there can be no question of the boost this gave it, but by enacting as no one else was doing at the time the particular definitions of sexuality for which *Playboy* was proselytizing.

Some idea of the double impact of Monroe on *Playboy* and of *Playboy* on Monroe can be gained by considering that *Golden Dreams* centerfold. It was already an object of scandalous interest. The photo had been taken in 1948 by Tom Kelley, and it had been used for several different calendars, one of hundreds of such images. However, in March 1952, the fact that this image was of an important new Hollywood star became a major news story. At this time, despite the wide circulation of the calendars, relatively few people had actually seen the photo except in small, black-and-white reproductions accompanying the news items about it. Its scandalousness made it in December 1953 still an object of much interest, and printing it in a full-color two-page spread in the first issue of a new magazine was a marketing coup.

What is important here is the nature of the scandal *Playboy* so unerringly turned to. On the one hand, there was the fact of a Hollywood star doing the kind of a pin-up *Golden Dreams* is; and on the other hand, there was the widely reported reaction of Monroe when the scandal broke.

There had long been pin-ups of the *Golden Dreams* variety, but they were not the variety in which Hollywood and, up to 1952, Monroe specialized in. The early pin-ups of Monroe belong not to the highly wrought glamor traditions of Hollywood, associated with photographers such as Ruth Harriet Louise and George Hurrell; they belong rather to a much simpler and probably far more common tradition, both in style and choice of model. The style is generally head-on, using high-key lighting, few props, and vague backdrops; the model is always young, generally white, the "healthy, American, cheerleader type"[7] and she is not individualized. The key icon of this tradition, certainly in the forties and fifties, was the one-piece bathing costume, whose rigors make all bodies conform to a certain notion of streamlined femininity. But *Golden Dreams* is not like these pin-ups or the glamor type; it belongs rather to a tradition known as "art photography" (since it was ostensibly sold to artists, whose responses to naked women were supposedly less coarse than other men's). In this tradition the model is invariably nude, and, though the lighting and the camera position are often quite straightforward, the model is usually required to pose in willfully bizarre positions that run counter to most established notions of classical grace and line. Clearly few were fooled by the art label for this unpleasantly dehumanizing tradition of photography—and it was indeed a disreputable form, associated quite correctly with the dirty talk of men's lockerrooms and toilets.

The scandal was the association of a Hollywood star with this tradition, but Monroe's reported reaction took the sting out of the scandal and made the photo just the one *Playboy* needed for its "new" ideas about sex. In an interview with Aline Mosby, Monroe said that she'd done the photo because she needed the money, that Kelley's wife was present at the time, and besides, "I'm not ashamed of it. I've done nothing wrong."[8] This sense of guiltlessness was picked up by *Time* magazine, whose wording was, as we'll see, significant—". . . Marilyn believes in doing what comes naturally."[9] They also quote her reply to being asked what she had on when the photo was taken—"I had the radio on." A classic dumb blonde one-liner, it implies a refusal or inability to answer the question at the level of prurience at which it was asked—indeed, it suggests an ignorance of prurience altogether.

Guiltless, natural, not prurient—these were precisely part of the attitude toward sexuality that *Playboy* was pushing. *Playboy*'s "philosophy" was not formally articulated as such until 1962, but it was clearly developing through the magazine in the fifties, and it combined two reigning ideas concerning sexuality in the twentieth century. The first is what Michel Foucault has called "the repressive hypothesis," namely the idea that sexuality has "been rigorously subjugated . . . during the age of the hypocritical, bustling and responsible bourgeoisie."[10] The second has been termed by John Gagnon and John Simon "a drive-reduction model" of sexuality, positing the sex drives as "a basic biological mandate" seeking "expression" or "release."[11] It is common enough to see this "biological mandate" as a fierce and disruptive drive that really needs repression, but *Playboy*'s view of it was that it was benign, that only repression itself turns the sex drive malignant, and that left to its own devices, it will bring nothing but beauty and happiness. Sex exists with and without love and in both forms it does far more good than harm. The attempts at its suppression, however, are almost universally harmful, both to the individuals involved and to society as a whole.[12]

The force of these ideas for the mid–twentieth century, especially in America, lies in their appeal to the idea of naturalness, the idea that you can justify any attitude or course of action by asserting it to be in accord with what people would really like if they lived in a state of nature. Sexuality is peculiarly amenable to this kind of argument, since it is at first glance (our habitual first glance, anyhow) so "biological," so rooted in the flesh.[13] Monroe, so much set up in terms of sexuality, also seemed to personify naturalness. Her perceived naturalness not only guaranteed the truth of her sexuality in much the same way as the imputed qualities of sincerity and authenticity, spontaneity and openness, guaranteed the personality of other stars; it also defined and justified that sexuality, exactly in line with the playboy discourse.

The assertion of Monroe's naturalness in relation to sexuality has been made so often I do not need to establish it at length. At the time, critics and observers referred to it constantly, and retrospectively many of the people involved with her have ascribed it to her. Jayne Mansfield, when asked to appear nude at a nudist colony in Rio de Janeiro, refused, reportedly saying, "It's too bad I'm not Marilyn Monroe. She's a naturalist. But I would not feel right."[14]

Although she was always thought of as an also-ran to Monroe, Mansfield clearly recognized the particular ingredient in Monroe's image that she herself did not have. Immediately following Monroe's death, Diana Trilling wrote an article about her that is in many ways emblematic of this widely held view of Monroe. "None but Marilyn Monroe could suggest such a purity of sexual delight."[15] And Monroe herself said in her last interview: "I think that sexuality is only attractive when it is natural and spontaneous."

We have to tread carefully here, since ambiguities crowd in that I'll just signal here—for instance, the fact that most of those who ascribe this natural sexualness emanating from her are also clearly describing their responses to her, or the presence in so much of the writing about her of an endless raking over of the possible perversities (or unnaturalnesses) of Monroe's "real" sexuality. What we need to keep in focus is the degree to which the Monroe image clearly offered itself to be read in terms of (benign) naturalness and with the impact of being something new.

Monroe combined naturalness *and* overt sexuality, notably in a series of gags that became known as Monroeisms. Though in form they were typical of the dumb blonde tradition to which she in part belongs, they are different in nearly always having to do with sex. One of the most striking was the one she delivered to the troops in Korea in February 1954: "I don't know why you boys are always getting excited about sweater girls. Take away their sweaters and what have they got?" Though overtly referring to other women stars, she also effectively refers to herself, her own body, and perhaps even to her own breasts, so recently, finally, exposed in *Playboy*.

Though a clever gag, it is also, in context, dumb, because Marilyn Monroe is a dumb blonde. The dumbness of the dumb blonde is by

tradition given as natural, because it means that she is not touched by
the rationality of the world. But the dumb blonde is also untouched by
the corruption of the world. She's a figure out of Rousseau, but some
way from his conceptions of the essential nature of the human being,
before civilization gets to her or him. The dumb blonde's ignorance of
the world is brainlessness, seldom the superior wisdom of Rousseau's
"natural" woman; and her innocence is above all a sexual innocence, a
lack of knowledge about sexuality. She is a figure of comedy, because
she is also always extraordinarily and devastatingly sexually attractive—the comedy resides either in the way her irresistible attractions
get men tied up in her irrationality or else in the contrast between her
sexual innocence and her sexual impact. The most interesting play on
these comic possibilities comes about when ambiguities are acknowledged—maybe (as with Judy Holliday in *It Should Happen to You*), the
dumb blonde's irrationality is wise in its way; maybe (as with Carol
Channing in the stage version of *Gentlemen Prefer Blondes*), she is
using the dumb blonde image to manipulate men. But Monroe's image
does not really follow either of these directions. Rather she fundamentally alters the dumb blonde comic equation. Rationality hardly comes
up as a question in the comedy of her films at all; it is sexual innocence
that's the core of the gag—but that core is no longer a contrast between
sexuality and innocence, since with Monroe sexuality is innocent. So
the sweater girl gag is funny not because the blonde is being dirty
about herself without knowing it, but because it is a play on words that
cheerfully acknowledges her sexual impact. Monroe knows about
sexuality, but she doesn't know about guilt and innocence—she welcomes sex as natural.

Naturalness, which Monroe so vividly embodied and thereby guaranteed, was elaborated in *Playboy* above all at the level of its philosophy, its overt and proclaimed *Weltanschauung*. At this level, it is an
attitude that sees itself as socially progressive, as taboo-breaking. The
feeling it conveys is exactly the one noted by Michel Foucault as
characteristic of those committed to "the repression hypothesis":

> we are conscious of defying established power, our tone of voice shows
> that we know we are being subversive, and we ardently conjure away the
> present and appeal to the future, whose day will be hastened by the
> contribution we believe we are making.[16]

Foucault's irony stems from his proposition that we should not think so
much in terms of sexuality being repressed, but rather in terms of its
form being constructed, with an ever-renewed insistence, as an instru-

ment of power. Similarly the feminist critique of the *Playboy* discourse points out that what it is concerned with are new definitions of male power within sexuality. From these perspectives, what the *Playboy* discourse was doing was simply another variation on the regime of sexual power.

David Standish, writing in *Playboy's* twenty-fifth anniversary edition, suggests that *Playboy's* aim was to present "a pin-up as something other than a porno postcard," as, in fact, "the girl next door" (art photography meets June Allyson and becomes Marilyn Monroe), and he takes the July 1955 centerfold of Janet Pilgrim as the turning point in this project.

> At the time, the idea that a 'nice' girl would appear in the four-colour altogether was shocking! . . Suddenly, here were girls, *a* girl, Janet Pilgrim, who looked like a good, decent human being and worked in an actual office . . . not some distant, bored bimbo with her clothes off but, perhaps, if God were in a good mood, she might one day be that girl you see on the bus every day who's making your heart melt.[17]

The Seven Year Itch, made in 1954, works off of just this fantasy. Monroe is the never-named girl upstairs, the kind of girl who appears in art photo magazines of the kind that Richard Sherman (Tom Ewell) buys—the kind of girl he has been slavering over just happens to move into the apartment upstairs. It's the *Playboy* dream come true. At the end of the film, as he is leaving to rejoin his wife, he calls after the girl, "What's your name?" "Marilyn Monroe," she jokes back, the film thus signaling that it knows how inextricable are the Monroe and *Playmate* images.

Janet Pilgrim, the July 1955 *Playboy* centerfold, is almost, in the way she is written about in the few pages featuring her, a rerun of Monroe's career. To quote Standish again, she is "an engaging blonde" (more on blondeness later), "shown first at work slaving beautifully over her typewriter, "then sitting two pages later wearing mostly diamonds at a fancy dressing table." Monroe had played a secretary in *Hometown Story* (1951), *As Young As You Feel* (1951), and *Monkey Business* (1952). Monroe's biggest number in *Gentlemen Prefer Blondes* (1953) was "Diamonds Are a Girl's Best Friend"; so big that it was also used for her appearance at the fashion show in *How to Marry a Millionaire* (1953). Pilgrim and Monroe normalize sex appeal (in the secretary image) while still associating it with something to be possessed, like a mistress bought with diamonds.

The secretary—to say nothing of the showgirl or model—be she

Janet Pilgrim in *Playboy* or Marilyn Monroe in *Monkey Business*, is not there to do a job or for her own advancement: she is there for men. This is the nub of the *Playboy* discourse—it is a demand for sexual liberation for *men*. Women are set up as the embodiment of sexuality itself. As Hollis Alpert put it at the time (and presumably without any intended feminist irony):

> Hollywood has given [audiences] the Hollywood Siren—the woman who simply by existing, or at most sprawling on a rug or sauntering up a street—is supposed to imply all the vigorous, kaleidoscopic possibilities of human sexuality.[18]

Women are to *be* sexuality, yet this really means as a vehicle *for* male sexuality. Monroe refers to her own sexualness—her breasts in the sweater girl gag, or her buttocks in the line near the beginning of *The Seven Year Itch*, "My fan is caught in the door." But read through the eyes of the *Playboy* discourse, she is not referring to a body she experiences, but rather to a body that is experienced by others, that is, by men. By embodying the desired sexual playmate, she, a woman, becomes the vehicle for securing a male sexuality free of guilt.

Desirability

Monroe not only provided the vehicle for the expression of the Playboy discourse's project of "liberating" sexuality, she was also the epitome of what was desirable in a playmate. "Desirability" is the quality that women in the fifties were urged to attain.

Monroe conforms to and is part of the construction of what constitutes this quality. It is a set of implied character traits, but before it is that, it is also a social position, for the desirable woman is a white woman. The typical playmate is white, and most often blonde; and, of course, so is Monroe. It is not the case that Monroe could not have been some sort of star had she been dark, but she could not then have been the ultimate embodiment of the desirable woman.

There is nothing particularly white about Monroe, no more than there is about, say, Jean Harlow, or Doris Day. Equally, being white is no guarantee of Monroe's particular kind of stardom; it is a necessary but not a sufficient explanation of it. Nor does Monroe's image specifically refer to her whiteness by explicitly setting her over against black women, or women of other ethnic backgrounds. On the one hand, the image doesn't need to do that because she is so indelibly, blondely white; and on the other hand, to make a point of that whiteness would be to draw attention to her particular racial qualities, whereas she is offered as *the* ideal of woman, not regardless of race, but rather, without reference to race. To recognize her racial specificity would be to acknowledge racial differences in a culture that seeks to deny the significance of such differences (even while being fundamentally based upon them).

To be the ideal, Monroe had to be white, and not just white, but blonde, the most unambiguously white you can get. This race element conflates with sexuality in (at least) two ways. First, the white woman is offered as the most highly prized possession of the white man, and as the envy of all other races. American imperialist and Southern popular cultures abound in imagery playing on this theme, and it has been the major source of all dominant race images in the twentieth century. There is the notion of the universally desired "white Goddess" explicity adumbrated in Rider Haggard's *She* and its several film versions; there is the rape motif exploited in *The Birth of a Nation* and countless films and novels before and since; and there is the most obvious playing out of this theme in *King Kong,* with the jungle creature ascending the pinnacle of the Western world caressingly clutching a white woman. (In the remake, Jessica Lange affects a Monroe accent for the part.)

Blondeness, especially platinum (peroxided) blondeness, is the ultimate sign of whiteness. Blonde hair is frequently associated with wealth, either in the choice of the term platinum to describe the effect of peroxide, or in pin-ups where the hair color is visually rhymed with a silver or gold dress and with jewelry. (We might remember too the title of Monroe's nude calendar pose, *GOLDEN Dreams.*) And blondeness is not racially ambiguous. It keeps the white woman distinct from the black, brown, or yellow woman, and at the same time, it assures the viewer that the woman is the genuine article, that she is definitely really white. The hysteria surrounding ambiguity on this point is astonishing. This is why films return so frequently to the figure of the mulatto, whose racial ambiguity and ability to "pass for white" so disturb the white patriarchal order.

The white woman is not only the most prized possession of white patriarchy, she is also part of the symbol of sexuality itself. Christianity associates sin with darkness and sexuality, virtue with light and chastity. With the denial of female sexuality that pervaded the late nineteenth and early twentieth centuries (except as, by definition, a problem), sexuality also became associated with masculinity. Men are then seen as split between their baser, sexual, "black" side and their good, spiritual, white side. That split is specifically redeemed in Victorian imagery by the chastity of woman. Thus the extreme figures in this conflation of race and gender stereotypes are the black stud/rapist and the white virginal maiden. By the fifties, such extremes were becoming less current, and they did not necessarily carry with them all the strict moral associations of sexuality = bad, nonsexuality = good; but the associations of darkness with the drives model of masculine sexuality and of fairness with female desirability remained strong.

Monroe's blondeness is remarked upon often enough in films, but the first saloon scene in *Bus Stop* seems to make something special out of it. Beau storms in and at once sees Cherie on stage, the angel that he has said he is looking for. His words emphasize her whiteness— "Look at her gleaming there so pale and white." He finds in her the projection of his desires, and the song she sings might be her acknowledgement of this—"That old black magic that you weave so well."

Monroe was not a natural blonde (she started dyeing her hair in 1947), but for her to be the epitome of desirability, she had to be a blonde white woman. She also had, or seemed to have, several personality traits that together summed up female desirability in the fifties. She looks like she's no trouble, she is vulnerable, and she appears to offer herself to the viewer, to be available.

She embodies what the *Reader's Digest* in 1957 declared "Every Husband Needs" in a wife, namely, "good sex uncomplicated by the worry of satisfying his woman."[19] She does not make a man feel inadequate; she is not the ballbuster or castrator of male fears. Norman Mailer articulates this way of reading of Monroe: "Marilyn suggested sex might be difficult and dangerous with others, but ice cream with her. . . ."[20] Monroe, whose image was so overdetermined in terms of sexuality, is nevertheless not an image of the danger of sex: she is not the *femme fatale* of *film noir* and of other such hypererotic stars as Clara Bow, Marlene Dietrich, Jean Harlow, and even Greta Garbo, all of whom in some measure bespoke trouble for the men in their films. In her later roles especially, the slightly disruptive quality that any introduction of a highly sexual (which is almost the same thing as saying any) woman into a male character's life always involves, is defused; indeed, it almost becomes the point of these films that Monroe takes the sting out of anything that the fact of her sexuality seems at first likely to stir up. So Richard (Tom Ewell) in *The Seven Year Itch* goes back happily to his wife, Beau (Don Murray) in *Bus Stop* gets his girl (Cherie/Monroe) and goes back to his ranch, Elsie (Monroe) in *The Prince and the Showgirl* reconciles the king (Jeremy Spenser) and his father, the regent (Laurence Olivier), and so on. It's a standard narrative pattern—a state of equilibrium, a disruption, and then a return to equilibrium through resolution of the disruption; only here the cause of the disruptions (Monroe, just because she *is* sex) and the resolution are embodied in one and the same person/character, Monroe.

If Monroe's desirability has to do with her being no trouble, it also has to do with being vulnerable. Susan Brownmiller has discussed the importance of this quality in her study of rape, *Against Our Will*. There is, she suggests, a "deep belief . . . that our attractiveness to men, or sexual desirability, is in direct proportion to our ability to play the victim." Women live "the part of the walking wounded," and this is something that "goes to the very core of our sexuality."[21] She names Monroe as perhaps "the most famous and overworked example" of "the beautiful victim" syndrome.[22] This can be seen in the way she is treated in films and in the way her biography is constructed.

Monroe is not characteristically physically abused in films. She is, rather, taken advantage of or humiliated. Very often this means little more than putting her in situations where she is exposed to the gaze of the male hero, but in two of the films that are also considered her best, *Bus Stop* and *Some Like It Hot*, this goes much further. In *Bus Stop*, for instance, she plays Cherie, a showgirl who wants to get out of the cheap barrooms where she works, to be a success and "get a little respect." But even though this was the film that was set up for her return to Hollywood (after she walked out and went to study at the Actors' Studio in New York), and even though she is undoubtedly the star of it, the project that carries the narrative is not Cherie's, but Beau's (Don Murray). He is looking for his "angel" and finds her in Cherie/Monroe; the trajectory of the narrative is the defeat of her project in the name of his (getting her to marry him). One of the turning points in the film—and one we are obviously meant to find funny—occurs when Beau, an expert cowboy, lassoes Cherie as she is trying to escape him on a bus. It is not just that the narrative shows her as helpless before the male drive to conquer; the film invites us to delight in her pitiful and hopeless struggling, precisely in vivid gags such as this one with the lasso.

Monroe's vulnerability is also confirmed by aspects of her offscreen image. Indeed, all of that image could be read as a neverending series of testimonials to how easily, and frequently, she is hurt. A brief list of the main points that were so often raked over in the publicity surrounding her will suffice to indicate this, always bearing in mind that some of these things never happened or were very exaggerated:

Bus Stop, Twentieth Century Fox Productions
Courtesy of Museum of Modern Art/Film Stills Archive

(a) born illegitimate to a mother who spent her daughter's childhood in and
out of mental hospitals;
(b) fostered by several different couples;
(c) spent time in an orphanage (sometimes presented in positively Dicken-
sian terms in the biographies, articles, and interviews);
(d) indecently assaulted at the age of nine;
(e) an habitual sufferer from menstrual pains;
(f) going through three unsuccessful marriages;
(g) unable to bear children, having a succession of miscarriages;
(h) a nymphomaniac who was frigid (oh the categories of fifties sexual theory!);
(i) a woman so difficult to work with that Tony Curtis said that kissing her
was like kissing Hitler;

(j) a suicide, or murdered, or died of an overdose of the pills she was so habituated to.

The appeal of this biographical vulnerability necessarily involves the power of the reader, but we need to get the emphasis right here. Vulnerability may call forth any number of responses, including empathy, protectiveness, or contempt. It is the way that the Monroe biography is ineluctably associated with sexuality that is significant. The elements of the biography that are heightened nearly all have to do with sex—not just sexual experience itself, but with the interrelations of sexuality with menstruation, childbirth, marriage, and so on. Monroe's problems are repeatedly related (often using her own words) to the need for love, and love, in the vocabulary of the fifties, is overwhelmingly identified as (hetero)sexual love. All this, plus the overwhelming emphasis on sexuality in her image anyway, means that the sexual dimension of her vulnerability was more likely to be taken as reinforced than as qualified by the biographical stories.

It is worth adding here a word about the possible deeply ambivalent effects of these aspects of her image for contemporary women audiences, who were much less clearly the addressees of her image than were men. Her vulnerability could have made her a sympathetic identification figure, but there is not much evidence of this. At least as much, Monroe's was an image that, at the time, women resented for embodying so impossible an image of female allure. There may then have been a certain satisfaction to be had from observing that this woman, the *ne plus ultra* of femininity, nonetheless failed as a woman by all the other norms of fifties womanhood—she was "unfulfilled" for lack of children, unable (and this might be a comforting thought) to keep a man, even while she progressed from the guy-next-door Jim Dougherty, through all-American sports hero Joe DiMaggio, to ace egghead Arthur Miller. Her "failure" at least suggested that that kind of desirability did not bring the happiness that women were assured was secured by that other feminine route, domesticity.

Unthreatening, vulnerable, Monroe also always seemed to be available, on offer. At the time, and even more since her death, many observers saw her career in terms of a series of moments in which she offered herself to the gaze of men—the *Golden Dreams* calendar, *The Seven Year Itch* subway gratings pose, shot before passing crowds in a Manhattan street, her appearances in revealing fetishistic gowns, her final nude photo session with Bert Stern, and the nude scene for *Something's Gotta Give*. All of these moments were taken as done by Monroe, the person, at her own behest. Each one a dramatic news story, they were not read as media manipulation, but rather as a star's willing presentation of her sexuality to the world's gaze.

Monroe appeared at a moment when feminism was at its lowest ebb in the twentieth century, and both her career decisions and her remarks in interviews could be and were read as confirming the male-serving myth of the desirable playmate. But so great an emphasis on her own purported involvement in the production of her sexy image is *also* an emphasis on the will and desire of the person who inhabits and produces the sexy image. It does actually raise the question of the person who plays the fantasy; in other terms, of the subject who is habitually the object of desire.

The image of the desirable playmate, which Monroe so exactly incarnated, is an image of female sexuality for men. Yet so much does it insist on the equation of women and sexuality that it also raises the question, or specter, of female sexuality for women. Monroe's image is much less clearly articulated in relation to this. Part of what makes her desirable, unthreatening, is that her image does not insist on a female sexuality for itself. Yet there is always the possibility of the other, woman-centered reading. On the one hand, she registers aspects of the fifties discourse on the "question" of female sexuality; and on the other hand, some of her actions and performances begin to articulate something of the drama and difficulty of being held to embody the desirable playmate. The first remains caught within the fifties' equal-but-different view of gender identities; the second can be seen as part of that general, beneath-the-surface, not-yet-articulable expression of discontent that Brandon French takes as an indication that in the fifties women were, as in the title of her book, "on the verge of revolt."

The most decisive discourse on female sexuality in the fifties stemmed from psychoanalysis. There was a massive spread and popularization of psychoanalytic ideas, both in magazines and fiction, and in the developing practices of counseling, family guidance, social work, and so on, to say nothing of the growth of therapy proper. This is very clearly marked in the films of the period, above all in the melodramas with their very direct acknowledgements of the unconscious, of repression, of drives, of the sexuality of family relations, of the sexuality of everything. The growth of the "psychological Western," the knowing gags of the sex comedies, and the development of method acting are further indices of how far psychoanalytic ideas, however garbled, had got under the skin of popular culture. Perhaps one of the most striking, because unexpected, indications of the trend is MGM's science-fiction extravaganza, *Forbidden Planet,* whose plot depends upon the audience being able to grasp the notions of the Id and the

Ego. This discourse can be termed one "psycho" discourse, since Hitchcock, whose films are so marked by explicit and implicit references to psychoanalysis, perfectly caught in naming *Psycho* the popularization of psychoanalysis such that a whole world of reference could be summed up in a jaunty abbreviation.

In one psycho discourse, female sexuality is always dependent on male sexuality, whether because it is seen purely in terms of a response to male sexuality or as an internalization of male desire, or else because it is seen as a kind of experience that can only be had in heterosexual intercourse. The first of these male-oriented views of female sexuality takes us back to desirability and to the idea of sexual "readiness"; the second leads to notions of narcissism, while the third raises the question of the nature of female orgasm.

Desirability means what makes a woman attractive to a man; but in psycho discourse it is also a source of pleasure and satisfaction for the woman herself. It is the concomitant of the playboy drive-reduction model of male sexuality, a model deriving from one version of psycho-analytical thought. Marynia Farnham and Ferdinand Lundberg in their influential tract, *Modern Woman: the Lost Sex,* published in 1947, remark that the "traits necessary to the attainment of sexual pleasure" in women include "receptivity and passiveness, a willingness to accept dependence without fear or resentment, with a deep inwardness and readiness. . . ."[23] Part of the pleasure psychoanalysts such as Helene Deutsch and Marie Bonaparte saw in female sexuality was in "surrender" to the male "as testimony to the women's own desirability."[24] We have already seen how much Monroe's image came to be understood in terms of her offering herself, her making herself ready.

Being found pleasing is part and parcel of the way that women, not men, are constructed as "the beautiful sex."[25] Since women were the beautiful ones, there was a kind of logic in representing female desire as being turned on not by men, but by their own bodies, as narcissism. From a psychological point of view, narcissism is both a normal aspect of female sexuality and an aberration or kink. This is characteristic of how psychology constructs the female—what makes her normal is also what makes her peculiar and therefore, implicitly, a problem or enigma for men.

There is a considerable emphasis on narcissism in Monroe's image. She is often shown caressing herself. One of the most reproduced stills from any of her films is a shot that lasts only a few seconds in the film itself, *How to Marry a Millionaire,* but it catches the idea of her narcissism in both the pose, her hand touching her shoulder, her cheek touching her arm, and in the multiple mirrors, offering her an orgy of delight in her own reflection. Magazine stories were fond of playing up this angle too,

> When she's alone, she often strikes art poses before a full-length mirror, admiring the beautifully distributed 118 lbs. that millions of moviegoers admire.[26]

Readiness and narcissism both work aspects of male sexuality into female sexuality; but there was also a discourse on female sexuality that sought to establish it as something distinct and on its own. This is not the autonomous female sexuality to which the seventies women's movement has relaid claim, but rather a sexuality that is implicitly dependent on men but is also quite different from male sexuality.

Clinically, in psychotherapeutic theories and practices, this kind of sexuality centered on the notion of the vaginal orgasm. Kinsey's female report contributed to the growth of an emphasis on female sexual satisfaction, but in one crucial regard, his findings had little impact. His evidence pointed ineluctably to the clitoris as the organ of female sexual pleasure, but, as Regina Maxwell Morantz points out, this evidence was systematically ignored both in the intensive media coverage of the report and in the psychotherapeutic world of counseling. "The persistent influence of Freudian theory on definitions of female nature and the absence of an organized feminist movement in the early 1950s softened the impact of this most radical of Kinsey's findings."[27]

Psychoanalysis insisted that the clitoral orgasm was "immature," or even, in Helene Deutsch's words, "malicious"; and that only the vaginal orgasm was "real" and "truly satisfying." But what was this orgasm like? Since women were supposed to achieve it, but yet somehow had great difficulty in doing so, it had to be described so that they would know what they were after. How to describe it?

Orgasms, female or male, are not amenable to description, but this has not stopped writers and artists in the age of sexuality. A common method has been to conflate the inner experience of orgasm with outward aspects of it, but this has proved easier with male penile orgasm than with female vaginal orgasm. The experience of male orgasm can be identified with both the actions of the man in intercourse (his orgasm typically thrusts, beats, stabs, sears, grinds and so on) and with the visible sign of it in the ejaculation of semen (which, in pornographic movies, is *de rigueur* as proof that you have "really seen" an orgasm). But in the psycho discourse with women, there are neither actions nor visible products. As a result, the orgasmic vocabulary becomes vague, formless, mysterious. Inevitably, it is oceanic imagery that predominates in the popular literature. For instance, from *Return to Peyton Place* (1960),

> Like a sea's retaining wall she lay and allowed herself to be buffeted, and felt the tidal pull that, at the end, seemed to draw her soul out of her body.[28]

Characteristic of such descriptions is that although they operate with a notion of a specifically (vaginally) located experience, they evoke an experience that suffuses the whole body in a buffeting, dissolving, waterfalling ecstasy. Where the visible–visual analogue for the male experience is definitely in, and out of, the penis, for the female it is everywhere. The visual analogue of the vaginal orgasm is the female body itself.

It is this that I want to argue in relation to Monroe. The presentation of her body, broadly in line with other traditions in Western culture but not in line with that of previous screen sex goddesses, is the analogue of the conception of female sexual experience that is expressed in the psycho discourse as the vaginal orgasm.

The most suggestive term through which to approach this idea is one proposed by Mary Ellmann in her book *Thinking About Women*, namely, the concept of formlessness.

> The impression of women's formlessness underlies the familiar, and often most generous, acknowledgement of their superficial form. . . . The flesh of women (as Sade would put it) is less resistant and less muscular than that of men. Pinched, it bruises more easily. . . . Solid ground is masculine, the sea is feminine.[29]

Margaret Walters, in her study of *The Nude Male*, likewise points to a fundamental distinction throughout Western art between the male and female forms. She compares two Greek statues, of a man and a woman, both in a similar posture—yet the male nude suggests potency and an upward reaching movement, the female passivity, a shrinking downward. Even the physical textures of the bodies, exaggerated here by the different materials used, contrast: the male body is tautened, the anatomy outlined; the female body is slack, with a textured surface that blurs its outline.

There are two stages to my argument so far. If traditionally a woman's body (and a man's come to that) is held to be the analogue of her inner self, then in a period when the inner self and sexuality are identified, the female body signifies ideas of female sexuality. And if the conception of female sexuality dwells on its dissolving, oceanic nature, then the visual form it takes is, paradoxically, formlessness, slackness, blur. Yet before Monroe it was not quite the case that the sexuality signified by female stars' bodies was of this soft blurred, "vaginal" kind. It's not that women were not represented with soft bodies, they were; but as soon as the question of their sexuality was implied, the imagery became tougher, harder, more "masculine," more "phallic." Supposedly male secondary sexual characteristics are emphasized—wide shoulders (Greta Garbo, Joan Crawford), deep voices (Marlene Dietrich), slim hips and flat chests (the flapper, such as Clara Bow) and a style that "hardens" them (Mae West's corseting, Jane Russell's brassieres and so on).

Monroe herself started out like that. The reinforced fabric of the one-piece bathing costume and the side-on tits and arse positionings in the early films do not create a blurred, formless look. But already the *Golden Dreams* calendar begins to move in that direction. Its tones are more soft and dissolving than the much more precise chiaroscuro of "art photography," its pose more rounded and langorous than their sharp, contorted positionings.

Nowhere is this more true than in her most characteristic facial expression, repeated in every film, endlessly reproduced, an expression that even in a still photograph suggests movement, and was well enough described by *Time* as "moist, half-closed eyes and moist, half-opened mouth." The repetition of "moist" hints at the obvious vaginal symbolism here, but that wetness isn't the only thing that suggests such symbolism. Monroe's mouth, open for a kiss, is never actually still, but is constantly quivering. Thus it forms not the neat round hole of Clara Bow's puckered lips, or the hard butterfly set of Jean Harlow's mouth, but a shape that never actually takes on a definite shape, that remains formless.

My argument is not that quivering lips must be vaginal symbols, but that they are of a piece with other formless aspects of her image that together can be read as the visual analogue for a basic conception of female sexuality as formlessness itself. But don't take my word for it, take Norman Mailer's. The language of Mailer's book on Monroe constantly evokes her in "vaginal" terms. Everything about her is soft, and she reaches her apotheosis, for him, in *The Misfits*, where his description could not corroborate more clearly what I have been arguing about sexuality and formlessness:

She is not sensual here but sensuous . . . she seems to possess *no clear outline* on screen. She is not so much a woman as a mood, a *cloud* of *drifting senses* in the form of Marilyn Monroe.[30]

Sexual Politics

I have been trying to read Monroe in the discourses current at the time she was a working star. To introduce, finally, the perspective of feminism and sexual politics more directly is to try to read her through a set of discourses from the past fifteen years or so. This is not centrally my concern. The question of the ways in which Monroe's image has been taken up and articulated in relation to changing patterns of ideas in the sixties, seventies, and into the eighties represents a whole different concern. Here I want to use feminist understanding to get at what, after all, is there to be read in the image, that not-yet-quite-articulated sense that all is not right with the position of women in contemporary capitalism, Betty Friedan's "problem that has no name," Brandon French's "verge of revolt."

The contemporary women's movement has seen Monroe, at worst, as the ultimate example of woman as victim and as sex object, and, at best, as in rebellion against her objectification. Susan Brownmiller, quoted above, gives us one of the clearest expressions of the former position; while Gloria Steinem's article "Marilyn—The Woman Who Died Too Young" in *Ms.* magazine, was one of the first statements of the latter position. Yet Steinem makes it clear that this is retrospective—"We are taking her seriously *at last*" (my italics)—and Molly Haskell makes the point directly,

Women . . . have become contrite over their previous hostility to Monroe, canonizing her as a martyr to male chauvinism, which in most ways she was. But at the time, women couldn't identify with her and didn't support her.[31]

I haven't done an audience survey, but I have presented this material to many groups of women who remembered Monroe as a star when she was alive, and by far the majority have confirmed what Haskell says. This is not to say that Monroe was never a figure of identification or sympathy for women; but it is to say, at the least, that the terms in which she may have been that, and the terms in which her image articulates the question of being a sex object, were *not* the terms of objectification, desire, and so on that have become familiar during the seventies. She is caught rather in what it was possible to say in the discourses of the fifties. The most we can say is that her image did at certain points crack open these discourses, but there was nothing to draw on to construct the kind of elaborated discourse on woman as sexual spectacle that feminism has since given us.

Two widely printed quotations may illustrate this. At first glance, they seem to come very close to the feminist woman-as-sex-object critique. In her first press interview after her break with Hollywood, she is quoted as saying

> I formed my own corporation so I can play the better kind of roles I want to play. I didn't like a lot of my pictures. I'm tired of sex roles. I don't want to play sex roles any more.[32]

and in her last interview, for *Life,* she said, "That's the trouble, a sex symbol becomes a thing—I just hate to be a thing."

It's possible to pick out quotations like this and make it seem that Monroe was articulating a prescient seventies feminist position—the alienation (thingness) of being treated relentlessly in terms of sex. But the context confuses this reading, or rather, it suggests how necessarily confused any such articulation is. In the case of the first quotation, Monroe's appearance at the press conference seemed to undercut what she was saying. Here is Maurice Zolotow's description, characteristically prurient, but also indicating how much Monroe's declarations were compromised by her apparent self-presentation:

> the "New Marilyn," when she arrived, didn't look as if she were a candidate for a convent or even for the role of one of Chekhov's sisters. She swished into the salon in a tight white satin gown which revealed forty per cent of her bosom, she was made up to the nines—hair in a new shade of "subdued" platinum and lips carmined to extravagance.[33]

Such self-objectification accompanying objections to being objectified was generally read in favor of the former, with the latter ridiculed in line with her dumb blonde image.

However, what does happen in some of the later films is that the effect of Monroe in them is to hint at the struggle, traps, and conundrums of living the fifties discourses of sexuality.

Bus Stop is probably the most extended example of this. It offers a space in which it is possible, without straining too much against the drift of the film, to read Cherie/Monroe not just as the object of male desire, but as someone who has to live with being a sex object. In the early part, the film offers something like a critique of sexual objectification in some of the dialogue and in Monroe's performance at certain points.

Cherie/Monroe's longest dialogue comes in scenes with other women characters, and it has thereby the quality of unburdening herself rather than of putting on an act or standing up to men. With the waitress, Vera (Eileen Heckart), she expresses her ambition to be a singer and a Hollywood actress, and this involves her in referring to the lack of respect she has had up to now. With the young woman on the bus, Elma (Hope Lange), she speaks of the ideal man she is looking for, and she formulates something like a notion of a man who combines both traditionally masculine and feminine qualities:

> I want a guy I can look up to and admire—but I don't want him to brow beat me.
> I want a guy who's sweet to me, but I don't want him to baby me.
> I want a guy who has some real regard for me, aside from all that loving stuff.

(It is immaterial who wrote these lines, what is significant is Monroe speaking them in a vehicle so much identified with her.) None of this is desperately radical or progressive; the ambition is mainstream individualism ("I'm trying to be somebody"), the ideal man is a sentimental fantasy. But both are given as the consciousness of a dumb showgirl type, and these sentiments are given a legitimate voice by the seriousness of the performance, by the way in which they are filmed, and especially by virtue of the fact that they are spoken to another woman. The ambition and the fantasy are not in the slightest ridiculed, and they have the effect of throwing into relief the showgirl role that Cherie/Monroe is playing.

This throwing into relief also works in aspects of her performance, notably those surrounding the "Old Black Magic" number. The choice of this song is appropriate anyway—Beau has been set up as looking for an "angel" and when he enters the saloon and sees Cherie for the first time, he lets out, "look at her gleaming there, so pale and white." She is his luminous angel—but the song is "That Old Black Magic," suggesting the opposite of angelic. As the number proceeds, we see how she is producing her image. She kicks light switches to change the color of the light in relation to the words of the song; and in close-ups we see her putting on an act, adopting an excessive classical posture for "I should stay away, but what can I do?" and exaggerated hand-to-mouth kissing gestures for "kiss, kiss, kiss." Before the first of these, she winks at Beau and smiles in a giggly way, implying a collusion with him in putting on this act.

Yet we must set all of this dialogue and this performance against a lot else that is happening in the film, and happening more insistently as it goes on. Cherie/Monroe is the butt of three sight gags that we are clearly meant to find funny, though they humiliate her and endorse male supremacy. The first occurs at the rodeo, when a journalist and photographer from *Life* come to take her picture (because Beau, from the arena, has just announced their marriage). She bends over to pick up her lipstick from her bag and the photographer snaps a picture of her backside, and leaves. "But I didn't have my lipstick on yet," she wails. At one level, this could be read as Cherie/Monroe wishing to be a glamorous object, but not quite in the dehumanizing terms of the photographer; but equally, the gag (especially the line) only works as a gag if we collude with the photographer, with the assumption that of course we'd rather see her backside than her face and only a dumb broad wouldn't see that. Later, in the saloon, when Cherie tries to get away from Beau, he graps her costume and its tail comes off in his hands—"Give me back my tail," she screams. Again, this could be mocking the absurd accoutrements of the showgirl, but the line, because she refers to it as "my tail," mocks her. The third gag (already discussed above) occurs at the bus station, where Beau lassoes her as she is trying to get on a bus to escape him. We are invited to laugh at least despite this gross humiliation, and probably at it.

Elements of dialogue and performance seem to open the showgirl image up for scrutiny, while the gags (and the ultimate working out of the story) invite us to laugh at her (and to endorse her final capture). The film shifts confusedly between one approach (crypto-feminist) and another (male chauvinist), and reveals thereby the sense in which, and the limits to which, the later Monroe image was opening up a discourse that the resurgent women's movement would finally fully articulate.

As to why Monroe should still have such a hold on popular culture, this question is outside of my concerns here. Yet it is at any rate in part related to what she meant in the fifties in the terms I have tried to suggest. She can be taken now as a talisman of what we are rejecting, of the price people had to pay for living in the regime of sexual discourses of the fifties. She flatters our sense of being so advanced. But perhaps too we are not so far from the fifties as we might like to think—fifties notions of natural sexuality, of repression, of the ineffability of female sexuality, of sexuality as the key to human happiness and truth, these are not notions we have left behind. As long as sexuality goes on being privileged in quite the way it is, Monroe will be an affirmation of that principle, even while also being a witness to the price we pay for it.

Notes

1. Betty Friedan, *The Feminine Mystique* (New York: W. W. Norton, 1963), p. 226.

2. Ibid., p. 289.

3. Brandon French, *On the Verge of Revolt* (New York: Frederick Ungar, 1978), p. xxii.

4. See Paul Delbert Brinkmann, "Dr. Alfred C. Kinsey and the Press," unpublished Ph.D. diss., University of Indiana, 1971.

5. Molly Haskell, *From Reverence to Rape* (New York: Holt, Rinehart and Winston, 1974), p. 25.

6. Compare the discussion of Twentieth Century Fox's conscious promotion of Monroe as "the ideal playmate" in Thomas B. Harris, "The Building of Popular Images: Grace Kelly and Marilyn Monroe," *Studies in Public Communication*, 1, 1957.

7. Thomas B. Hess, "Pinup and Icon" in Thomas B. Hess and Linda Nochlin, eds., *Woman as Sex Object* (New York: *Newsweek*, 1972).

8. Quoted in Maurice Zolotow, *Marilyn Monroe, An Uncensored Biography* (London: W. H. Allen, 1961), p. 105.

9. *Time*, 11 August 1952.

10. Michel Foucault, *The History of Sexuality* (New York: Vintage Books, 1980), p. 8.

11. John Gagnon and John Simon, *Sexual Conduct* (London: Hutchinson, 1974), p. 11.

12. Reprinted without date in *Playboy* (January 1976), p. 33.

13. For a summary of arguments against such a view, see Jeffrey Weeks, *Sex, Politics and Society* (London and New York: Longman, 1981), chapter 1.

14. Quoted in Martha Saxton, *Jayne Mansfield and the American Fifties* (Boston: Houghton Mifflin, 1975), p. 50.

15. Diana Trilling, "The Death of Marilyn Monroe," *Claremont Essays* (New York: Harcourt Brace Jovanovich, 1963), p. 236.

16. Op. cit., pp. 6–7.

17. *Playboy* (January 1976), p. 68.

18. Hollis Alpert, "Sexual Behavior in the American Movie," *Saturday Review*, no. 39 (23 June 1956), p. 38.

19. Quoted in Douglas T. Miller and Mary Nowak, *The Fifties, the Way We Really Were* (Garden City, N. Y.: Doubleday, 1977), pp. 157–58.

20. Norman Mailer, *Marilyn* (London) Hodder and Stoughton, 1973, p. 15.

21. Susan Brownmiller, *Against Our Will* (London: Secker and Warburg, 1975), p. 333.

22. Ibid., p. 335.

23. Marynia Farnham and Ferdinand Lundberg, *Modern Woman, the Lost Sex* (New York: Harper and Brothers, 1947), p. 142.

24. Quoted in Mary P. Ryan, *Womanhood in America* (New York: Franklin Watts, 1975), p. 283.

25. Cf. Una Stannard, "The Mask of Beauty" in Vivian Gornick and Barbara K. Moran, eds., *Woman in Sexist Society* (New York: Basic Books, 1971), pp. 187–205.

26. *Time,* op. cit.

27. Regina Maxwell Morantz, "The Scientist as Sex Crusader, Alfred C. Kinsey and American Culture," *American Quarterly,* 29, no. 5 (1977), p. 574.

28. Grace Metallious, *Return to Peyton Place* (New York: Frederick Muller, 1960), p. 183.

29. Mary Ellmann, *Thinking about Women* (New York: Harcourt Brace Jovanovich, 1970), p. 74.

30. Op. cit., p. 193. All emphasis save first added.

31. Op. cit., p. 254.

32. Op. cit., p. 191.

33. Ibid.

5

Sunset Boulevard: Fading Stars

LUCY FISCHER
University of Pittsburgh

> What happens to old movie stars,
> those faded queens of stage and screen?
> They move into hotels off Times Square maybe
> where they live among their souvenirs,
> near the lights, the people, the premieres
> that no longer know them—
> funny old ladies with hair a pink frizz
> salvaging old costumes for street clothes.
>
> —Edward Field

Over the past decade, with the advent of feminist film criticism, there has been a great deal written about the representation of women in the Hollywood cinema. A book on *film noir,* for example, analyzes the role of the forties *femme fatale* in works like *The Blue Gardenia* (1953),

Double Indemnity (1944), *Gilda* (1946) and *The Lady From Shanghai* (1947)[1]. Taking a broader perspective, Marjorie Rosen's *Popcorn Venus* and Molly Haskell's *From Reverence to Rape* examine Hollywood's stereotypes against the backdrop of American cultural history.[2] In recent years, criticism has taken a decidedly more psychoanalytic thrust. Laura Mulvey invokes the syndrome of fetishism in describing the male-oriented screen portrayal of women in the classical Hollywood narrative.[3] And Mary Ann Doane alludes to the psychology of masochism in explaining the female spectator's fascination with the American "woman's picture."[4]

But perhaps one of the most fruitful and neglected avenues for examining the position of women in the Hollywood cinema is by investigating the manner in which that institution depicts itself. In this regard it is useful to explore that subgenre of Hollywood melodrama that concerns the screen actress: works like *The Star* (1952), *The Goddess* (1958) and, most especially, *Sunset Boulevard* (1950).

But why is this genre so rich for a study of the representation of women in American film? First of all, because of its subject matter, it obviously focuses at the narrative level on the concrete issue of women in motion pictures. Thus, these films present a look at what life is like for female movie stars both on the screen and behind the scenes. Even more importantly, these films are interesting because the figure of the actress has come to be viewed by men as the quintessential woman, the paradigmatic female role. Molly Haskell comments on this issue by stating:

> The actress—whether as literal thespian . . . or as a symbol for the role-playing woman—is a key female figure throughout film history. . . . In one sense the actress merely extends the role-playing dimension of woman, emphasizing what she already is.[5]

In this way, the actress is seen by men to constitute a kind of metaphor for woman, since there is a perfect "match" between her perceived qualities and patriarchal attitudes toward the second sex. In her cinematic incarnation she is, then, both the archetypal woman and the exemplary woman in film.

There is yet a further level at which the subgenre of melodrama is intriguing, and it has to do with its dimension of self-reflexivity. When such films are made, a real actress must take the fictional star's role, thus superimposing the career of an actual performer over the dramatic text.

Given these various layers of meaning, the actress film accumulates

Sunset Boulevard, Paramount Pictures Corporation
Courtesy of Museum of Modern Art/Film Stills Archive

a resonant multiplicity of references to the broad topic of women in the cinema. But how, specifically, are these issues articulated in a film like *Sunset Boulevard*—the indisputable classic of the genre and a work that has been recently imitated by Rainer Werner Fassbinder in *Veronika Voss* (1982)? The answer to that question can be approached through a brief plot summary.

The film opens as a young, down-and-out Hollywood screenwriter named Joe Gillis (William Holden) is being pursued on the highway by some men trying to repossess his car. On an impulse, he veers into the driveway of an old Hollywood mansion in an attempt to dodge his creditors. There he encounters the residents of the estate: Norma Desmond (Gloria Swanson), a former silent screen acress, and her butler, Max (Erich von Stroheim). Mistaking Gillis for an expected guest, they usher him into the drawing room, and he and Miss Desmond begin to talk. She reveals that she has been working on a screenplay for a film called *Salome,* which she intends to submit to Cecil B. DeMille, and she confesses that she needs some editorial help to complete the script. Though Gillis knows the project is futile and her hopes delusional, he wangles himself the job, greedy for a regular salary. Miss Desmond insists that he move into the house with her, since she will not let the manuscript out of her sight. During the course of their work together, she falls in love with Gillis, and he gradually assumes the role of her gigolo. When he becomes infatuated with a young woman, Miss Desmond turns violent and suicidal. One night, in a crime of passion, she shoots him, and the police find his body adrift in her seedy pool.

There are several striking aspects to the narrative of *Sunset Boulevard.* First of all, we notice that the female star is portrayed as a particularly vicious character, a literal *femme fatale.* Furthermore, the story line is noteworthy for its emphasis on an aging actress—a movie queen over the veritable hill. *Sunset Boulevard,* in fact, shares this obsession with almost all backstage melodramas, which, similarly, focus on the female performer past her prime. Thus, in a film like *Dangerous* (1935) Bette Davis plays a declining stage star who attempts to kill her husband, and later, in *All About Eve* (1950), she takes the role of a Broadway actress jealous of an up-and-coming ingenue. Likewise, in *Torch Song* (1953) Joan Crawford plays a shrewish, middle-aged theater woman who has regrets about her loveless life, and in *The Roman Spring of Mrs. Stone* (1961) Vivien Leigh is cast as a pathetic mature actress who is prey to the machinations of a young Italian womanizer. But why, we might ask, this apparent fascination with the malevolent older female star?

The answer to that question would seem to reside in the fact that the figure of the aging actress tends to "violate" certain cherished cultural myths concerning both Hollywood and woman. As Edgar Morin points out in *The Stars,* onscreen we desire our performers to remain forever beautiful and beyond the ravages of time. Although this rule applies to both actors and actresses, it is enforced far more prescriptively in the latter case, because of general patriarchal attitudes toward feminine beauty. As Morin writes:

> In the American cinema before 1940 the average age of female stars was 20–25; their career was shorter than that of male stars, who may ripen, if not age, in order to attain an ideal seductive status.[6]

Consequently, the middle years for a screen actress are "fragile, always threatened, always ephemeral." And, ultimately, "the queen-for-perhaps-a-day fears waking."[7] *Sunset Boulevard,* then, is a film about such a movie princess, whose decades of somnambulatory existence are disturbed by the appearance of a Prince-Not-So-Charming.

How does *Sunset Boulevard* articulate its message concerning woman and her relation to the cinematic medium? Perhaps the first clue to the film's attitude comes from its rather bizarre mode of narration. Although the story line is rendered in a flashback that begins after the writer's murder, it is he who narrates the film—posthumously, as it were—from beyond the grave. It would seem that this paradoxical break with realism serves only one function—to insure that the text is mediated by a man. The narrative voice is entirely denied to Norma Desmond, who remains (in a typically feminine posture) a "silent" movie star.

Within the narrative, told from the writer's point of view, we get a decidedly masculine vision of Norma Desmond. This is hardly surprising, since, as feminist theorist Claire Johnston points out: "within a sexist society . . . woman is presented as what she represents for man."[8] In this respect, Norma Desmond is handled by the film's director, Billy Wilder, in a manner consonant with other filmmakers' treatments of the female actress. As Molly Haskell has noted, she constitutes "not just the symbol of woman, but the repository of certain repellent qualities which [the male director] would like to disavow."[9]

But how is such a patriarchal viewpoint manifest in Joe Gillis's response to Norma Desmond? In *The Second Sex* and *The Coming of Age,* Simone de Beauvoir formulates the concept of the "other" to characterize the male attitude toward the female, as well as the youthful response toward age.[10] She talks, for example, of how men view females as their opposite: "In woman is incarnated in positive form the lack that the existent carries in his heart."[11] Man's attitude toward this other is marked by deep ambivalence: although he worships woman for her unique and positive qualities, he dreads her for her difference. Similarly, in discussing youth's view of aging, de Beauvoir calls it "the Other within us"—thus emphasizing our estrangement from the experience of growing old.[12]

Both of these senses of otherness inform Joe Gillis's reaction to Norma Desmond. She is the quintessential alien, both in terms of her sex and of her advanced maturity. Thus the view of her presented is hardly sympathetic; rather it is marked by distance, loathing, and fear.

The particularities of Gillis's response are worthy of analysis because of what they disclose about social attitudes toward aging women. He initially sees Norma as some strange "antique," some anachronistic "curio" that has outlived its proper epoch and use. This posture is revealed in his characterization of her house as a "big white elephant of a place," and in his amazement at her vintage 1932 car, with its leopard-skin upholstery. He is similarly disdainful of her baroque bedroom, with its "satin and ruffles and . . . bed like a gilded rose." He finds it eccentric that she still watches silent films, and callously refers to her old movie friends as "the waxworks."

It is clear, of course, within the terms of the film, that Norma Desmond is mentally unbalanced and that she has hermetically sealed herself into a closed nostalgic domain. But that fact does not entirely explain Gillis's contempt. For while older men may be venerated as sagacious patriarchs, the keepers of important traditions, older women are thought simply to be obsolete—past their biological and social prime.

Further attitudes toward aging women are revealed in Gillis's response to Norma Desmond's house, which is alternately described as "rundown," or "neglected." Gillis points out its "ghost of a tennis court with faded markings and a sagging net." It is clear from these descriptions that a horror of bodily decay lies at the root of Joe Gillis's attitude toward the mansion—a fact that emerges when he refers to the place as "crumbling apart in slow motion." Thus the aging process is viewed as somehow repulsive, to be shunted away.

It is apparent, however, within the context of the film, that Norma Desmond's house is, indeed, more than a home. Rather, it functions as an extension of the woman herself. This identification of Norma and the mansion comes out clearly in one scene, when Gillis compares it to a character in *Great Expectations*. He says: "[the house] was like that old woman. . . . Miss Havisham in her rotting wedding dress and torn veil, taking it out on the world cause she'd been given the go-bye."

In Gillis's statement, we sense the particular revulsion he feels when bodily deterioration is enacted on the female. From the male point of view, woman's essence is defined as the "Eternal Feminine," a concept that is incompatible with age. Thus it is with extreme repugnance that Joe Gillis views the aging of this movie queen—this glamor girl devoid of her youthful sexual allure. She is not, like Max, merely an eccentric old person, mired in a past era. Rather she is an object of special horror, an affront to the male conception of the female.

This sense of disgust is communicated in various ways. During his initial meeting with Norma, when he plows through her screenplay, he says he becomes "sick to his stomach" at her "script and sweet champagne." Later, as they watch movies together in her screening room, he talks of how she would draw close to him, squeezing his hand in excitement. "She'd smell of tube roses," he remarks "which is not my favorite scent by a long shot." Opposed to Norma is his young girl friend, Betty, who smells like "freshly laundered handkerchiefs" and a "new automobile."

When he does not find Norma sexually repellent, Joe finds her ridiculous—particularly on the night of her New Year's Eve party, which she has arranged solely for him. As she romances him, she perceives his condescension and queries: "Do you think this is funny?" Again, Gillis's attitude conforms to a stereotypical view of the older woman—that of the ludicrous "bawd," or the "shameless old lady."

But aside from this particular stereotype, there is another more pernicious image that underlies Gillis's conception of the aging Norma Desmond—that of the vampire.[13] This theme comes out early in the film when Gillis first approaches the house. Norma is seen, initially, quite indirectly, as a mysterious silhouette behind a slatted shade or screen. As he enters the house she exists as an offscreen voice—ordering Max to ready a coffin for the burial of her pet chimpanzee. When she is finally glimpsed, she is dressed in black, lurking in a dark shadow, exuding an ominous presence.

Upon reflection, this scenario has a familiar aura to it and a haunting sense of *déja vu*. For it is a variation on the classic horror story of the innocent approaching the vampire's castle. Norma Desmond is like Dracula or Nosferatu, waiting to ensnare her next unsuspecting victim. Hence our suspicion when Norma suggests that Joe move in to the mansion with her, and our terror when we learn that Max has made up the bedroom for him before he has agreed to stay. With the wind blowing through the organ pipes, Joe's reference to the place as a "grim Sunset castle" seems most apt.

This sense of Norma as a vampire is also advanced in her visual presentation. She wears dark glasses, as though to protect her eyes from the dangerous rays of sunlight, and she smokes cigarettes from a sinister wire holder, perched on her gnarled finger. Norma's ghoulish quality is also apparent in the sequences of her watching old movies, as the projector light illuminates her face in a fiendish manner. There is even a way in which she seems vampiristic toward her own self-image. For as she watches the silent films, she seems almost to "feed" on her youthful persona.

This horrific portrayal of Norma is also accomplished by an emphasis on her old age. For vampires are, typically, ancient creatures, unable to die—destined to be, forever, "undead." No better word can characterize the position of Norma Desmond, who is technically alive, yet mired in a state of suspended animation. This monstrous view of

Norma Desmond is encapsulated in the final shot of the film, when, in a state of shock following the murder of Joe, she sinuously approaches the newsreel cameras, thinking herself on the set of a Hollywood picture. For here, her presence is no longer mediated through the eyes of Joe Gillis; here she makes a direct and threatening advance on the audience.

Although this perverse portrayal of Norma Desmond in *Sunset Boulevard* is informed by general attitudes toward aging, it is clear that her special status as a maturing woman is central to an understanding of the film. It is this that makes her eccentricity more offensive than that of Max, and this that makes her presence more repugnant than the male members of the "waxworks." As Molly Haskell has written:

> There's nothing reprehensible in showing an older woman in love with a younger man and growing old ungracefully. Women do it all the time. But so do men! Yet where are the male grotesques.[14]

Clearly, this emphasis on female excess, in *Sunset Boulevard,* foregrounds the problem of aging women in our culture. We have already mentioned Edgar Morin's view that the screen actress has more to lose with maturity than does the leading man. He writes:

> Gary Cooper, Clark Gable, and Errol Flynn, approaching their sixties, are not old, but real men. Their wrinkles come from interesting experiences, not dilapidation. These rough trappers of movie space are more virile than ever.[15]

Obviously, the female star can look forward to no such eloquent denouement. But, then, as de Beauvoir makes clear, neither can the average woman. As she notes:

> Whereas man grows old gradually, woman is suddenly deprived of her femininity: she is still relatively young when she loses the erotic attractiveness and the fertility which, in the view of society and in her own, provide the justification of her existence and her opportunity for happiness. With no future, she still has about one half of her adult life to live.[16]

Because of this prevalent attitude, the process of aging is more psychologically painful to women, who, as de Beauvoir so aptly puts it, are "haunted by the horror of growing old."[17] But if women are "haunted" by the prospect of aging, it is clear that they "haunt" men, whose imaginations turn them into figures as grotesque as Norma Desmond.

De Beauvoir's discussion of women and aging also provides a broader framework in which to understand Morin's observations concerning the screen actress. For de Beauvoir sees the movie queen as a descendant of the prostitute or *hetaira* class: "women who treat not only their bodies but their entire personalities as capital to be exploited."[18] As the ultimate female sex object, the *hetaira* experiences the coming of age as most painful and devastating.

> The *hetaira* depends strictly on her body, which suffers pitiless depreciation with time; for her the struggle against growing old assumes its most dramatic form . . . maintaining the renown that is her most dependable property puts her under the worst of tyrannies: that of public opinion. The subjection of Hollywood stars is well known.[19]

Clearly, Norma Desmond is a woman within the *hetaira* class. In her youth, she was a glamor queen, a movie goddess, who came to depend on male adoration. Max tells us how fans fought for a lock of her hair, and even now he must preserve her illusions by writing her phony fan letters.

As de Beauvoir has noted, the *hetaira*'s role is quintessentially a theatrical one. Her "whole life . . . is a show . . . intended to produce an effect . . . with public opinion."[20] Thus, it is fitting that when Norma Desmond fears Joe's attentions are slipping, she puts on a skit for him: the "Norma Desmond Follies." But her need to be a showgirl, both in her personal and professional life, makes the aging process a special threat.

Throughout the film we see Norma enact the "struggle" against aging that de Beauvoir describes. When she fancies that she is on the verge of a Hollywood comeback, she enlists the aid of an army of beauty experts. As Joe Gillis remarks: "She went through a merciless series of treatments like an athlete training for an Olympic game." Images of Norma appear on the screen: sweating in steam baths, getting massages, having facials. Morin speaks of this Hollywood obsession with taxidermy as well in discussing make-up departments, which "[devote] themselves to rejuvenation with increasing skill . . . suppress [ing] wrinkles and restor [ing] the complexion to its springtime freshness." Yet, he remarks: "a day will come when the wrinkles and puffiness corrected by ceaseless combat will be ineffaceable. The star will join her last battle, after which she must resign herself to giving up being in love, i.e., being young and beautiful, i.e., being a star."[21]

It is at precisely this moment that we encounter Norma Desmond, and it is clearly no surprise to us that she finds Joe Gillis's indifference to her most unnerving. She needs to feel that she can still attract a man, and when this fantasy fails, there remain but two options: suicide or murder.

The final shot of the "beauty sequence" reveals yet another issue in the psychology of the star/*hetaira:* narcissism. For it depicts Norma in a close-up, as seen through the lens of a magnifying glass. Clearly, if one's worth is invested in allure and surface beauty, it is one's image that will be valued and its preservation that will become a lifelong task. Although the cultural emphasis on female appearance tends to impose on all women a narcissistic frame of mind, the pressure is particularly acute for the screen actress, who lives under the harsh scrutiny of the camera eye.

This aura of vanity surrounds the characterization of Norma Desmond. She experiences a quasi-erotic frenzy watching her own silent films, her "celluloid self," as Joe Gillis terms it. And she lives in a mansion that also functions as a photographic archive of her cinematic presence. Joe Gillis asks: "How could she breathe in that house so crowded with Norma Desmond, and more Norma Desmond—and still more Norma Desmond?" Furthering this theme, throughout the film we are shown sequences of Norma gazing in the mirror: when she makes up in the car for her visit to Paramount, when she peels off her cosmetic facial mask before begging Joe to stay, when she sits in her boudoir after the murder, contemplating her image mesmerically, as the police give her the third degree.

Because Norma Desmond represents the typical woman in our culture—Woman, as it were, writ large—she also experiences the most ruinous sense of dislocation when her surface appearance changes through the maturation process. Since her life has been invested in the cult of image, it is she who suffers most when her looks are cruelly transformed. Once more, de Beauvoir is most articulate in describing this phenomenon:

> One of the outstanding traits of the aging woman is a feeling of depersonalization that makes her lose all objective bearings. . . . This cannot be *I,* this old woman reflected in the mirror! The woman who "never felt so young in her life" and who has never seen herself so old does not succeed in reconciling those two aspects of herself . . . *her double no longer resembles her.*[22]

Whereas all aging women experience this sense of "doubling," of a youthful image superimposed on their visage in age, it is clear that for the movie actress, the awareness would be more extreme. Although most of us possess photographs that remind us of our past appearance, the movie star has a motion-picture record of her glorious youth. Thus she would experience the disjunction of aging more acutely than would the average person. We perceive this trauma in the scenes of Norma Desmond watching her larger-than-life film image, animated on the screen. We share with her a poignant sense of "doubling," of being face-to-face with her youthful presence.

In a way, Norma Desmond confronts the opposite situation of a figure like Dorian Gray. While he is plagued by a portrait that ages mercilessly with the passing years, while he himself does not, she is haunted by a screen image that refuses to grow old, which perversely "embalms time," as André Bazin once noted.[23]

For most individuals, the process of synthesizing old and youthful selves is gradual, but for a movie star it is abrupt and brutal. This sense of the film actor's peculiarly vulnerable position can be understood in

Sunset Boulevard, Paramount Pictures Corporation
Courtesy of Museum of Modern Art/Film Stills Archive

terms of de Beauvoir's image of the shock of recognition at the aging process. She writes:

> If at the age of twenty we were taken to a mirror and shown the face that we should have . . . at sixty, comparing it with that of twenty, we should be utterly taken aback and it would frighten us.[24]

For Norma Desmond, the cinema is such a mirror, operating in reverse. As an elderly woman she must confront her youthful self, preserved or frozen in time—then liberated, as it were, from cryogenic storage, revitalized into a figure of apparent life.

There is yet another sense in which Norma's screen image reflects her youth and it has to do with certain issues raised by the psychoanalyst, Jacques Lacan. In much of his writing, Lacan speaks of the crucial "mirror stage" through which each person passes during infancy. As described by Sherry Turkle in *Psychoanalytic Politics,* it is at this time that

> the child comes to see its body, which is still uncoordinated and not fully under its control, as whole rather than fragmented by identifying with its mirror *image* in much the same way that it identifies with its mother's body and with the bodies of other children.[25]

Furthermore, Lacan believes "that all of these unmediated one-to-one identifications are *alienating.* The child is actually subordinated to its image, to its mother and to others."[26] It is through this process that "the subject constructs the alienated self which Lacan calls the *ego* or *moi.*"[27]

According to Lacan, however, the importance of the mirror stage extends well beyond the period of infancy. Rather, it becomes paradigmatic for how one views oneself throughout life. As he states, the mirror stage leads "to the assumption, finally, of the armour of an alienating identity which will stamp with the rigidity of its structure the whole of the subject's mental development."[28]

But what is the relevance of this theoretical insight to *Sunset Boulevard?* If we examine the position of Norma Desmond as she spends her aging years fused with her girlish movie image, it is not difficult to see her as perpetually reexperiencing the mirror stage, and to find parallels between her and Lacan's immobile infant. Both are involved in constituting a sense of self by identifying with an illusory external image, and both are alienated from their sense of self, which they experience as an other. While the infant has only begun this process—confronting a true mirror likeness—Norma Desmond has developed a more extreme dissociation, preferring her youthful image to her present self. Clearly she is "subordinated" to her screen persona, and, like the Lacanian infant, stands "jubilant" in the "assumption" of her specular image.[29] While the infant has only commenced to be distanced from its true identity, Norma has had a lifetime to experience the radical loss of self visited upon women in our culture.

Although we have examined how the character of Norma Desmond is tormented by her movie image, that youthful "doppelganger" who taunts her from the screen, there is another kind of "doubling" involved in the film that pertains to the real actress, Gloria Swanson. In his book on the star system, Edgar Morin talks of the female performer's bondage to her film persona. He writes:

> Like her admirers, the star is subjugated by this image superimposed upon her real self: like them, too, she wonders if she is really identical with her double on the screen. Devalued by her double, a phantom of a phantom, the star . . . can amuse herself only by imitating her double, by miming her movie life. . . . Thus the screen mythology extends itself behind the screen and beyond it.[30]

Elsewhere Morin speaks of how the "characters of [the actress's] film infect the star" and of how "reciprocally the star herself infects these characters."[31] It is just such a phenomenon of mutual contamination that Gloria Swanson experienced around the making of *Sunset Boulevard*.

The film was released in 1950, when Swanson was fifty-one years of age. Like Norma Desmond, she had once been a silent movie star, starting out in pictures with the Essanay Company of Chicago in the mid-teens. But the parallels with her screen persona run even deeper. Like Norma Desmond, she had been a Mack Sennett bathing beauty and had made several films with Cecil B. DeMille: *Male and Female* (1919), *Why Change Your Wife* (1919), *Don't Change Your Husband* (1919), *The Affairs of Anatol* (1921) and *Adam's Rib* (1923). While Norma Desmond only did an imitation of Charlie Chaplin, Swanson herself had worked with him in the early Essanay days. Like Norma Desmond, she had once been directed in films by "Max," or Erich von Stroheim. In fact, the clip that we see of "Norma Desmond" on the screen is actually Swanson in *Queen Kelly* (1928), a film that von Stroheim directed and that she herself produced.

Like the fictional actress, Swanson herself did not fare so well when the movies began to talk. Between 1928 and 1934 she made a series of less-than-monumental pictures: *Indiscreet* (1931), *Perfect Understanding* (1933) and *Music in the Air* (1934). By 1934, the Hollywood press regarded her as a "has-been" and spoke frequently of her executing a "come-back." As Swanson recollects in her recent memoirs, that was an

> . . . ominous [phrase] . . . for someone just turning thirty-six. . . . For the first time the real image and the created image seemed to be at war. On the one hand, I was a lucky American girl—who had succeeded admirably. . . . On the other hand, I was a legend—a sacred monster, in Jean Cocteau's phrase—a fading star the public had worshipped long enough.[32]

Unfortunately, the specter of a comeback would continue to bedevil Swanson into her later years. In 1941, after being out of pictures for nearly a decade, RKO offered her a role in *Father Takes a Wife*. As Swanson recalls, it was: "A comedown as well as a comeback," but she accepted the offer, which was $35,000 more than any other studio had offered her in seven years.[33] As Swanson admits, the film "was not quite in the marvelous category." So she pocketed the money and "returned to cinematic oblivion."[34] It was from this oblivion that she was called in 1950 to do *Sunset Boulevard*, a film about an actress in oblivion.

Beyond the parallels between Norma Desmond and Gloria Swanson, there are other self-referential aspects of the film. Made as a Paramount production, it enacts Norma's return to that very studio. Furthermore, the film casts Cecil B. DeMille playing himself, at a time when he was still successful in the industry. Consequently, he is shown on a set directing films. Erich von Stroheim, on the other hand, seems more demeaned in the role of Max, as though the part bespoke his failed career. Swanson recollects sadly how von Stroheim tried to supervise Billy Wilder's shooting of the film, harking back to his own directorial days. Similarly, Swanson knew all the members of the "waxworks" from her early Hollywood years: Anna Q. Nilsson, G. B. Warner and, of course, Buster Keaton. Thus the film surrounds Swanson not only with fictive characters, but with her real-life acquaintances. As she remarked, she had to use all her past experience for "props" in a film, that was "akin to analysis."[35]

The manner in which Paramount initially approached Swanson for a role in *Sunset Boulevard* is also worthy of examination. Like Norma Desmond, she began receiving mysterious phone calls from the studio at a time when she was completely out of circulation. Unlike Norma's calls, however, these turned out to be legitimate, and the studio asked her to fly out to do a screen test. She was somewhat miffed and humiliated by their audition request, but went out nonetheless, at-tracted by their offers of a healthy salary.

As it turns out, it was Montgomery Clift who had insisted on Swan-son's test at a time when he was being considered for the writer's role. Eventually, however, he backed out of the film, feeling it was not good for his career to play romantic scenes with an "older woman." When the studio gave the lead to William Holden, the opposite problem emerged. Holden, at thirty-one, was afraid that Swanson would look too *young* to be credible as his senior by twenty-five years. Aging make-up for Swanson was then considered. Fortunately, Swanson informed Billy Wilder that women of fifty frequently look quite good. She suggested instead that they make William Holden look younger—and leave her appearance alone.

Sunset Boulevard was, in many respects, a great triumph for Gloria Swanson. Having descended into the depths of Hollywood obscurity, she had returned to the screen in a role that won her an Academy Award nomination. But her euphoria was short-lived, as she realized the price she had to pay for her successful "come-back." She recalls the evening that the awards were announced, and her name was not among them:

> I honestly didn't care but I could see in the faces of everyone . . . that people wanted me to care. They expected scenes from me, wild sarcastic tantrums. They wanted Norma Desmond as if I had hooked up unsym-pathetically, disastrously with the role by playing it.[36]

For years after that, scripts arrived at her door containing imitations of *Sunset Boulevard*, "all featuring a deranged superstar crashing toward tragedy."[37] As she commented: "I could obviously [have gone] on playing [the part] . . . until at last I became some sort of creepy parody of myself, or rather of Norma Desmond—a shadow of a shadow."[38] As a fine middle-aged actress, it seemed there were no other roles for Swanson than a distorted version of herself.

Thus, in making *Sunset Boulevard*, Swanson experienced a bizarre melding of the real and the unreal, a "reciprocal infection" of art and life. Though the character she played was conceived as a reflection of Gloria Swanson, their roles were ultimately reversed. For by the end of *Sunset Boulevard*, Norma Desmond had not only achieved dominance over the writer, Joe Gillis, but over the actress, Gloria Swanson, as well. As Swanson puts it, she had become a mere "shadow of a shadow"—a specter of Norma Desmond, and of her own younger self.

If Hollywood had worshipped the actress, in youth, for her glamor and beauty, its only use for her in maturity was mercilessly to divest her of those very traits, conducting a prurient, onscreen "striptease" at the very site of her former triumph. For aging woman then—the situation has somewhat changed now—was viewed by man only as a figure of profound loss. And her sunset years stretched out as bleakly as the desolate Hollywood boulevard that presciently opens the film.

Notes

1. E. Ann Kaplan, ed. *Women in Film Noir* (London: British Film Institute, 1978).

2. Marjorie Rosen, *Popcorn Venus* (New York: Avon, 1973) and Molly Haskell, *From Reverence to Rape* (Baltimore, Md.: Penguin Books, 1974).

3. Laura Mulvey, "Visual Pleasure and Narrative Cinema," *Screen,* 16, 3 (Autumn 1975).

4. Mary Ann Doane, "The Woman's Film: Possession and Address." Unpublished paper.

5. Haskell, *Reverence,* 242.

6. Edgar Morin, *The Stars,* trans. Richard Howard (New York: Grove Press, 1960), 46–47.

7. Ibid., 67.

8. Claire Johnston, "Myths of Women in the Cinema," in *Women and the Cinema,* ed. Karyn Kay and Gerald Peary (New York: E. P. Dutton, 1977), 410.

9. Haskell, *Reverence,* 244.

10. Simone de Beauvoir, *The Second Sex,* trans. H. M. Parshley (New York: Random House, 1974) and *The Coming of Age,* trans. Patrick O'Brian (New York: Warner Books, 1970).

11. De Beauvoir, *Second Sex,* 160.

12. De Beauvoir, *Coming of Age,* 426.

13. Molly Haskell also used the image of the vampire to characterize Norma Desmond, *Reverence,* 246.

14. Ibid.

15. Morin, footnote on 47.

16. De Beauvoir, *Second Sex,* 640.

17. Ibid., 640–41.

18. Ibid., 631–32.

19. Ibid., 634.

20. Ibid., 636.

21. Morin, *The Stars,* 47.

22. De Beauvoir, *Second Sex,* 645.

23. Andre Bazin, "The Ontology of the Photographic Image," in *What Is Cinema?* trans. Hugh Gray (Berkeley and Los Angeles: University of California Press, 1967), 1: 14.

24. De Beauvoir, *Coming of Age,* 425.

25. Sherry Turkle, *Psychoanalytic Politics* (New York: Basic Books, 1978), 57.

26. Ibid.

27. Ibid., 58.

28. Jacques Lacan, "The Mirror Phase as Formative of the Function of the I," *New Left Review* (September 1968): 74.

29. Ibid., 72.

30. Morin, *The Stars*, 67.

31. Ibid., 37.

32. Gloria Swanson, *Swanson on Swanson* (New York: Random House, 1980), 444–45.

33. Ibid., 466.

34. Ibid., 467.

35. Ibid., 481.

36. Ibid., 488.

37. Ibid., 489.

38. Ibid., 259.

6

The "Woman's Film" Genre and One Modern Transmutation: *Kramer vs. Kramer*

ANCA VLASOPOLOS
Wayne State University

I

Despite its popularity at the box office and in the collective memory of filmgoers, the woman's film has been both neglected and abused as a genre. Perhaps the chief reason for that neglect and abuse is that the woman's film does not quite fit into either the auteur theory or the post-structuralist analyses that dominate current film criticism, whereas primarily male genres, such as the western, the detective film, the *film noir*, and the gangster film, do much more neatly. Moreover, famous directors, whose work attracts critics' notice, try

114

their hands at these male genres.[1] Few such directors direct woman's films, and when they do, they understandably object to being "tagged as a 'woman's director'";[2] these directors risk being overlooked by critics because, as Andrew Sarris explains, of "an inbred prejudice to what . . . has [been] called the genre of the female weepies."[3] Although generally derided as a tearjerker, the woman's film has throughout its history attracted major stars and has shown greater versatility than more prestigious genres; it has ranged from tragedy, *Dark Victory* (1939), (1963 as *The Stolen Hours*) (1976, the tv-movie version); through melodrama, *Madame X* (1929), (1937), (1966), (1982), all sound versions, the last a tv-movie version; to comedy, *Woman of the Year* (1942), (1976, as the tv-movie version).

The intellectual challenge of defining the woman's film as a genre resides in the very resistance of this genre to decontextualization. While some critics study these films as "texts," they tend to overlook them as "shows," and so they concurrently reach improbable conclusions about the spectators of these films.[4] Formalist, strictly semiotic, and psychoanalytic approaches might be ultimately defeated by this genre because of its special place as a subculture myth. Social history seems to provide the richest areas of investigation for understanding that myth. The woman's film, until recently, has been a female-star vehicle. A star, particularly in Hollywood, was a woman who kept or invented her name, no matter whether or how many times she married; a woman who earned vastly more money than the average male; a woman whose presence and charisma could command the type of adulation that allowed her (with some notable exceptions) to fly in the teeth of convention. In the woman's film, the star became the goddess, taking human form, and enduring the common female lot, while having at all times ready access to immortality. Did the women in the audience respond to this type of film because it captured their lives and their painful compromises, or did they say to themselves, "I too am a goddess in disguise with an unbreakable core of self that remains unaltered by mundane experience"? Does the iconography of the genre, e.g., Bette Davis's strong chin, uplifted in the close-up of the *Now, Voyager* finale (1942); Barbara Stanwyck's jaunty walk at the end of *Stella Dallas* (1937) manage to subvert the explicit message of the script ("Why reach for the moon when we have the stars")?[5] Or does that iconography generate the kind of ambivalence intrinsic to female heroines' quests, in which personal fulfillment comes to mean death, and life means settling for a great deal less than the stars?[6] Prompted by the thematic and structural elements of the genre, these questions show the need for continued study of the woman's film and for specific analyses of such contemporary transmutations of it as *Kramer vs. Kramer* (1979).

The principal feature of the woman's film is that it focuses on a female or on a number of female heroes. It covers a fairly extensive timespan; this characteristic tends to give the woman's film an epic, or, sometimes less gloriously, an episodic scope. Thus, many films trace the life of the female hero from late adolescence or early adulthood to old age—*The Old Maid* (1939), *Old Acquaintance* (1943), *To Each His Own* (1946), *Stella Dallas* (1937). The drama reveals a mythic dimension, which is the source of its power and tenacity as a genre, and which provides a filmic and worldly parallel to a kind of *Paradise Lost* and *Regained,* with woman squarely at the center. While few members of the audience can be expected to respond to such Miltonic allusions, the myth of temptation, fall, suffering, and redemption has immense resonances for members of a predominantly Christian culture. Eve transgresses by intruding into masculine territory, either by her behavior—polyandrous, sexually aggressive, sexually adventurous—or by her ambition for a career, for power, or for worldly goods that can be used to manipulate men rather than to nest. Eve falls and begins her suffering. Her travail appears as inner turmoil and/or (oftener and than or) societal censure. Eve is redeemed from the brink of catastrophe (often represented as divorce or single-woman loneliness) by reintegration into society, which follows her refeminization. Reintegration sometimes takes place only after the female hero's death, since death in many a woman's film is the only acceptable path to regained respectability.

Woman's films from the twenties through the forties have reflected the conflicts emerging in women's lives from the choices available with few exceptions to ordinary women only in the twentieth century. These choices ranged from the old-as-time pre- or extramarital fling— *Now, Voyager, The Letter* (1940), *Humoresque* (1946), *Nora Prentiss* (1947) to nontraditional careers, *Christopher Strong* (1932), *Woman of the Year, Mildred Pierce* (1945), to the downright revolutionary possibility of life without the protection or financial support of a father or husband. The birth scenes in *The Great Lie* (1941) and *To Each His Own* (1946) as well as the solitary death scene in *Dark Victory* (1939) suggest that the most profound transformations undergone by women can be achieved without men's assistance. Yet the film, like the nineteenth-century novel, remains a form of art that both subverts middle-class values and reinforces them; the hero defies established customs but is ultimately crushed by his/her society or absorbed into it.

Woman's films of the twenties, thirties, and forties faced, more bravely than other genres, the undeniable fact that women's roles were not so much changing, perhaps, as being challenged. They created memorable female heroes, embodied by Helen Morgan in *Applause* (1929); Bette Davis in *Jezebel* (1938), in *Dark Victory* (1939), in *A Stolen Life* (1946); Joan Crawford in *Mildred Pierce* (1945); Barbara Stanwyck in *Stella Dallas* (1945); Olivia de Havilland in *To Each His Own* (1946); in *The Heiress* (1949); Katharine Hepburn in *Christopher Strong* (1933) and in the remarkably feminist *A Woman Rebels* (1936), which failed at the box office and earned her the unmerited reputation of being box office poison.

However, the primarily male screenwriters, directors, and producers of these films made sure that the full weight of societal judgment would crush these independent spirits by having them come to a bad end, showing them to be unprincipled and sexually voracious, or denying them their children or their children's affections, until the women paid their dues in deep and prolonged suffering. Many of these female heroes died of mysterious illnesses or in grotesque accidents, *Dark Victory* (1939), *Beyond the Forest* (1949), committed suicide, *Humoresque* (1947), *Applause* (1929), *The Strange Love of Martha Ivers* (1946), exiled themselves physically or spiritually from society and especially from sex, *Jezebel* (1938), *Dangerous* (1935), *Stella Dallas* (1937), or were converted to dependence upon men or on men's view of women, *To Each His Own* (1946), *The Hard Way* (1942), *A Letter to Three Wives* (1949). These films retain their hold on modern audiences because the female heroes they present are exceptional women who challenge existing norms, and we have come to regard the necessity of their physical or spiritual destruction as extraneous to their characters, as merely part of the Hollywood formula. Those of us who are women, moreover, recognize in the inflexible formula the diehard traditions and attitudes that to a greater or lesser extent still constrict our lives. This awareness, rather than female sensibility, is the reason that our handkerchiefs are wetter at the end of these films.

Accounts of the decline of the woman's film in the fifties and sixties remain gender-determined: male critics either ignore the genre entirely or see its near-disappearance as a return to normality after the hardships of the Depression, from which presumably women needed cinematic escapes of their own, or after the anomalous war years, characterized by the absence of younger men and the emergence of women in the workforce.[7] Female critics have regarded the virtual death of the studio-produced woman's film as symptomatic of a backlash against women's rights, a reactionary attack that not only submerged the genre but destroyed the limited power of women in motion pictures by doing away with the star system.[8] Yet, although few woman's films were made during the two decades following the war, television, through its early morning, noon, and early afternoon movie programs, kept the genre alive, especially for housebound women. Consequently, when the seventies and early eighties revived the genre, audiences felt a shock of recognition rather than surprise. Little wonder that the recent woman's film, *Rich and Famous* (1981), a remake of *Old Acquaintance* (1943), was directed by a veteran women's director, George Cukor.

Relatively recent films, both American and foreign, have attempted to soften the blows dealt to "fallen" women, *An Unmarried Woman* (1978), *The Turning Point* (1977), *No Time for Breakfast* (1978), *Moscow Does Not Believe in Tears* (1979). Careers, such as the famous ballerina in *The Turning Point,* the renowned doctor in *No Time for Breakfast,* the top executive Katerina in *Moscow* seem to allow these women a full, if not an unrealistically large, share of a man's world. Yet, but for the unexceptional heroine Jill Clayburgh of *An Unmarried Woman,* who holds her own against the wind and the flopping gigantic canvas with which her painter-lover has burdened her, the others succumb to or are rescued in the nick of time from the same old chestnuts: single-woman despair, appearing in such various guises as child-envy and success-envy (neither the loosely married Shirley Mac-Laine nor the single Anne Bancroft character in *The Turning Point* is allowed the satisfaction of her choice); terminal illness, such as cancer in *No Time for Breakfast;* and helpless tearful breakdown at the loss of a lover, as in *Moscow,* in which the most stable and happy of the three women is the one who had no masculine ambitions and married young. The change in the genre toward more career-women as heroes and fewer fatal denouements probably came about because of changes in attitudes among the public of the late sixties and the seventies as to how women sin and how much they should suffer if they do, while the revival of the lovable but lethally punished adulterer (another cancer case) in *Terms of Endearment* (1984) signals the reactionary climate of the eighties.

II

Kramer vs. Kramer is a film that could have been made successfully in the forties and fifties with the wife in Dustin Hoffman's role. In retrospect, one can see *Kramer vs. Kramer* as the training ground for Hoffman as the implicit sex-role reversal that became explicit in *Toot-*

sie (1982). The film follows the generic pattern of a person (sex female in the forties) who is too involved with her career and is punished by being abandoned by her long-suffering husband. See Miriam Hopkins in *Old Acquaintance* and Bette Davis as sister Pat in *A Stolen Life* (1939). She can also be punished by having to undergo a process of refeminization; see Maureen O'Hara in *Miracle on 34th Street* (1947), Myrna Loy in *The Bachelor and the Bobbysoxer* (1947) or punished through the agency of a child, who is often in collusion with a man or a group of men, as in *Miracle* and *The Bachelor*. Despite the inability or unwillingness of modern filmmakers to break through the conventions of earlier woman's films, I strongly suspect that a film like *Kramer vs. Kramer* with a woman in Hoffman's role would have been unpalatable to contemporary audiences; the formula would have been seen as threadbare, the myth reduced to a cautionary tale about the career-and-family conflict, and the box office receipts would have suffered.

By showing the drama with a reversal of sex roles, *Kramer vs. Kramer* underwent a fascinating process of feminization from novel to film. Screenwriter and director Robert Benton left out many trivializing and even ugly details about Joanna and Ted, their in-laws, parents, ex-husbands, lovers, and prospective housekeepers. Some of these deletions naturally fall within the province necessitated by the economy of genre, but the excisions are so consistent with changes of emphasis from novel to film that we must credit Benton for creating far more interesting and sympathetic characters than those who populate Avery Corman's novel and thereby for enhancing the economics of film production. In the novel, Joanna and Ted marry because they are at loose ends and bored with single life. She is exceptionally pretty; he is a good provider and the only unmarried man in her life. His career is a string of uninterrupted successes, an aspect that initially makes him attractive to Joanna. He is let go only when the entire company founders and is shortly rehired by his old boss at a new company, which also dissolves, through no fault of Ted's. He is able to find another job within twenty-four hours, but in the novel, his motivation is the insecurity he feels about his male image as provider, not the desire to keep Billy. Joanna has a college degree, but she never rises above the position of executive secretary. Her new career, found after her separation, is "sort of a girl Friday" at a Racquet Club, where she gets some free court time as part of her fringe benefits.[9]

In the novel, Ted's parenting gets considerable help from a Mother-Earth figure in the shape of a middle-aged, plump Polish woman whom he hires as a housekeeper. His preoccupations with running the house and taking care of a young child at the same time that he is holding down a job are therefore relegated to a rather insignificant level. Similarly, the novel's Joanna has a mouthpiece, her lover, who offers her emotional support, as well as financial support perhaps, and who acts as mediator between her and Ted in the matter of Billy's custody. As a consequence of the traditionally confined sex roles to which Ted and Joanna subscribe in the novel, we see a great deal of bitterness and anger in Ted, and of deviousness and irresponsibility in Joanna. For instance, Joanna leaves Ted the task of telling not only his parents but her own about her desertion. Her return to New York and her contact with Ted are presented as having been orchestrated by a clever attorney who is working for Joanna's custody suit.

In his internal monologues as well as in his conversations with Joanna, Ted uses a generous amount of verbal violence against her, none of which is transferred to the screenplay. Ultimately, Ted's suffering is righteous, and his final triumph registers as the triumph of a man who has won a game, or, perhaps more appropriately, a war against the other sex. It is significant that Ted's selection of his lawyer comes about through a football friendship; Corman has the two men exchange comments about strategy through football metaphors. After Shaunnessy, the attorney, does his best to destroy Joanna's image on the stand, he says, "Motherhood is tough to score against. . . . But we drew blood" (222). As for Joanna, she is indeed the weaker sex; she does not even come to tell Ted or the boy that she is giving up custody. She deserts, once more, because she is not "together" and cannot handle the responsibilities.

In the film, the writer-director presents us with a definite case of sex-role reversal. All the additions and deletions that illuminate Ted's character as the traditionally feminine one belong to the film, not the novel. The most telling points about Joanna's character, which remains somewhat mysterious, are also made exclusively in the film, and they reveal traits that have traditionally been associated with masculinity: self-possession, the ability for long-range planning, steadfastness of purpose, career ambitions and success, good sportsmanship, and, most important in view of the ultimate failure of nerve of the typical female hero, courage. The novel's Joanna, like most female heroes, conceals her identity by denying her forsaken marriage and the existence of her child for a time, whereas the Joanna we see on screen, despite Meryl Streep's credible tears, is too forthright, too self-possessed for such subterfuges.

We see Joanna break down to the point where she makes personal revelations only at the end, and even then, the nature of her insight

concerns the child's environment and well-being rather than any il-
lumination of her own character. We, along with Ted, are told by
Margaret about Joanna's unhappiness and sense of frustration, but
what we see is a woman who knows precisely what she is doing. She is
putting a child to bed tenderly and unhesitatingly. She confronts Ted
and manages to elude his questions and his anger, even his short-lived
attempt to detain her forcibly, and, as she bids him good-bye, she
sounds like a person who has reflected deeply about a major decision
and has planned well for it: "I took two thousand dollars out of the
bank because that's what I came into the marriage with." In her next
scene, when she announces her intention of regaining custody, she
again acts according to a well-thought-out plan, a plan of her own
making, not that of a lawyer behind the scenes. Ted's anger and
sublimated violence do not scare her. She says she has anticipated and
prepared for his reactions, and she convinces us that she has, even if
she starts when he smashes his wine glass against the wall. Her first
meeting with Billy, instead of being a sentimental, tearful one, shows
her picking up this solid youngster of seven and rocking him in her
arms, more in the manner of a muscular father than of a fragile-
looking mother. Her courtroom appearance reflects the same self-
possession. Of the witnesses we see (Ted, Joanna, and Margaret), she
is the only one who does not provoke the judge into repeated gaveling
by straying from the questions or becoming hysterical. She tosses
aside such embarrassing questions as "Do you have a lover?" with an
ironic smile and with silence. Even the defense's hard-won admission
from Joanna that the longest relationship of her life is a failure makes
her drop silent tears and leaves her dignified. We see none of the
accusations and outbursts of emotion that mark Ted's behavior on the
stand.

As for her career and her ability to provide for Billy, she clearly has
Ted, and, by implication, many other men beat. She earns more than
$2,000 a year over Ted's income, and she does so after having been in
the job market for at most a couple of years. Her profession as a
designer of sportswear for a major company is a far cry from the
demeaning and irresponsible situation of the novel's Joanna.

Joanna exhibits the other virtue often associated with males: she is a
good sport, even a good loser. She refuses to play dirty, and, when
others do, she dissociates herself from them. She stays after a court
session to apologize to Ted about her lawyer's harassment of Ted
regarding the child's accident in the park. At the end, she braves both
Ted and the boy, then bows out of the female role as mother for good,

not because she cannot accept the responsibilities, but because she courageously accepts the unexpected bond her departure has created between Ted and the child.

Ted, by contrast, becomes more and more of an "honest" woman as the film unfolds. What makes *Kramer vs. Kramer* unique, to my knowledge, is its treatment of a male's moderate desire to succeed as the unpardonable sin of woman, namely, overreaching ambition. All we see Ted doing and all he is charged with is spending a great deal of time at his work, a type of behavior glorified in other films in which men excel because of their drive and their commitment to a given pursuit.[10] Generally, men's ambitions become sinful only when men use unscrupulous means for attaining their goals. Often, their growing ruthlessness is reflected in their rejection of domestic bliss, their choice of a "loose" woman over the childhood sweetheart next door, or their denial of their ethnic or socioeconomic origins.[11] In *Kramer vs. Kramer* Ted merely wants to provide a more comfortable living for his family by thinking up catchier ad campaigns and by maintaining his good standing in the boss's eyes by behaving like a good old boy.

However, for the first scene, we are invited to judge Ted as if he were the heroine of a typical woman's film. These first scenes emphasize his camaraderie with men and his inability to communicate with women and children. Ted tells stories in which the boss takes avid interest. He confides in the boss and expresses a traditionally male view of women when trying to account for Joanna's break with him: "She's got this friend, Margaret . . . tatata . . . women's lib." When Margaret comes to his apartment, he accuses her of having encouraged Joanna's estrangement from him. Their exchange seems to leave them confirmed enemies. While bungling the first breakfast after his wife's departure, Ted desperately repeats, "We're having a great time, aren't we," and the camera cuts to Billy's unconvinced, sullen face. He has no patience for Billy's anxiety ("Who's going to pick me up from school if you get hit by a truck?") or for the child's clumsiness, which results in red soda splattered all over his ad campaign presentation. Later, during the custody hearing, we learn that part of Joanna's dissatisfaction with the marriage had to do with Ted's insensitivity to the boy's needs, and Margaret admits that Ted was guilty of Joanna's charge at the time.

Ted begins to suffer the consequences of ruinous ambition as soon as his transgression is established in the minds of the audience. When he returns home from work, he announces almost in the same breath his recent success and possible promotion as well as a co-worker's suicide. As soon as he comes home, Joanna leaves, easily brushing aside his exasperated explanations and entreaties. Instead of offering sympathy, Margaret (Jane Alexander) drily summarizes Ted's attitude about the crisis: "She [Joanna] loused up one of the best five days of your life." When Ted apprises the boss of his domestic problems, the boss's advice gives Ted a clear choice between career and parenthood; the "one-hundred-and-ten-percent, seven-days-a-week" effort on the job leaves no room for "a kid with a runny nose." The rest of the film presents Ted's expiation for his sin, namely putting himself in the position of having to make such a choice.

An important structural device that emphasizes Ted's feminization appears in the parallel scenes of breakfast-making and taking Billy to school. In the French toast breakfast sequence, Ted exhibits a comic-pathetic inadequacy as a homemaker, strongly reminiscent of Katharine Hepburn's frenzied attempts to make breakfast for Spencer Tracy in *Woman of the Year* (1942). The child's kibbitzing (he knows where the pan is kept; he reminds Ted about the milk in the batter) serves to make us regard Ted as a comical failure rather than as a poor put-upon male whose wife walked out on him. He knows less about cooking, and, later, about shopping, than a five-year-old boy. On the way to school, Ted rushes the boy along to the refrain of "I'm going to be late for work," hands him over to a young woman at the school door with the injunction that she take care of him, and hails a taxi. A parallel scene, which comes much later in the film, shows Ted's successful feminization. Ted knows Billy's friends and greets them by name as he walks his son to school. He lingers to listen to his child's story until Billy interrupts himself, saying "I don't want to be late for school." (This episode is also a nice inversion of the first scene in which Ted appears in the film, where he is late getting home due to his storytelling for the boss.) He kisses the boy goodbye.

Similarly, the breakfast scene on the day Joanna is to take Billy away is matched almost shot for shot with the initial one in order to emphasize Ted's growth as a woman; he and Billy work in unison, and the French toast he prepares sizzles toward a golden-brown perfection while son and father cry in each other's arms.

Apart from the ruinous ambition and the inadequacies as a homemaker Ted must learn to overcome, he exhibits another trait typical of redeemed heroines in the woman's film: women who are to be reintegrated into society abstain from sex after their fall. Similarly, Ted virtually abstains from sex. The episode with Phyllis, Ted's only and one-time sex partner, and her nighttime encounter with Billy, exposes the preposterous and precarious nature of Ted's sex life. When, on his lawyer's advice, he draws up a list of pros and cons in order to determine whether he really wants to fight Joanna about custody, the con

Kramer vs. Kramer, Columbia Pictures Industries, Inc.
Courtesy of Museum of Modern Art/Film Stills Archive

side shows "NO PRIVACY, NO SOCIAL LIFE, NO LET-UP." The camera
zooms in for a close-up of a blank pro side; then, as if the camera's
movement is to fill in the blank, the camera follows Ted, walking to
Billy's room and cradling the sleeping child in his arms.

The sex-role reversals achieved by character delineation and development receive further emphasis from the structure of *Kramer vs.
Kramer.* Although the film's timespan, eighteen months to two years, is
considerably shorter than that of many woman's films (I assume

because of an unwillingness to substitute an older child for the winning Justin Henry, who plays Billy), development through time is an
essential feature of the film, as parallel scenes other than the ones
discussed indicate. Ted sheds his overmasculine personality, accepts
the feminine persona in which circumstances and choice have placed
him, suffers societal opprobrium for his past sins, and is redeemed
from the brink of catastrophe at the last minute.

Gradually, we see a more and more feminized Ted. He refuses a
drink after office hours and cuts the boss short in order to pick Billy up
from a children's party. He maternally covers the sleeping child, and,
sensing Billy's feeling of loss, he replaces Joanna's picture, which he
had removed in anger immediately after her leaving, on the child's
nightstand. He appears late at the office laden with grocery bags. He
discusses discipline matters with Billy on the phone, having taken the
call in the boss's office during a chewing-out by the boss about Ted's
family problems interfering with his work. After he puts Billy in his
room for trying to eat ice cream instead of a home-cooked dinner, he
cries over his drink; then, when the child calls for him, they have a
heart-to-heart talk, and father and son go through the "good night,
don't let the bedbugs bite" routine that we saw Joanna doing with Billy
at the beginning of the film.

That Billy begins to think of Ted as his mother is evident from a line
that occurs twice in the movie. Angry because Ted is late in picking
him up from a birthday party, Billy says, "All the mothers were there
before you." When Billy demands something over the phone, Ted
responds, "I don't care what the other mothers do!" When he informs
Billy that he is to live with his mother, the child's greatest sorrow is
that "You're [Ted] not going to kiss me good night any more."[12]

In addition to learning how to mother his son, Ted develops a fine
sisterly relationship with Margaret. Theirs is an equal partnership,
devoid of sexual tension, but not of physical contact and comfort. By
contrast, in the novel Ted abstains from making sexual advances that
Thelma (Margaret) is likely to accept, because he opts for an uncomplicated, not a deeper relationship. In the film we see Ted and Margaret
at the park, watching their children play; at Ted's apartment, washing
dishes together after Billy's accident; on the street, meeting by chance
and walking home together; the two are companionable in a deep,
loving, yet nonromantic way. Margaret's passionate defense of Ted in
the courtroom centers on Ted's change, his redemption, the feminization that Joanna cannot know about. Joanna herself looks with intense
wonder at a Ted who defends his leaving work, his coming in late for a

crucial presentation before a client, with arguments such as "My child was sick, he was running a temperature of 104° . . ." and "There was a problem at school about a boy who hit him."

Later, Joanna experiences firsthand Ted's new-found nurturing persona. Before going to Billy to tell him that she will not take him away from home and his father, she asks Ted, "How do I look?" and he generously replies, "Terrific," not so much in tribute to Meryl Streep's beauty but as a gesture of support for a human being who seems childishly vulnerable at that point and who needs adult reassurance.

Ted's increasing acceptance of a feminine persona takes him through the suffering required of a female hero before she can be redeemed. Like many heroines, caught up in his ambition, he gradually realizes that he loves; unlike many of them, he loves a child, not a member of the opposite sex, although several memorable woman's films revolve around the same love: *To Each His Own* (1946), *Mildred Pierce* (1945), *Stella Dallas* (1925, 1937), *The Old Maid* (1939), *Madame X* (1965). He experiences a loss of drive and in turn loses his accustomed place in society. His identity becomes subsumed to another's needs. Consequently, the office workers whisper behind his back. His secretary admonishes him. Clients give him the severest looks. Finally, his boss fires him over an elegant luncheon. The Christmas Eve job-getting episode is not the resounding success it appears to be on first viewing. Ted is told in no uncertain terms that he must have a job in order to have even a slim chance in the custody suit, and he does what many a female hero has done: he fights without regard to his self-esteem to get a position for which he is vastly overqualified and much underpaid. In *To Each His Own*, Olivia de Havilland, tortured by her separation from her son, is shown ready to accept an office job from a man who is a successful traveling salesman; in *Mildred Pierce,* Joan Crawford sells homemade pies to advance her children's fortunes; in *Moscow Does Not Believe in Tears*, Katerina works as a fitter in a factory; these women's vertiginous rise indicates that they were vastly superior to their initial employments, which they accepted in order to support or regain their children.

But Ted's real suffering, the sense of exclusion from society and ultimately from the life of love for which he has sacrificed himself, is the custody suit and the court's decision in Joanna's favor. In the courtroom, Ted, more than Joanna, has to defend his reputation and his respectability. Joanna's lawyer questions him about his loss of status and salary at his new job and presents evidence of Ted's "negligence" in his former position. Ted's answers about his son's illness and so forth bring him close to being held in contempt, literally and figuratively. The scene in Central Park, when Ted discusses the meaning of the change in custody with Billy, echoes similar scenes in woman's films in which the heroine has to be the braver, stronger one, in which she gives up the man she loves for his sake, for the sake of his wife, or of his family.[13] In *Kramer vs. Kramer,* Ted needs all his courage for the sake of the child. However, his loss and his sense of isolation are so great that he refuses even Margaret's companionship the evening after the court's verdict.

Ted's attempt at cheerfulness under the December sun in Central Park does not hide his bitterness, the desolation that he sees henceforth as his lot: "I'm really lucky 'cause I get to have dinner with you [Billy] once a week. . . ." The time in between, we sense, will be filled with longing for Billy. Then, as occasionally happens in the woman's film if the hero has suffered enough, Ted is restored to life—with Billy—through the miracle of Joanna's change of mind, or, should we say, of sex.[14] For in the final instance, the questions posed by *Kramer vs. Kramer* are the ones voiced by the two Kramers, whose sexual identities are hidden on the legal briefs: "Why can't a woman have the same ambitions as a man?" asks Joanna, and "What says that a woman can be a better parent by virtue of her sex, that a man can't have the same emotions and feelings?" asks Ted. The generic structure of the film gives the answers. The sex-role reversal in *Kramer vs. Kramer* is more of an acquiescence toward what audiences could accept in 1979 than a radical departure toward androgyny, because, despite the slight increase in the number of women who leave their children in their husbands' care, the film's message—that raising a child is far more important and rewarding than professional success—applies and has been forcibly applied mostly to women.

Ted's feminization from young business go-getter into a nurturing, vulnerable, and self-sacrificing parent reinforces the notion supported by the structure of the woman's film that a woman who becomes the hero of her life rather than a supporting or bit player falls prey to sin, censure, and suffering, and may be redeemed from misery only by a miracle, a change outside her control. In *Kramer vs. Kramer* the myth remains unchanged, even when the woman happens to be a man.[15]

Notes

1. See the treatment of the Western by Robert Altman, *McCabe and Mrs. Miller* (1971); of the gangster film by John Huston, *The Asphalt Jungle* (1950); of the detective film by Roman Polanski, *Chinatown* (1974). These

examples, as well as those given in the text and in subsequent notes, are meant to be representative rather than exhaustive.

2. George Cukor, quoted in Gavin Lambert, *On Cukor* (New York: Capricorn Books, 1973), 28.

3. Andrew Sarris, *The American Cinema: Directors and Directions, 1929–1968* (New York: E. P. Dutton, 1968), 110.

4. Recent articles, such as Tania Modleski's "Time and Desire in the Woman's Film," in *Cinema Journal* 23 (Spring 1984): 19–30, and Mary Ann Doane's "The 'Woman's Film': Possession and Address," in *Revision: Essays in Feminist Film Criticism,* ed. Mary Ann Doane, Patricia Mallencamp, and Linda Williams (Los Angeles: University Publications of America, 1984), 67–82, concentrate respectively on the melodrama as a psychoanalytic text and on the medical (i.e., psychiatric) discourse that in the woman's film replaces the legal discourse of the *film noir.* Yet surely the Biblical, more than the Freudian model, informed and continues to inform spectators' reactions to the woman's film, despite many critics' penchant for filmic psychoanalysis.

5. I am indebted for this insight into iconography to Judith Gustafson, who discussed its implications at the MLA special session on the woman's film, at which I presented the first version of this chapter in December 1981.

6. See Annis Pratt, *Archetypal Patterns of Women's Fiction* (Bloomington; Indiana Unviersity Press, 1981).

7. Stuart Kaminski's study, *American Film Genres: Approaches to a Critical Theory of Popular Film* (New York: Dell Publishing Co., 1974), for instance, ignores the existence of woman's films; Ted Sennett in *Warner Brothers Presents* (n.p.: Castle Books, 1971) groups woman's films under the chapter title "Sob Sisters: The 'Weepers,' " and regards their disappearance as a return to normality.

8. See Molly Haskell, *From Reverence to Rape: The Treatment of Women in the Movies* (New York: Holt, Rinehart & Winston, 1974), 153–88, 230–34; and Marjorie Rosen, *Popcorn Venus: Women, Movies and the American Dream* (New York: Avon Books, 1973), 259–62.

9. Avery Corman, *Kramer vs. Kramer* (New York: Signet Books, 1978), 177. All further quotations are from this edition.

10. Any number of films would serve as examples, but sports films, e.g., *Rocky* (1976) and biographies, e.g., *Dr. Erhlich's Magic Bullet* (1940) and *The Story of Louis Pasteur* (1936) are two notable genres.

11. Types of ambition gone sour are Michael in *The Godfather I* and *II* (1972, 1974), J. J. Hunsecker in *The Sweet Smell of Success* (1957), and Joe Gillis in *Sunset Boulevard* (1950); note also the parody of the ambitious youth's corruption in the "Dynamite Hands" episode of *Movie, Movie* (1978).

12. Joanna says in court, "I have been his [Billy's] mommy for eight years. Mr. Kramer took over that role for eighteen months. I don't see how anyone could believe that I have less of a stake in *mothering* that little boy than does Mr. Kramer" (italics mine).

13. Examples of this kind of courage come more often from love stories than from woman's films: *Camille* (1936), *Love Affair* (1939) and its remake,

An Affair to Remember (1957), but also *Now, Voyager* (1942) and *Humoresque*.

14. Films in which "sinful" women get to see their children or finally have their children know them are plentiful: *Madame X* (1965), *To Each His Own* (1946), *The Old Maid* (1934), and so forth.

15. For the background research of this paper, I am most indebted to Anthony Ambrogio, who has generously shared his knowledge and film library with me; I also wish to thank Ava and James Collins for their help.

7

Woman as Genre

ROBERT PHILLIP KOLKER
University of Maryland

The function of much feminist film criticism is to reveal a lack. When dealing with American commercial cinema, the critical project has unmasked the absence of woman as a viable, active force and discovered instead an empty space that has been filled in and articulated by filmmakers with the stereotypes created out of male fantasy and fear. Women do not exist in American film. Instead we find another creation, made by men, growing out of their ideological imperatives. Gaye Tuchman has called the phenomenon the symbolic annihilation of women, the replacement of reality by the patriarchal fantasies of subservience or its opposite, the fantasy of the voracious, destructive woman (who must, in her turn, be destroyed).[1] Recently, in reaction to the feminist struggle, this annihilation has strained the bounds of the symbolic. Women in film have become increasingly frequent targets of physical attack, the knife-wielder on the screen acting as surrogate for a masculine sensibility enraged at the notion of female assertiveness.

130

Before women achieved a clear and active voice "in reality," their annihilation could be achieved through the creation of images that denied their existence as independent entities, that figured them as appendages to or destroyers of men. Now that such denial is being denied in its turn, the makers of the images can hold on to the stereotypes, turn upon them angrily, or attempt in one way or another to align them with the new reality of feminist sensibility. In a form of expression as reactionary as commercial American film, the latter option is taken rarely, usually half-heartedly, sometimes semi-consciously, buried in or by the text, needing excavation to get dis-covered. This essay will attempt some small amount of excavation, examining how a few major American directors have tried to come to terms with the old ideologies and the new realities of women over the past decade.

Feminist critics ought no longer to be surprised at the degree of symbolic annihilation women have undergone in the course of film history. Nor should that history be looked at in any way as the unique embodiment of sexist ideology. From its beginnings, American film-making has been part of the economic structure of the society, sharing its images of the world, creating images for it, aiding the process of manufacture and the turning of the human figure into a commodity. Ideology, however, is not something necessarily imposed from the top. Although it may originate in the industrial, legal, political, educational, and communications structures of a society, it must be believed and participated in by a majority of the people in a culture in order to exist as an ideology.[2]

The ideological interchange between film and culture is not subtle, but it is complex, operating through a system of images and assent. The images and narratives of women that filmmakers create must be shared by both sexes in order to exist. If audiences did not assent to the images, they would not go to see them; if they were not seen, they would no longer be made. That they were made and continue to be made, that the varieties of subordinate, passive, or pacified women, of women as sexual objects, of killer women, or women who are killed, have persisted throughout the history of American film indicates ei-ther that the producers' cliché—"we give the public what it wants"—is true, or that the "public" accepts whatever it is given and in that acceptance is molded into a state of assent. Since women constitute more than half of that public, we are faced with the troubling reality of an audience passively, even willingly, accepting images of its own degradation.

Troubling, but not necessarily surprising. The fact of our social-economic system is that belief is created and assent manufactured (a phenomenon apparent in the recent struggle over the Equal Rights Amendment, when many women opposed their own liberation). When the world is perceived as a marketplace, consumers and commodities "positioned" to the best advantage, the visual and aural space of the society articulated to create the best context for exchange, and cognition structurally engineered, a structure of assent is all but inevitable. Film is part of the exchange process. Formally and contextually, it has created itself as part of—a major creator of—the structure of assent that makes the culture possible. Film (and now television, which uses the same language) teaches us how to see and understand from the point of view of the dominant, male-oriented ideology. Woman has been figured as the center of the male "look," its object and fetish, the cause and recipient of desire, pity, and cruelty.[3] These representations (picked up by film from painting and literature) were sealed in a "reality" that could not be questioned because it did not question itself. The diegesis created by American film, the very signifiers that created the diegesis, never exposed themselves as the productions of an economic-ideological system and therefore never risked exposure for what they were—not reality, but an ideological deformation of reality, in service to the dominant voice of the culture that spoke of women as objects of desire and needful of either marriage or destruction.

Deviations from the ideological stereotypes are so rare or slight that they constitute only variations upon a predictable structure, so predictable that the way women are figured in American film narratives constitutes a genre—a transgeneric genre, if you will—as predictable in form and content as the more immediately recognizable genres like the Western, the romantic melodrama, the horror film or science fiction. Though I call it "transgeneric," "intrageneric" might be more appropriate, for the codes of the female narrative and character not only cross the boundaries of conventional genres, but they exist within the representatives of any one genre. The paradigms are almost invariably the same: woman as helpmate; as careerist waiting for the right man; as forgiving or unforgiving; as sacrificer of local pleasure for a greater happiness (the paradigm of "why ask for the moon when we have the stars?"); woman as bitch; as lonely and confused (without a man); as happy and in a position of strength, but ready to yield that position for a man. In the 1948 film *June Bride* Bette Davis plays a strong and self-assured magazine editor; by the end of the film, however, she is carrying the suitcases for her reporter-lover, Robert Montgomery, promising to be his wife and follow him wherever he goes). Like a genre, the narrative forms in which these paradigms are placed and worked out into syntagms create a circuit of expectation and affirmation; there are rarely any surprises. The voice is persistent and undaunted.

For a brief time in the late sixties and early seventies, the voice faltered somewhat. Or, put more positively, other voices were briefly heard. For that moment, between the rigorous control that was exercised by the studios through the fifties and the more deadening control of corporate ownership that asserted itself in the late seventies, some filmmakers emerged who were able to break down the old conventions, question the generic codes, and reevaluate the "woman" who had dominated American cinema in her oppression. Some women were allowed entry into filmmaking. In *Girlfriends* (1978) Claudia Weill created a woman-centered narrative that was able to eschew some of the male definitions of the female character. Unfortunately, that film's success led her to make a more commercial product, *It's My Turn* (1980), which fed on conventional structures (a woman mathematician chooses romance between an architect and a baseball player). There were few other female directors of merit during the period; the field remained dominated by men, and the revisions of the genre came from them.

And they were really revisions only, most of them minor, none very long-lasting. The descriptions and analyses that follow, however, indicate that, no matter how slight and brief, changes were (and are) possible in the tedious and degrading clichés fostered by American film. The suggestions in these works of alternative possibilities for female and male characters, and the relationships between them, proved at least that conventions are alterable, codes able to be changed, the dead air cleared somewhat.

The work of Robert Altman is inconsistent in its treatment of women. But in some of his films, he manages to take an unidealized view, and his female characters appear neither pure nor sullied, not beyond the masculine world or dependent upon it, but rather within it, sharing the same field as men. One of these characters, Constance Miller (Julie Christie) in *McCabe and Mrs. Miller* (1971), outstrips the men around her with a thorough hard-headedness and an ability to deal strongly with the world. Her strength and business acumen make the men who surround her appear childish by comparison. Mrs. Miller is a brothel owner in a wretched frontier town. She is, however, not a whore with a heart of gold (though she has a box in which she keeps the gold her customers pay her for her favors) and she shows very little sympathy or motherly care, particularly for the town's would-be entrepreneur and her would-be lover, McCabe (Warren Beatty), who wishes to play the conventional role of Western hero and save her and the town—in this instance from the forces of exploitation who would buy them out. McCabe attempts to act the role the genre assigns to him and goes to fight the mining company's hired guns, dying alone in the snow. Mrs. Miller withdraws to an opium den and ʃ ˙ okes herself into oblivion as McCabe kills and is killed by the intruders.

The traditional heroic patterns are disarranged. The male figure tries to draw upon the Western's paradigms: self-sufficiency, strength, romantic isolation, bravery, duty. But he only manages to parody them and dies for his pains. The female character inverts the codes. She has none of the conventional characteristics of the Western woman, except perhaps for a well-developed sense of self-protection. In the shoot-out she demonstrates no heroism or sacrifice. The woman who would ordinarily be directed by the conventions of the woman's genre to help her man (think of *High Noon*) merely leaves him to his own stupidity and the brutalities of history. But in her withdrawal, there is also a denial. Her antiromantic position is so strong that it turns on itself and becomes self-annihilation. Altman allows Mrs. Miller to remove herself from the futile and destructive action; but her action is itself futile. Altman tends to see history as a force that pushes men and women into themselves and away from communal endeavors. Mrs. Miller saves herself, but the community around her dies. She saves herself only for herself, and while this act constitutes a major challenge to the convention of the self-sacrificing woman, it is not permitted to advance any further than a challenge. Altman cannot envision an alternative to the patriarchal order. The corporate takeover of the town will occur (it is suggested) despite McCabe's heroics and Mrs. Miller's withdrawal.

In *Three Women* (1977), one of the very few films by a male director to concentrate almost exclusively on women characters, Altman places them as hostages to the dominant culture. They are deformed by it, violated by it, and in the end they reduplicate it. Like Mrs. Miller, they withdraw; but here they form an isolated family unit that mimics the patriarchal hierarchies of the society outside. The three women are depicted as empty vessels, filled by the order they cannot control. Altman, despite his dedication to generic inversion and recodification (a dedication that now prevents him from getting money for new projects), has been unable to create female characters who endure by positive action. When they do attempt to impress themselves upon the world, they tend to become lost and isolated figures, like Keechie in *Thieves Like Us* (1974), or figures of parody, like many of the female characters in *Nashville* (1975), *A Wedding* (1978), and *Health* (1981), who become mere objects of derision.

Martin Scorsese would seem, at first glance, to be the last director one would turn to for a convincing reappraisal of the woman genre. But on a closer look, his films manifest an almost schizophrenic tension, a struggle between his Lower East Side, Italian Catholic attitude toward women as either madonnas or whores, most clearly realized in *Who's That Knocking on My Door* (1969), *Mean Streets* (1973), and *Taxi Driver* (1976), and a somewhat more enlightened perspective that pushes through *Alice Doesn't Live Here Anymore* (1973), *New York, New York* (1977), and *Raging Bull* (1980). Scorsese shares Altman's intelligence and understanding of film genres and of the attitudes and images they persistently generate. Despite, or in the face of, his worst instincts, he knows on some level that the symbolic annihilation of women is part of the machinery of American film. The central characters in all of his films, with the exception of *Alice*, are male working-class figures (a lunatic, in the case of *Taxi Driver*); and in the face of these dominant and domineering characters, Scorsese demonstrates an understanding of the female figure who is oppressed by them. It is a measure of his talent that he has often been able to keep the struggle between his male and female characters in the foreground, to admire and be critical of the behavior of the male through the perspective of the female character.

The effect is most subtly achieved in *Taxi Driver*. The two women who become snared in Travis Bickle's madness never achieve the individuality of traditionally "well-motivated" characters. Instead, they remain projections of his crazed sensibilities. But rather than diminish them, this process enlightens us about the ways in which we perceive women in film. Travis's mind is a great junk receptacle. He believes unthinkingly in the images of the woman genre, the ideologies of purity and dependence, of masculine strength and protectiveness. Travis perceives a violent world all around him, into which one woman, Betsy the campaign worker, descends, and from which Iris, the young whore (Jodie Foster) must be rescued. Travis sees Betsy as an angel in white, whom he quickly soils and scares away by taking her to a porn movie. Iris emerges directly from the ugly world Travis inhabits. An East village prostitute, she comes to represent for Travis a means of salvation and cleansing.

From Travis's madness, a certain truth emerges: a revelation of the way films present woman either as a pure creature or as soiled property—as an idol for man or as something either to be discarded or saved. That these dichotomies exist in a madman's mind raises them almost to the level of allegory, for it is madness—certainly a willful error of perception—that has perpetuated these myths and taken them for reality. The grotesque simplicity of Travis's vision clarifies the error, though at the same time, Scorsese indicates the ease with which the error is perpetuated. Travis, deciding that he must save Iris from her wretched life (after he has unsuccessfully attempted to assassinate a presidential candidate), kills her pimp and client in an orgy of violence, gets shot up himself, and is made, upon his recovery, a hero. Madness is shown to be a general quality, and Travis's distorted perceptions of the world are shown to be shared at large. The lunatic is admired and his lunatic vision of woman as virgin or whore endures inside and outside the fiction.

In *Raging Bull*, Scorsese attempts a somewhat more restrained view of a similar problem. The film is a meditation on the strong male character, which offers some important questions about generic clichés. To a greater extent than in *Taxi Driver*, Scorsese refuses in this film to ascribe precise motivations to his central character, the boxer Jake La Motta (played, as was Travis Bickle, by Robert De Niro). He forms the character from a combination of the things and the events he sees (and the way he sees them) and the way we as viewers are permitted to see him. At the intersection of these perceptions arises a shadowy, somewhat bewildering and frightening figure, full of sexist brutality. Scorsese's La Motta sees the woman of his affections either as a distant figure moving in slow motion, or (once he owns her) as a figure upon whom he can take out violently his frustrations and insecurities. There is no mistaking the admiration Scorsese has for this character; but the way he structures our perception of him, the distance he creates between the character and any easy comprehension of him, provides a space for reflection and perhaps for deflection. La Motta's treatment of women is both a part of his character and a critical comment upon that character. His jealousy of and violence toward his first and second wives are part of the reduced emotional equipment that makes him a good boxer and a diminished human being. But his diminution is not unique. Out of the fragments that make up La Motta's character, we discover the contradictions of woman-needing, woman-fearing, and woman-hating, qualities that stand out clearly here, but that go unquestioned in most films.

If *Taxi Driver* and *Raging Bull* provide some clarity as to the conventions of the woman genre (indirectly, obliquely), then *Alice Doesn't Live Here Anymore* and *New York, New York* attempt a major break with its codes. Each of these films deals with a specific and recognized genre—*Alice* with the "woman's picture," the thirties and forties melodramatic form in which a woman suffers in love, often attempts a career, and usually discovers that marriage is the only salvation; *New*

York, New York with the show business biography, in which a performer works his or her way up to the top. Both forms conform to the codes of the larger woman genre, even though in the show business film, women are occasionally permitted a larger field of action. In his traversal, Scorsese attempts to rearrange a number of codes, particularly those governing the interchanges between male and female characters. *Alice* was very much a film of its time, when the popular arts came to reflect (or distort) some lines of thought in the woman's movement. The narrative of a woman breaking out of a suffocating domestic environment became a standard device, and the single mother would soon emerge as a new cliché in the narratives of film, television, and the novel. In 1974 there was still a measure of surprise in this structure, and Scorsese played it up fully, turning melodrama into comedy, describing the energy manifested by a woman who launched herself out of an oppressive domestic situation (partly by accident—her husband dies) to take to the road with her son in search of a new life.

Despite the freedom and self-confidence of its central figure, the film comes to rest firmly within the bounds of generic convention. Alice (Ellen Burstyn) finds a charming and malleable man with whom to settle down. But within these bounds, the character is permitted some unusual latitude in her choices and actions. She is also given two unusual relationships, one with her son, the other with another woman, a waitress at a diner at which she gets a job. In both instances, Alice is allowed to act as a component rather than as an opponent in the grouping. There is an equality between mother and child and a lack of condescension and sentimentality here that is as unusual in a film presentation as it is in reality. The relationship between Alice and her woman friend, Flo, emphasizes an important element in the feminist argument: the need for the portrayal of relationships between women that is equal to the portrayal of those men have enjoyed. It provides a special response to the "male-bonding" or "buddy" films that sprang up in the late sixties and continued through the seventies (a subgenre Scorsese himself indulged in with *Mean Streets*, the film made prior to *Alice*). The "buddy" film is explicitly antifemale, denying women (and its latent homosexuality as well), celebrating male victory over the bothersome other.[4] The relationship of Alice and Flo (as well as women's groupings in other films, notably Paul Mazursky's *The Unmarried Woman*) does not deny males; it is not antimale as much as it is profemale, offering each character the other's support: help rather than an implied hatred.

The strength of *Alice Doesn't Live Here Anymore* lies within its reorientation of expectations, its vital attempt to give the female character her own narrative.[5] In *New York, New York,* Scorsese does something different again. Rather than breaking out of old codes, he breaks into them. Recreating the artificial world of the Hollywood musical, using studio sets, which through the fifties had signified "reality" but by now only signify the reality of Hollywood production, employing the skeleton of the conventional narrative of the burgeoning show business career, Scorsese sets up a structure of expectations that he then refutes at every point. Within this artificial world, he breaks apart the artifices of conventional film relationships. (An interesting comparison can be made between *New York, New York* and Coppola's *One From the Heart,* another attempt to refashion the musical genre. Whereas Scorsese uses artificiality to comment upon the signifying system of the old Hollywood *mise-en-scène,* Coppola only creates a technologically interesting set of signifiers that do not form any system; his narrative remains rooted in the old conventions of romance and romantic sexuality, uninformed by the *mise-en-scène.*)

While the artificial sets and pastel colors set up a complex visual field in *New York, New York,* the refutation of conventional romantic expectations is handled rather simply. Jimmy and Francine Doyle (Robert De Niro and Liza Minnelli) both achieve success as entertainers and in the conflict caused by that equality, masculine hegemony is broken down. The male character is permitted to show the usually female traits of jealousy and insecurity, anger and resentment. The female character is allowed to remain strong and independent. But Jimmy does not go into decline because of this; *New York, New York* is not a remake of *A Star Is Born.* Both characters endure and prevail, but not with each other. An American film narrative is able, finally, to admit that marriage is not the answer to a woman's existence and that a dependent woman is not necessary for a man's survival. Historically, the one event that Hollywood melodrama cannot abide is an individual existing successfully without a mate—a curious fact, given the culture's obsessive belief in the ideology of individuality. But ideology is, by definition, a complex of contradictions, and the convention of romantic need and dependency, especially when founded in a man's desire for a woman's support, easily overtakes the clichés of individualism. The culture's need to be reassured that the nuclear family will prevail, isolated from an apparently unmanageable world, the woman as its passive center, is stronger than any notion of independent or group action.

Very few American films have found—or have even cared to search for—an adequate response to this structure. The separation and survival of Jimmy and Francine in *New York, New York* is a small, important narrative event that has had little follow-up in recent film. Works of male self-satisfaction and reassurance like *Ordinary People* and *Kramer vs. Kramer* have continued the myth of the nuclear family. The woman who leaves it, or who proves incapable of emotionally supporting the family unit, calls forth heretofore unknown strengths from the male member who keeps the unit operative. Such films turn out to be not so much celebrations of individual capability (the "survivor" code, something of a recent introduction), nor even demonstrations of how adequate men are to "female" tasks. They are in fact antiwoman narratives. Less evident reactions to the feminist movement than the rape-and-slash films, more subtle in their defiance of female individuality, they still deny it through a narrative focus on the strong male figure.

It would be foolish to point to Martin Scorsese as a feminist director. I would only indicate that here is a filmmaker willing to probe the generic patterns, to demand some accounting for them, to demand the active attention of the audience in coming to terms with the conflicting details he presents. At the moment, he is the only commercial filmmaker in America actively using visual form and narrative structure to build a mutually interrogating relationship between viewer and film. The economic retrenchment that occurred in Hollywood in the mid-seventies, the reassertion of the commodity status of movies, and the reduction of the major distributors to holdings of large corporations assured the return of the "realist" mode that had always been dominant in American film, and with it the reassertion of the woman genre. (Neither, of course, has ever actually disappeared.) If a few directors in the late sixties and early seventies were able to break away from these codes, to deny simple continuity to a variety of stereotypically motivated characters, by the end of the last decade all of these structures had returned with a vengeance. This retrograde process was part of the reactionary movement in the culture at large, and with it, of course, women in film were returned to their passive secondary roles. There were a few exceptions, some comedies in the screwball vein— *Fun With Dick and Jane* (1976), *A Touch of Class* (1973), *Continental Divide* (1981) that permitted vitality and independence in their female characters; Jane Fonda introduced a new and (happily) short-lived convention of the free-spirited woman reporter; and there was a return of the *film noir* killer woman (*Body Heat* (1981) is a recent example). But mostly women retained their roles as helpless fools, as bitches, and especially as victims.

One filmmaker, Brian De Palma, has made his reputation by brutalizing his female characters, constructing narratives whose main goal is the stabbing or strangling of a woman. Reviewers compare his work to that of Hitchcock, without understanding that Hitchcock, though a misogynist to his core, at least opened his films to an interrogation process, invited the viewer to comprehend the errors made by his characters and by the viewer's own perceptions. Hitchcock's misogyny was part of a greater misanthropy (which does not excuse it). The point is that like Scorsese (who is very much influenced by him), Hitchcock was the rare filmmaker in America who questioned the very narratives he was making and did not accept conventions and stereotypes without either acknowledging them as such or questioning their status as stereotypes. Those filmmakers, like De Palma, who copy Hitchcock's violence against woman without comprehending the intricate patterns of perception and deception out of which the violence emerges are guilty of abusing their audience in a way Hitchcock rarely does.

I will return to this notion of audience abuse later on. But it is important to recognize again the importance of *formal* inquiry that makes the work of Altman and Scorsese able to question the codes of the woman genre. While it may be possible to create some new perspectives through content alone, presenting a progressive character or situation that may go beyond the destructive norms, the fact is that in general form determines content. A film made in the conventional manner, following standard patterns of continuity cutting, linear narrative development, conventionally motivated characters, will only recreate the most conventional attitudes. In order to alter attitudes, the formal apparatus necessary for producing that content must be altered. That alteration will in turn alter all other texts, which will then have to be seen in the context of the new forms and new codes. (One reason we can recognize the reactionary content of recent film is precisely because there was a brief period of work that formally and thematically questioned the old material.) The more radical the change in the form, the greater the possibility for a radical change in content—a phenomenon apparent in the work of many independent feminist filmmakers. In commercial cinema, there is no longer the possibility for such change, and once again the critical viewer is forced to look into the absences of a text to find in what is *not* stated that which needs to be stated, and to stand the text on its head if need be, in order to make it yield useful information, to make it account for the reality it keeps denying in the name of the "reality" of conventional patriarchal ideology.[6]

One recent film provides an excellent example of the "double text," revealing a pattern of conventional stimulus and response on an immediate level, and upon a careful rereading, a response to, or at least a questioning of, those conventions, a recoding that does not yield a feminist text, but marks out the lineaments of conflict, demonstrating the stresses in the dominant ideology. The film is *The Shining* (1980), directed by Stanley Kubrick, a filmmaker whose attitude toward women in his work is a considerable rank below his attitude toward men—very poor. Women always play a secondary role in Kubrick's films. In *Paths of Glory* (1957) and *2001: A Space Odyssey* (1968), they are all but nonexistent. In *Dr. Strangelove* (1963) there is one female character seen lounging in bed. The title character and her mother in *Lolita* (1961) are the cause and foil of Humbert Humbert's despair and obsession, not stereotypes but caricatures. *A Clockwork Orange* (1971) blatantly displays women as sexual objects: naked, abused, murdered.[7]

The antifeminism of Kubrick's work is a kind of baseline, an ongoing, almost unconscious support for the central structure of his films, a satirical structure that plucks out significant aspects of human behavior, exaggerates them, and sets them in an enormous symbolic space—the American road in *Lolita,* a chateau near the Maginot Line in WWI in *Paths of Glory,* an air force base and a SAC bomber in *Strangelove,* the vastness of space itself in *2001,* a decayed future society in *A Clockwork Orange,* a decaying past society in *Barry Lyndon* (1976). In these spaces, his men act out doomed rituals of self-reduction and destruction, a slow process moving toward impotence and imprisonment within political, social, or psychological systems that they have set up and over which they have lost control. In Kubrick's universe, things, places, and social structures diminish the male figure; the woman is already always lost.

Kubrick's misogyny is buried within a general misanthropy, which is itself lodged within an attitude of hopelessness and despair. Kubrick does not so much hate men and women as find the former helpless in exercising any control in their world, and the latter, reduced already as women, as of almost no consequence except as they receive the anger and violence of the suffering and helpless males or as they cause them further pain. Kubrick's attitude toward all this is not entirely uncritical. On a certain level, at least when his satirical apparatus is functioning, the harm his male characters do to their women is recognized as a reflection of their own diminished state and of the harm they are doing to themselves. A key to this is General Jack D. Ripper's infamous comments in *Dr. Strangelove* about women robbing him of his vital bodily fluids. Here is a figure so maddened by rigid militarism and fears of Communist plots that it distorts his sexuality, blanks out his basic knowledge of sexual mechanics, and permits him to interpret intercourse as something that weakens him and that therefore must be avoided. *Strangelove* uses misdirected sexuality as a metaphor for a system that has become dysfunctional on all levels. In the vastnesses of their fears and obsessions, Kubrick's men displace their oppression down along the line. In their inability to act upon the world that does them in, they enact violence upon each other and upon women.

Kubrick is a brilliant formalist, able to create his trapped figures in articulate images through a thoughtful and energetic use of color, movement, and spatial dynamics, controlled enough to allow the viewer comprehension of the situation through its visual manifestations. The problem is that he is either not intelligent enough or not concerned sufficiently to pursue these images and the narrative they create in such a way that the relationships between his male and female characters are clarified and articulated. The late German filmmaker, Rainer Werner Fassbinder, spent his career defining the intricate patterns of cross-reference between the oppressions that are visited upon an individual by his or her society and absorbing and reworking those oppressions into the relationships of a couple or a family. Kubrick, like all American filmmakers, refuses to see in detail the analogue relationships between the larger political structures and the smaller structures of domestic and sexual hierarchies. His films indicate their presence but refuse to detail or analyze them. In *A Clockwork Orange,* Alex's violence toward women is stated unquestioningly as an expression of masculine freedom. When the State conditions away his violent impulses, he demonstrates a sexual revulsion, a problem that disappears once the conditioning has been reversed. Nowhere in the film does Kubrick question why women in this future world are the objects of male aggression or why this aggression is assumed to be a "natural" sign of masculine vitality. It is barely implied that this sexual cruelty is part of a larger cruelty in the society, whose politics are barely alluded to. Alex's behavior is shown as a reaction to the society's deadness, but no dialectic is formed about this reaction. Why is nonrevolutionary violence an appropriate response to the restraints of society? Why should it be exhilarating to see a young man rape and beat women? What does this say about the film—all film—its audience, and Kubrick himself?

A Clockwork Orange appears almost as an act of liberation for Kubrick, a way of delivering himself of his misogyny under the guise of discussing the ethics of freedom and restraint. He in fact discusses neither of these and seems to indulge in cruelty for its own sake. In the film that followed, *Barry Lyndon*, Kubrick expresses a greater sense of understanding and understatement. This is a work of meditative calm and compositional intensity in which a somewhat critical gaze at sexual and romantic relationships is undertaken; the scurrilous behavior of the central character toward his wife is seen as part of his attempt to mimic the rituals of the late eighteenth-century aristocracy. Barry attempts to attain status in a devitalized and convention-ridden world; he fails, and in the process hurts and is hurt by those around him. The criticism of the male-female relationships is still minimal. Barry receives the most sympathy, and the elegant compositions and elegiac rhythms of the film develop a structure of pain and loss for him. His wife becomes one more destructive figure in a pantheon of cruelty.

Formally the most complex film Kubrick made, *Barry Lyndon* was not a commercial success. He needed a film to reestablish his commercial viability, the only thing that permits him the freedom to work in England without the pressures and interference most American filmmakers face. *The Shining* was that film. Visually and aurally loud and unsubtle, whereas *Barry Lyndon* was quiet and recessive, set in the contemporary world, whereas *Barry Lyndon* was set in the past, the film was fully involved in the popular conventions of the horror film: a frightening house (or hotel in this instance) visitations from ghosts, premonitions, acts of violence. *The Shining* ranks with *Spartacus* (1960) as the most conventional and least interesting films Kubrick has made. Yet, within the context of Kubrick's treatment of women in his films, it works out a most intricate textual counterpoint of convention and contradiction, a site of such confusion that it becomes both intriguing and unresolvable.

In the character of Wendy Torrance, Kubrick creates the strongest female character of any of his films. No nymphette or predator like Lolita and her mother, hardly a sexual object, Wendy is a plain, popeyed, perfectly ordinary woman (played by Shelly Duvall) placed in rather extraordinary circumstances. This blank, slightly goofy, ultimately hysterical figure suffers the rage of a crazed husband and still prevails. Through her ordeal, a curious investigation of the family unit takes place, for beneath its generic trappings, its ghosts and violence and ESP, *The Shining* is a domestic comedy-melodrama about a man's hatred for his wife, incorporating in it some remarkable iterations of masculine insecurity and the brittleness of marriage and the domestic alliance.

Jack Torrance (Jack Nicholson), an itinerant schoolteacher and would-be writer, takes his wife and child to spend the winter as the caretaker of a Colorado resort hotel that is closed for the season. He is anxious for the isolation so that he can start a new writing project (its exact nature is never announced). In the course of their stay, he goes mad and attempts to kill his family—as a previous caretaker had done—only to be foiled by them and left to freeze to death in a maze outside the hotel. Jack is a violent man, who once dislocated his child's shoulder in a drunken fit. From the beginning of the film, his attitude toward his family is condescending and taunting. His descent into madness constitutes the apex of his frustration as the head of the domestic unit, which finally breaks into a violent fit of revenge. He lives out a male fanatasy of destruction, a one-man wish-fulfillment of destroying his family that all men are supposed to have, the family that secretly they despise because of the inhibitions it places upon them. His "writing project" becomes itself the statement of his mad perceptions of marriage's imprisonment and devitalization. The only words he writes, obsessively, filling pages and pages of manuscript, are "All work and no play make Jack a dull boy."

In the course of his torment, he plays out a parody of all the roles the patriarchy allows the male. He is the family's sole source of financial support; he provides shelter (the huge, deserted resort that engulfs the family, dwarfs the domestic enclave). He is master and overseer: as wife and child play in the maze outside the hotel (which will be the place of Jack's death), he goes to a model of the place in the great hall of the hotel. He peers down at the model, and Kubrick cuts to his point of view, though this time his gaze is at the maze itself, as Wendy and her son move around in it, under the omniscient patriarchal eye. He can pretend to be a little boy seeking comfort: to keep him from killing her and their son, Wendy beats him with a baseball bat and locks him in a storeroom. He whines at her, "Wendy, I think you hurt my head real bad. I'm dying. I think I need a Doctor. . . . Honey, don't leave me here." He is the dutifully returning husband: upon his release from the storeroom he bashes down the door to their living quarters with an axe, looks through the wreckage, and announces with murderous glee, "Wendy, I'm home!"

But mostly he is the long-suffering, woman-hating man, the clichéd figure of the slob at the bar complaining that his wife does not understand him. Jack plays out the cliché literally as he stands at the hotel bar, the ghost of the hotel's barman listening to his complaints. Jack whines about the "white man's burden." "Just a little problem with the old sperm bank upstairs," he says. "Nothing I can't handle though. . . ." As every beleaguered husband must, Jack looks for an affair. Entering the mysterious, forbidden hotelroom where his son

The Shining, Warner Brothers, Inc.
Courtesy of Museum of Modern Art/Film Stills Archive

was just assaulted, he discovers a naked lady in the bath. She comes to him, they embrace, and in his arms she turns into a scabrous, laughing old crone. Women abuse poor Jack, mock him, or (he thinks) imprison him. He is undone and unforgiven—even by the very ghosts of the hotel who wish him to reenact a domestic slaughter of old. Jack is driven to act out the contradictions of an ideology that speaks of the necessity of a man taking on the burden of being a provider and protector even while this burden is shown to be oppressive. In this light, Jack Torrance is just a distant relation of Jack D. Ripper in *Dr. Strangelove.* Instead of the draining of precious bodily fluids, this Jack fears his inability to control his life and hates the smothering of his life by his family. In place of Communist subversion, this Jack sees supernatural forces guiding his destiny and his revenge.

The difference between this Jack and the others of Kubrick's crazed males, is, as I've said, the active presence of a woman whom the man believes is causing all his trouble. In her reactions to his madness, one would like to think that Kubrick was creating a woman of some strength and resourcefulness (or that perhaps his co-writer, Diane Johnson, was able to furnish some strength for the female character). Generically however, Wendy merely manifests a number of the horror film's major paradigms. Gérard Lenne points out some of these: the woman in a horror film may act as the instigator of evil; as the subjugator of the male character (the ogress figure); or as the object of the horror.[8] Wendy takes on all three functions, but in order to understand how, once again we have to separate the texts of the fiction. In the horror narrative of *The Shining*, the "instigator" of events is the supernatural aura of the hotel and its various manifestations. But in the narrative of domestic terror, the "secret" narrative that informs the whole, it is Wendy who pushes Jack over the edge. He sees her as the subjugator of his talent, passion, and liberty. She instigates his need for revenge and becomes the object of it. Her status as object is defined by the formal codes of the horror film, especially those insinuating tracks of the camera, the movement and cutting that intricately arrange the reactions of the audience by inscribing the woman as object of danger. She becomes in fact a triple object: of Jack and the horrifying "forces" of the hotel, of the filmmaker's camera, and of the viewer's response, which is tuned to her fear and danger so that we are unsettled and desirous of them.

But the monster threatening Wendy is, finally, not the ghost of past events at the hotel, but Jack's own misogyny, which turns him into a raving thing. In her fight against him, she calls up great reserves of strength and a (conventional) maternal instinct to save herself and her child. At one point she arms herself with a baseball bat, in effect stealing the phallus and outmaneuvering Jack with it. But the final victory is not hers. This is not to be a narrative of the woman triumphant. Danny, the son, ultimately destroys the father by trapping him in the snow-covered maze where he freezes to death, a grimace of hate on his face. And despite his terrifying presence—perhaps even because of it—Jack himself becomes more sympathetic the deeper he slips into lunacy, while Wendy merely becomes hysterical. She remains active in her and her son's defense, yet at the same time she remains helpless, increasingly the object of Jack's game, no matter how bad he is at playing it. In other words, she is never permitted to be heroic and just manages to assume the status of clever mouse fleeing the mad cat. The audience is asked to take pleasure in the pursuit, joy in the possibilities of destruction. When Jack finally takes after his son outside, Wendy is left alone in the hotel with the body of the cook (whom Jack has killed) and with various apparitions, as the hotel comes to supernatural life. She is no longer needed by the narrative, except to continue her role as object, further terrified by ghosts and visions, one of which is particularly curious. She sees—through a partially opened door—a bare-assed man in a rabbit costume, apparently engaging in oral sex with another man in a tuxedo. This brief encounter gives a final inflection to the domestic horror rippling beneath the other conventions of the film. *The Shining* is very much a film of heterosexual fear and loathing. Jack's reference to his wife as "the old sperm bank," his horrifying experience with the naked lady who turns into an old crone, present a notion of woman as thing and threat. His violence toward Wendy, her need to defend herself with a baseball bat, limns out the horror of destruction threatened when the patriarchal unit and its oppressive sexual domination collapses under its own dead weight.

The homosexual event witnessed by Wendy is by no means offered as an alternative to the sexuality that Jack can no longer abide. Given Kubrick's attitude toward such things, it is meant as a frightening "perversion," another sign of the chaos that follows the family's breakdown. For in the end, everything "normal" has been turned around: the provider has become destroyer; the passive woman has become the unwilling protector of herself and her child; the child himself has withdrawn into a schizophrenic world of visions and fears. No hero or heroine emerges from the film. Wendy disappears into the snowy night with her son, escaping the immediate terror, but not freed from the subordinate position of a despised object. Jack is left a frozen corpse in a maze, the body dead, but misogyny and misanthrope surviving. The notion entered at the end of the film that Jack has always been at the hotel, that this scene is acted and reenacted, confirms Kubrick's sense of an eternity of despair. He is excellent at suggesting the terrors of destructive hierarchies and their collapse, but he is never able to analyze them or to suggest that their demise might be permanent. His is a vision of the way things are, and, apparently, always will be.

There is yet another text embedded in *The Shining*, even more vicious than the one I have just examined. I mentioned earlier that Kubrick's previous film, *Barry Lyndon,* was a commercial failure—too restrained and complex to create the critical reaction necessary to bring in an audience. *The Shining* was a response to that failure and an allegory of Kubrick's own revenge. Wendy very much signifies the film audience and Jack the filmmaker himself, terrorizing that audience, coming after it, screaming at it, threatening violence. "Wendy," snarls Jack at one point, "I've let you fuck up my life so far, but I'm not going to let you fuck this up." If the audience will not accept contemplative images of loss and despair set in the past, it will be forced to accept screaming images of violence and brutality set in the present; it will be manipulated and abused into reacting appropriately. If an audience will not bring patience and intelligence to a film, then, like Wendy, it will be harrassed and pummeled.

To be fair, the manipulation and pummeling that Kubrick works in this film is not as severe nor as condescending as that practiced by other American filmmakers, like Steven Spielberg, for example. But the attitude is not much different in quality. In *The Shining,* as in most recent American films, the audience is treated like a "girl," as the stereotypical film signified of woman: passive, stupid, "wanting" to be abused. Filmmakers have spent over eighty years creating this image in their films; they now believe it exists outside, in the people for whom they make them. The woman genre not only subsumes the films we see, it now incorporates the audience—male and female—as well. A circle as vicious as that drawn in Kubrick's work seems to have enclosed the relationship of viewer and filmmaker. Perhaps the only way out is to stop looking from within its circumference.

Notes

1. Gaye Tuchman, "Introduction: The Symbolic Annihilation of Women by the Mass Media," in *Hearth and Home: Images of Women in the Mass Media,* ed. Gaye Tuchman, Arlene Kaplan Daniels, James Benét (New York: Oxford University Press, 1978), 3–38.

2. See Louis Althusser, "Ideology and Ideological State Apparatuses," in *Lenin and Philosophy,* trans. Ben Brewster (New York and London: Monthly Review Press, 1971), 127–86.

3. The central statement on women in film as the object of the male gaze is Laura Mulvey, "Visual Pleasure and Narrative Cinema," *Screen* 16 (Autumn 1975): 6–18.

4. Joan Mellen provides an excellent discussion of "buddy" films in *Big Bad Wolves: Masculinity in the American Film* (New York: Pantheon Books, 1977), 311–25.

5. And much credit must be given to the film's writer, Robert Getchell.

6. The notion of "structuring absences" comes from the editors, *Cahiers du Cinéma,* "John Ford's *Young Mr. Lincoln,*" in *Movies and Methods,* ed. Bill Nichols (Berkeley and Los Angeles: University of California Press, 1976), 493–529. Another important theoretical basis for this article is Fredric Jameson's *The Political Unconscious* (Ithaca: Cornell University Press, 1981).

7. See Beverly Walker, "From Novel to Film: Kubrick's *Clockwork Orange*," *Women and Film* 2 (1972): 4–10.

8. Gérard Lenne, "Monster and Victim: Women in the Horror Film," trans. Elayne Donenberg and Thomas Agabiti, in *Sexual Stratagems: The World of Women in Film*, ed. Patricia Erens (New York: Horizon Press, 1979), 31–40.

PART
III

WOMEN AS
IMAGE MAKERS

8

Dietrich:
Empress of Signs

MICHAEL WOOD
University of Exeter

I

Films fragment and fetishize the body, invite us to gloat over pieces of persons.[1] Particular fetishes may be marks of style, or just ineptness: the director cuts to wringing or fluttering hands to signal anguish or nerves. But the longest lasting, most eloquent film fetish of all, transcending style and cliché, gathering the most heterogeneous actors and directors into its dominion, is the face.

Roland Barthes wrote of a "moment in cinema . . . when one literally lost oneself in a human image as one would in a philtre, when the face represented a kind of absolute state of the flesh."[2] I'm not sure the length of this moment can be determined with any precision. It began, no doubt, with Mary Pickford and Lillian Gish, and matured with

Keaton and Chaplin and Valentino. It is alive and well in *Casablanca* (1942). When Bogart on the airstrip gruffly says to Bergman, "You'd better hurry. You'll miss that plane," his face, sagging, soulful, a mask of toughness pitted with sentiment, says everything his voice cannot pronounce. The whole film is in that face; if we can't read it, we don't understand the film. For Barthes, the moment ends when the faces change, when Garbo gives way to Audrey Hepburn, "when the archetype leans towards the fascination of mortal faces."[3] I think the moment ends rather when the face itself loses its preeminence in the cinema, when it fades back into a general repertory of signs, becomes just a means of expression, no longer a fetish or a language. I don't mean that the movies abandoned faces and close-ups of faces. I mean faces ceased to speak with the peculiar, all-encompassing authority they possessed for a whole age. In this period all the major meanings of a film circulated among faces. The show didn't really start until a famous, hazy face filled the screen.

Charles Affron[4] details a number of instances with loving attention. Another good example is *Shanghai Express* (1932). We see a crowded, jumbled Peking station, east and west, old and new jostling for room, a camel backed by a huge steam engine, cows and chickens on the line. Characters come and go, bits of dialogue are spoken. Then the film seems to begin. Dietrich appears in a taxi, presents her ticket at the barrier. But her eyes are cast down; when she raises them, glances across the station with a flicker of curiosity, they remain hooded. This is only a prelude; the film is playing with us. We soon hear from a soldier of Shanghai Lily, the famous "coaster." "What's a coaster?" Clive Brook asks in scorn and disbelief. "A coaster's a woman who lives by her wits along the China coast." Lily, needless to say, turns out to be Dietrich, and she and Brook turn out to be old friends, estranged by his diffidence and her flirting with his rivals. "I wish you could tell me there had been no other men," he says mournfully, when they have met up again. "I wish I could, Doc," Dietrich replies, with an impressive absence of anything resembling regret, "but five years in China is a long time." When she speaks this lamentable line, the film really has begun, since we have seen, are seeing, the face we have been waiting for. Dietrich has joined Brook on the observation platform of the train, and Sternberg has unfurled all his overwrought artistry in effects of light and shadowy composition. The blonde hair makes waves against a large halo of fur, the eyes are wide enough now to swallow a man, and the famous sculpted features shimmer in the soft focus of the myth. This is not Shanghai Lily, this is Marlene-Dietrich-in-the-movies, an elaborate icon, fragile, remote, lost, lethal.

My guess is that the dominion of the face in films ended in the early 1960s. Why? For many reasons, no doubt, involving a whole sociology of expression, but principally, I would suggest, because we no longer believed in faces, or in our ability to read them. Contemporary faces became masks for us, and the old faces were just too legible for an age of paranoia. It was also true that the rest of the body was liberated, or at least was made visible and acceptable. This is to say that the face, in and out of films, had been not only the privileged field of meaning and beauty, but also the repository of a repression, the realm into which all the hidden, unspeakable meanings of the body were displaced—not a state of the flesh at all, in Barthes's phrase, but a refusal of the flesh. The faces of Garbo, Gish, Dietrich were almost always curiously dissociated, free-floating, unattached to shoulders and trunks, not to mention even more fearful or alluring parts. They used to hang in the air like lanterns, or (why resist the tug of the obvious?) like stars. A star was in one sense just this: a human image removed to a celluloid heaven. Of course Dietrich had legs too, which were frequently displayed and were thought, at least in the studio's wistful propaganda, to give her an edge over Garbo, who was *only* a face. But the land of sexual fantasy is full of altered routes, and Dietrich's legs became not an extra fetish but a complication of her disguise, a cancellation of certain signs of mannishness. Her face, like Garbo's, continued to rule—it was a sister face, in fact, often looking remarkably similar— and it was at the center of all her films.

II

Can we really read faces, even those that come at us so plainly crying their meanings? Can it be right to speak, as Charles Affron does, of Garbo's acting, when he seems to be describing what he finds in her face?[5] Large questions about interpretation, and not only of faces, hover here. I shall say for the moment that I think we really can read faces, but that accounting for our reading is a quite different story—rather like explaining a joke, as distinct from getting it. I want to read, to register a reading of, Dietrich's face, particularly as it appears in *Shanghai Express* and *The Scarlet Empress* (1934); but I also want to confess to a feeling of helplessness, because that is part of the reading.

Let's go back to the shimmer of the myth, the fur-haloed head. What is the myth? The general myth of stardom, as I've said, of a perfection so stylized and mystified that it scarcely seems human. But there is also a particular Dietrich myth. She is not just a star, but *this* star; the star she is, as Bishop Butler nearly said, and not another one. This myth has to do with the lure and the durability of an impossible innocence, an innocence, what's more, which finally turns into something else, an odd mixture of endurance and independence.

Much of what Dietrich "means" in films is caught between her two most frequent looks: her eyes are wide open, trusting, she is a woman who dares to be a child; her eyes are hooded by the heavy lids, she is smoking, shut away in her worldliness and scorn. Does she endure by becoming hard and cynical? No, because then she wouldn't be able to go back to her vulnerable look. She endures by being able to travel between the two looks, or to hint at the one hiding in the other.

The Devil Is a Woman, Paramount Pictures Corporation
Courtesy of Museum of Modern Art/Film Stills Archive

The heart of the myth, it seems to me, is this. Dietrich's beauty is so refined and geometrical, so *abstract,* so much a matter of smooth skin, carved cheekbones, and eyebrows that owe everything to draughts-manship and nothing to hair, that she seems untouchable and there-fore untouched—whatever the implications of the plots of her movies, or of the fact that she had a daughter in 1925. It is worth comparing this face with those of the pudgy vamps of an earlier generation, or indeed with that of the much pudgier Dietrich herself in *The Blue Angel* (1930). Sternberg, seeing Dietrich in Berlin, was first attracted, he said, by her air of "cold disdain," and he helped turn her face into a mask with this meaning: Andrew Sarris, writing about *The Scarlet Empress,* identifies a "glacial guile" in Dietrich. She herself told Max-imilian Schell in *Marlene* (1983) that she was sure Sternberg was interested in her apparent lack of interest: since she was sure she wouldn't get the part he was recruiting for, she decided not to care.

All this finds its way into her screen presence. Of course "disdain" and "guile" are ways of moralizing the curious distance that every viewer perceives in Dietrich's performances. We see her absence, so to speak. Her heart is not in the movie, and the lurid narrative form of this perception is to say that the character she plays has no heart. I don't doubt that Dietrich's rumored sexual preferences have a role here,[6] although I would also guess that even a heteromaniac could be less than wild about Clive Brook; and some of her aloofness is plainly just metallic bad acting. She is not in Garbo's class as a stylist. But I am interested here in the icon and its compulsions. Marilyn Monroe projected an alarming, almost hysterical innocence. Dietrich projects nothing of the kind, but we lend her innocence, because we can't bear to suspect such beauty—or at least the beauty presented to us in certain romantic shots. And yet of course—here is the contradiction that gives the myth its life and trouble—this kind of beauty is a treasure and a temptation, a goldmine, both in countless movie plots and in an actress's life, and it is impossible to believe that the world's collectors and prospectors have not had their hands on it. "It took more than one man to change my name to Shanghai Lily." I suppose this famous sentence, as written, was meant to conjure up the sad, soupy story of the fallen woman, unhappy victim of poverty and rampaging male desire. As Dietrich says it, it suggests a fine, barely damaged superiority, as if anything men could do to her could only be done by sheer force of numbers. The same crushing quality, the note of inso-lence verging on indifference, appears later in the same film, when Werner Oland, as a prosperous revolutionary leader, invites Dietrich to come and live at his nearby palace. "In time you will weary of men," he says, playing the man who knows the human condition and the mutability of the passions. Dietrich, with a mildness that is itself an insult, says, "I'm weary of you now."

She is not innocent after all, and she is not invulnerable. She has been hurt, and her very kindnesses show traces of pain. But her story is not that of the brave defeat Garbo so wonderfully portrayed,[7] and it is not that of the warm-hearted whore Dietrich was so often, especially in her later films, asked to embody. It is the story of weathering out storms that destroy nearly everyone else, preserving a purity where most people are smudged, and her continuing stage appearances confirmed this piece of the myth. The slurred, drooping voice did the old songs well, but the main feature of the spectacle was the visible conquest of time: a taut, trim woman of sixty putting flabby forty-year-olds to shame. Dietrich disappeared into her own shape the way Garbo disappeared into her New York City hiding.

Within the films, though, this extraordinary endurance of the chosen self is expressed as a change of face, a replacement of the romantic, "feminine" aura by a jaunty, mocking "male" gaze. As I shall suggest a little later, this change of face is the whole subject of *The Scarlet Empress*. In *Shanghai Express* the soft-focus furs give way to Clive Brook's peaked cap, which Dietrich lifts off his head and places on her own, flicking it back to settle at a raffish angle. She looks at such moments, if I may step carefully into a thicket of un-deconstructed assumptions, not like a woman dressed as a man, but like a boy trying to ape the heavy gestures of manhood—or better, like a brilliant parodist of a boy's attempts at such apery. She doesn't impersonate males, she turns them into language, assemblages of signs of malehood. The trick is so complicated that I don't entirely trust my account of it, but I *think* Dietrich's persistent femininity—small bones, smooth skin, faint eyebrows—makes it clear that the parody *is* a parody; while her aloofness, her obvious distance from all the easy conventions of womanliness, makes the trick really eerie, since it seems simultaneously to underscore sexual difference and to cause it to wobble. A test of this reading is to ask whether Dietrich ever really looks like a man, whether we are ever in any doubt about her sex (or even her gender). If she doesn't (if we aren't), then several recent interpretations of the icon need to be revised.

For Claire Johnston, a film like *Morocco* (1930) concentrates on woman as a sign in order to dispose of her as a reality:

> The real opposition posed by the sign is male/non-male, which Sternberg establishes by his use of masculine clothing enveloping the image of Dietrich. This masquerade indicates the absence of man, an

absence which is simultaneously negated and recuperated by man. The image of the woman becomes merely the trace of the exclusion and repression of Woman.[8]

There is a certain amount of muddle here, but it is a fair description of what may well have been Sternberg's project. We can see the seven films he made with Dietrich, or *on* Dietrich, as Herman G. Weinberg says,[9] as an attempted exorcism of the ghost he had himself eagerly raised. He was to be the governing male, the unavoidable master of an invented star. "Marlene is not Marlene," he said. "I am Marlene."[10] But this is not what the films themselves show. They insist, quite unequivocally, that Marlene *is* Marlene, and critics, not looking hard enough, have too readily accepted Sternberg's version of what he did. Dietrich may have been Sternberg's creation, but she quickly got away—or rather, she refused to get away, but stayed and haunted and mocked. When she dresses up in top hat and tails, she is not a sign of the non-male. On the contrary: the absent male (the director, if you like) is the flimsiest of signs, a matter of wardrobe and gesture, and when Dietrich, in this rig, suddenly kisses a woman on the mouth, we gasp not because women have been excluded but because there are only women here. I hasten to add that this is not a case of female bonding; it is a dashing usurpation of the male role, a bit of piracy.

The issue is actually broader than this, and has to do with Dietrich's freedom of movement within our sexual and cultural lexicon. Her legs and her face, as I've suggested, are the signs of her femininity—incontrovertible signs, I think most people would feel, although just why they are so incontrovertible would be a case for further study. She suggests not a person wanting to be a man, or even properly to imitate a man, but a person dressing up, playing with the outfit and the role.[11] And on this basis, she can play with the predictable or controvertible badges of femininity too: she makes up while facing the firing squad in *Dishonoured* (1931), toddles off into the desert on high heels in *Morocco*. She can even dabble with her more generally human identity because she is, finally, always Marlene and no one else. In *Blonde Venus* (1932) she leaps out of a shaggy gorilla suit. I'm still puzzling over the implications of this famous gag, but it seems lightly to reshuffle the chief ingredients of *King Kong*: the monster with Fay Wray in his fist turns out to *be* Fay Wray. The woman here surely figures not the repressed but the irrepressible.

It is likely that female *desire* is rarely represented in what Stephen Heath calls the masquerade of the cinema.[12] But this might be an advantage for Dietrich, as I've hinted—you can want to evade desire as well as express it—and certainly her image, whatever Sternberg thought he was doing, never panders to male desire. It taunts and troubles it. Dietrich's irony, her spinning of the signs, is her freedom.

I am not suggesting that the gaze in *Morocco,* or in many other films, is *not* male. We (men) have all brooded far too long and far too often over pictures that seemed to place women in our possession. I am suggesting that the male gaze in *Morocco,* if it is looking for its customary deck of submissive female images, is being cheated.

Dietrich is good at unsettling categories, at unsettling them and at the same time making us see how avidly we cling to them. She is a creature of the border, and for this reason, in films like *The Spoilers* (1942) and *Destry Rides Again* (1939), she is so curiously suited to the American West. Isn't it a long haul from Berlin cabaret to *Rancho Notorious* (1952)? Not if you're at home in places where identities and definitions slip. Confusion is Dietrich's element, rather as Thomas Pynchon says riot is V's. Other people's confusion, that is.

Early in *Shanghai Express* Dietrich pretends to mishear a lady's description of her home as a boarding-house. "What kind of house did you say?" "A boarding-house." Dietrich says, "Oh," pursing her lips, hollowing out her cheeks even more than usual, a faint smile appearing at the end of the pout. The exchange focuses a whole conversation about respectability, and Dietrich's amused expression doesn't particularly suggest the lady's house is not respectable, only that the very notion of respectability is perhaps an illusion or a joke. It implies a frontier that is both fiercely patrolled ("I suppose every train carries its cargo of sin," a parson says in the film) and easily crossed (how many respectable men have found their way to Shanghai Lily?).

It is interesting that Welles should have picked up so much of this in *Touch of Evil* (1958), making Dietrich a weary witch of a border town, keeper of a man's past, and teller of his nonexistent fortune. "Tell me my future like you used to," Welles says as the obese, corrupt, gifted, failing detective. "You haven't got any," Dietrich says, hooded eyes smoldering, cigarette dangling from her lip. "Your future is all used up." At the end of the film she speaks Welles's epitaph: "He was a great detective and a lousy cop"—a refinement of categories that are often confused. Then, refusing all categories except the most inclusive, she says, "He was some kind of a man." Was he a man because he had to be right? Because he was haunted by the thought of the murderer who got away, the one that killed his wife? The solver of riddles, the avenger of wrongs—these are dream identities for men. But Dietrich is not saying any more. "He was some kind of a man." It took more than one film to give her this banal and lugubrious wisdom. But she was not a man-eater. Quite the reverse: she was a survivor of men's attentions.

III

I am suggesting then that Dietrich's story is one of conquest—conquest of time, of signs, of sentiment, of Sternberg, of all would-be invaders of her dignity. She cannot be humanized, or feminized, according to submissive conventions. The failure of the attempt is caught most clearly perhaps in *The Devil Is a Woman* (1935), the last film she made with Sternberg. We see her at one point, for example, with the half-smile and dangling cigarette that are to reappear in *Touch of Evil*. She says to her forlorn suitor, "I kissed you because I loved you—for a minute." Later she wants to know why the police are after another of her lovers. "What did you do?" "Politics," he says, sounding rather grand about it. "A little bit revolutionary." "Is that all?" Dietrich drawls. "I thought it was something important." She is not a sadist in any of her movies, but she plainly likes power and is entertained by weakness in others. Her dominion is so harsh and so entire in this film that one wonders whether the male director can really have wanted to command at all, except as author of the *mise-en-scène*. The male fantasy—and this goes for most of Dietrich's work—seems to be more about groveling than about ruling, and it stares out at us with almost embarrassing clarity in this movie. Dietrich is playing with her hair, too busy to pay attention to her desperate admirer. "Concha, I love you," he says. "Life without you means nothing." Without turning her head or ceasing to play with her curls, Dietrich says in her tough, android voice, "One moment, and I'll give you a kiss." Toward the end of the film, she is supposed to repent of all her cruelties, to understand how much this poor old chap loves her, and what such love really means. This is what the script and the plot say, but we cannot *see* this in the film, and I return to the importance of the face. Dietrich in the long close-up Sternberg offers at this crucial point doesn't look at all like a woman who has repented of her cruelties. She looks like a person who has other plans, even when other plans are just what she is said to have given up. She looks like her own person, not a man's nurse or slave; she looks like Marlene Dietrich. "But what about her own life?" Angela Carter asks about Dietrich in *The Blue Angel*. "That is a gap in the scenario which . . . she must fill in herself."[13] There is always a gap in a Dietrich scenario: the space between the often maudlin plot and the privacy of the untroubled face.

This is the story that Dietrich carries into all her films, whether the plots will it or not; but it *is* the plot of *The Scarlet Empress,* a legend that was waiting for Dietrich, so to speak. It is the story of a woman whose life becomes her own. The film is said to be based on a diary of Catherine the Great, a German princess who married the crazy Prince Peter of Russia, and whose role, a title card informs us, is to "temper the madness of the holy Russian dynasty." She tempers it by stealing a march on it. "Now that I have learned how Russia expects me to behave," Dietrich says with sly pleasure, "I like it here." She becomes the famous female philanderer known to history and to Byron, "the Messalina of the North," as another card has it. Yet another card tells us she has deserted her "youthful ideals." What ideals were those?

This is where Dietrich really possesses herself of the Catherine story. The plot of the film requires an innocent, unknowing maiden who is corrupted by disappointment (marriage to a madman who hates her, the discovery that her surly, long-haired lover is also doing night duty with the empress her mother-in-law) and by the violence and faithlessness of the court she has come to. I doubt whether this version of things fits the historical situation at all well, but in any case Dietrich can't play it. Not only because she can't act young and innocent in an entirely straightforward way, but because by 1934 her face and style on the screen were haunted by the irremediable worldliness of her previous roles. In a series of shots early in the film she shakes her ringlets, opens her eyes wide, miming inexperience. She looks young enough; she looks bewildered and helpless. But there is a curious quality of travesty about the performance, as with her games with male attire. This is a parade of signs—the signs of youth, disarray, naiveté—and the face hints at the sign system, discreetly reveals how much it knows, how thoroughly this ignorance is simulated. It would simply be bad acting, and a disaster, if Dietrich didn't already have a screen identity that easily absorbs this sort of imposture as one of her charades.

I suggested earlier that Dietrich's face bore an implication simultaneously of innocence and of the impossibility of innocence. But *that* innocence was innocence in the midst of presumed guilt or obvious experience; an innocence sustained against the odds and perhaps against the facts, like that of Hardy's Tess. The innocence Dietrich can't project at all—and this is an interesting limitation and definition of her screen character—is the innocence *prior* to experience. There never was a time when she didn't know what she knows now. She was always already, to use a rapidly fraying phrase, in a position to tell Orson Welles's fortune.

The Scarlet Empress, Paramount Pictures Corporation
Courtesy of Museum of Modern Art/Film Stills Archive

The question of innocence comes up again at the wedding of Dietrich-Catherine to what the film calls "the royal half-wit." We see her face in a veil, in huge close-up, a candle flickering in the corner of the frame. The eyes are sorrowful, vulnerable, deep. She is looking at Alexei, her lover, knows she is being sacrificed to interests of state, poor little girl. Her eyebrows are faint, thin lines, pure pencil—*has* she any eyebrows of her own? She wears an elaborate headdress, which makes her look even more like an icon than usual. Another shot shows the half-wit grinning stupidly. Their hands are joined, and a card says that Catherine is now taking the first "innocent step" toward becoming a "sinister empress." This sequence is much harder to read than the earlier shots with the ringlets, because Dietrich's personality is muted by the elaborate composition and the static quality of the shots, and because Sternberg is doing everything he can (which is quite a lot) to make her into an image of innocence being bought and sold. But the effect finally is very close to that of the fur-haloed shot in *Shanghai Express*. This is a beauty that is both breakable and dangerous; dangerous because breakable perhaps; a form of vulnerability and a form of power. The promise of power comes, I think, from the fact that the vulnerability is *not* ignorance.

For this is what the film ultimately celebrates: the excited triumph of the so-called weaker sex. A lady-in-waiting asks the old empress what would have happened if she had not been a woman. "I would have had less trouble," the old lady says, with notable insincerity. "We women are creatures of the heart, aren't we, Catherine?" Dietrich says yes demurely, but is already beginning to look very much like her mischievous, close-to-heartless screen self.[14] When the empress dies, Catherine stages a coup and takes over the realm from the hapless and now extremely malevolent half-wit. She reviews her troops on horseback, wearing a resplendent white cossack uniform complete with fur shako and muff. She rides across the screen like something out of an allegorical painting of liberty, races her horse clattering up the internal steps of the palace, breathlessly rings the great bell proclaiming her victory. She is out of breath several times in this movie, panting with various forms of thrill and conquest. "There is no Emperor," she says. "There is only an Empress." And she sits herself on the throne, the little ringletted girl who has become ruler of all the Russias. There is no flavor of the "sinister empress" here, only an image of an extraordinary exultation.

Sternberg, it seems to me, often needs Dietrich's cruelty and irony for his own narrative purposes. "You have ice where others have a heart," is one of his less felicitous lines in *The Devil Is a Woman*, whose title alone says plenty. But in *The Scarlet Empress*, there is no male masochism that I can see, and no sorry stuff about the *femme fatale*. Dietrich-Catherine is the woman of destiny, and a figure for the destiny of women. Not because, as Andrew Sarris rather luridly puts it, "Dietrich's rapturous ride up the palace steps at the head of her Imperial cavalry is the visual correlative of soaring sexual ecstasy."[15] This is to translate sexuality too directly into politics, or back again, and once the metaphor is unraveled, it leaves the woman locked in the bedroom after all. It is true that Catherine, in the films, likes to sleep with her more handsome officers, but this is part of the legend, not a serious aspect of her power. What the magnificent principal images of the movie suggest—Dietrich's fragile face, her uniform, her fur hat and muff, her horse, the marvelous ride, the ringing bell, the breathless victory—is an exuberant freedom from the ordinary roles of women, creatures of the heart and the boudoir, and possibly a freedom from the constraints of sexual identity altogether, since Dietrich doesn't have to become a man to conquer. She merely gives herself the pleasure of pilfering male styles. There is no emperor, only an empress, and she is empress of herself, because she is empress of signs, to adapt a phrase from Barthes. This is a sovereignty of which men and women no doubt dream equally; but women until recently were far more severely confined to their dreams.

It is curious—more than curious perhaps—that this same slippage and loosening of sexual identity should characterize the most famous facial fetish of all. "Was this the face that launched a thousand ships," Faustus asks, "And burnt the topless towers of Ilium?" The grammar makes the face the actual agent of war and destruction. Then Faustus, having played out the ready-made fantasies ("I will be Paris, and for love of thee/Instead of Troy shall Wittenberg be sacked"), rather strangely compares Helen to Jupiter descending on Semele—that is, to male violence consuming a woman in lightning—and to the royal sun ("monarch of the sky") bathing in a blue (female) spring. This is not the place to untangle the assumptions of this passage.[16] We need note only that if the grammar makes Helen's face epically active, the imagery rapidly turns her into a man. Is this to equate power with masculinity, and if so, is it an oppressive, compromised thought, or merely a sober estimate of the score under patriarchy? But what if Helen remains a woman, taking on a man's power, as Yeats wondered whether her mother might have done when she was raped by the swan-god? What if she is a woman in fact and in the myth; a man only in the imagery, like Dietrich wearing tails or the uniform of a cossack? "This is the true source of the fatality of the *femme fatale*," Angela Carter says: "that she lives her life in such a way her freedom reveals to others their lack of liberty. So her sexuality is destructive, not in itself but in its effects."[17] Helen's face burns the towers of Troy because men cannot allow it to roam the world. *The Scarlet Empress* offers something like the guiltless reverse of this tale, a strangely accepted freedom that pensions off the *femme fatale*, because her lesson seems to be learned. Her significance, as Carter says, "lies not in her gender but in her freedom."[18]

Of course, not every face can launch that many ships, and Dietrich's beauty was a form of fortune. But the independence that hides behind her beauty, rescuing her from its snares and deceptions, may be seen as a promise and an example. Even in the darkest and most strangling of Sternberg's fictions about women, she retained an impressive liberty, and in *The Scarlet Empress,* Sternberg allowed her to push right through his cluttered myth and to rise like a blue or only slightly soiled angel into the clearer air of her own.

Notes

1. Cf. Stephen Heath, *Questions of Cinema* (Bloomington: Indiana University Press, 1981), 183–84: "films are full of fragments, bits of bodies, gestures, desirable traces, fetish points—if we take fetishism here as investment in a bit, a fragment, for its own sake, as the end of the accomplishment of a desire. . . . Cinema can and does fragment the body . . . but the human person, the total image of the body seen is always the pay-off. . . ." I want to suggest that for a long spell of cinema history, the pay-off was the face, which gathered into its orbit all the associations of the body, indeed almost everything we attach to the idea of a person. I am using *fetish* in its anthropological rather than its psychoanalytic sense, to mean an object or a principle "irrationally reverenced," as the Oxford English Dictionary nicely puts it; but I assume the concept involves quite a large element of displacement, so that the fetish is only partly, or only apparently, treasured "for its own sake."

2. Roland Barthes, *Mythologies,* translated by Annette Lavers (New York: Hill and Wang, 1972),56.

3. Roland Barthes, *Mythologies,* 57.

4. Charles Affron, *Star Acting: Gish, Garbo, Davis* (New York: E. P. Dutton, 1977).

5. Charles Affron, *Star Acting,* 149, remarks of the wounded, reflective faintly hopeful face Garbo presents in *Grand Hotel* (1932) that it is "exempt from script, and, I suspect, from direction." I think it is probably exempt from acting too, in the intentional, theatrical sense. The film actor's talent has less to do with expressing an emotion, however unscripted, than with feeding the camera the miniature details it likes, so that emotion can bloom on the screen. This is not to deny the film star's gift, or the discipline and hard work that go into being Garbo or Dietrich or Crawford or Cagney. Stars, *pace* Janet Gaynor, Judy Garland, and Barbra Streisand, are made, not born. But they are made of strange, brittle, aleatory stuff, and the concept of acting tends to submerge the mystery rather than explore it.

6. A curious conversation in Schell's film suggests Dietrich had no sexual preferences. She claims not to understand the concept of the erotic. Men demand sexual activity, she tells Schell, so one has to comply from time to time. But "one can also do without it," *man kann auch ohne.* A person supposed, as Dietrich is, to be a lesbian might well speak in just this way about sex with men. But I am tempted to take her quite literally. What if the sexual object had no, or only very slight, sexual inclinations herself? It would give her tremendous power, and the situation exactly fits the mood Dietrich projects into movies.

7. Cf. Affron, *Star Acting,* 199: "she charts the geography of love lost. . . .

Garbo's generosity contains the slipping away of things and people." And 155: "Her understanding leaves nothing out."

8. Claire Johnston, "Women's Cinema as Counter-Cinema," in *Sexual Stratagems,* ed. Patricia Erens, (New York: Horizon Press, 1979), 136.

9. Herman G Weinberg, *Joseph von Sternberg* (Paris: Seghers, 1966), 53.

10. Quoted in E. Ann Kaplan, *Women and Film* (New York: Methuen, 1983), 52.

11. Kaplan, *Women and Film,* 51–52, catches this flavor when she writes of Dietrich "deliberately making herself object" of Sternberg's gaze "outside the frame, beyond the diegesis. . . . Her understanding of the extra-cinematic discourse she is placed in permits a certain distance from what is being done to her, providing a gap through which the female spectator can glimpse her construction in patriarchy." But a star's identity cannot be extra-cinematic in Hollywood, and I'm not sure that extra-diegetic as a concept makes all that much sense in film study. Photographed places and people come trailing all kinds of bits of the world with them, in the way that the more purely conventional alphabet, in a literary text, doesn't. This is to say, perhaps, that film signs are not as moveable, or as "textual," as some others. I am suggesting throughout this essay that Dietrich's irony and distance are clearly visible within the frame, part of who she is on the screen.

12. Stephen Heath, *Questions,* 187: "For psychoanalysis . . . the masquerade is the assumption by the woman of a 'femininity' as the representation of desire. . . . she . . . becomes—in that 'rejection' which is the very fact of her as woman, the necessity of her existence in desire—his image as her femininity, a whole cinema."

13. Angela Carter, *Nothing Sacred* (London: Virago, 1982), 123.

14. The empress, played by Louise Dresser, a fast-talking American woman mysteriously elevated to the Russian throne, has about as much heart as Groucho Marx. "That's my chancellor," she remarks. "Steals more money from me in a week than I collect in taxes in a year." Addressing her Privy Council, she says, "Sit down, you fools, or I'll send you to Siberia." I suppose this is just galloping anachronism and American chauvinism. But the gag may be more delicate. "Russia," in this film, is obviously an American fantasy, a region of the frightened mind.

15. Andrew Sarris, *The Films of Joseph von Sternberg* (New York: Museum of Modern Art, 1966), 40.

16. Christopher Marlowe, *The Tragical History of Doctor Faustus,* in *The Complete Plays* (Harmondsworth: Penguin Books, 1969), 330–31. The passage in full runs as follows:

> Was this the face that launched a thousand ships,
> And burnt the topless towers of Ilium?
> Sweet Helen, make me immortal with a kiss.
> Her lips suck forth my soul: see where it flies.
> Come, Helen, come, give me my soul again.

Here will I dwell, for heaven is in those lips,
And all is dross that is not Helena.

I will be Paris, and for love of thee
Instead of Troy shall Wittenberg be sacked,
And I will combat with weak Menelaus,
And wear thy colours on my plumed crest.
Yea, I will wound Achilles in the heel,
And then return to Helen for a kiss.
Oh, thou art fairer than the evening's air,
Clad in the beauty of a thousand stars.
Brighter art thou than flaming Jupiter,
When he appeared to hapless Semele:

More lovely than the monarch of the sky,
In wanton Arethusa's azure arms,
And none but thou shalt be my paramour.

The image also appears in *Tamburlaine II, The Complete Plays*, 206: "Helen, whose beauty summon'd Greece to arms,/And drew a thousand ships to Tenedos. . . ."

17. Angela Carter, *Nothing Sacred*, 123.
18. Ibid.

9

"Shadows of the Substance": Women Screenwriters in the 1930s

MELISSA SUE KORT
Santa Rosa Junior College

Until recently, the words "Hollywood screenwriter" conjured up images of well-paid but vastly mistreated men in rolled shirtsleeves, fedoras thrown back over greasy hair, cigarettes dangling from mouths only recently removed from glasses of whiskey. We think of Scott Fitzgerald suffering and rarely receiving credit, of Ben Hecht and Charlie MacArthur rattling away at typewriters, of cramped quarters in backlots and stories being passed down an endless line of contract writers.

Unless one regularly pays attention to the credits on the late night movies on television or carefully reads film histories, one might assume that screenwriters, particularly in the thirties, were exclusively men. If one thought very hard, perhaps names like Dorothy Parker or Lillian Hellman would surface or the mention of Anita Loos would ring a bell. One might remember hearing whistles at Mae West's dialogue credit. But few people outside the film industry would immediately picture the screenwriter of the 1930s as any of the following: a well-established female veteran of silent films that she might have directed and produced as well as written; a woman who progressed from acting scripts to dictating them; or a woman who was lured to Hollywood from an award-winning, audience-pleasing career writing for the New York stage or magazines by promises of fame, freedom, and above all, hard cash—and lots of it.

Auteur criticism, brought to this country in the sixties by Andrew Sarris,[1] focused attention on the male directors of the 1930s and 1940s (only one woman had created enough films to study—Dorothy Arzner) and away from other aspects of film production. In response, a decade later, Richard Corliss in *Film Comment* began a wave of concern for screenwriters.[2] Still, although there were more women writing movies during the thirties than in any other period before or since, their contribution was almost entirely ignored.

Reestablishing these women in film history is a difficult task for a number of reasons. Fifty years later, few of them are still alive to recount their experiences. Film history tends to depend too heavily on personal accounts published in flashy editions, so if a woman wasn't involved in some sort of scandal, she would probably escape mention. Most of these stories also parrot the publicity vocabulary all Hollywood employees were reared on—the glamor is solidly in place, while a true picture of working conditions is almost impossible to construct. And women were not the ones writing scathing reports of the devastating life of the screenwriter. Instead, they did their work, earned their large salaries, and served the studios well.

But a reconstructed history of Hollywood would have to include the image of Frances Marion in an elegant bedjacket, propped up on pillows on her huge, custom-made bed, surrounded by yellow pads and dictating to three stenographers for hours every day.[3] Between 1915 and 1953, Marion's name appeared on 136 films as actress, producer, director, or, most often, writer, and in the thirties she was one of the highest paid, most influential, and most respected writers in Hollywood. Yet those who could quickly recognize the titles of her films—her Academy Award winners *The Big House* (1930) and *The Champ* (1931), *Anna Christie* (1930), *Min and Bill* (1930), *Dinner at*

Eight (1933), and *Camille* (1933)—would be hard-pressed to name their writer.

Having spent some time as a cub reporter (with Adela Rogers St. Johns) on her hometown paper, the San Francisco *Examiner,* Marion visited Hollywood in 1913 as a commercial artist. She stayed, first as an actress, then as a protégé of Lois Weber, America's first important woman director. Weber is best remembered for her films on such controversial subjects as birth control, capital punishment, and racism. She offered Marion a training that would be impossible to obtain today in all aspects of film production: editing, costuming, set design, and maintenance. Marion's first writing work consisted of providing extras with appropriate responses in mob scenes, just in case deaf people in the silent movie houses were reading lips. This background helped her become an extremely cost-efficient writer. Knowing all elements of production, she knew how to write easily produced films. By the twenties, she was the highest paid scenario writer in town.

Marion was not the only woman enjoying success in Hollywood in the 1920s. Other women had achieved similar stature in the free-wheeling, pioneering days of the silents. Bess Meredyth began as an actress with Biograph in 1911 and started writing in 1917. By 1919 she had written ninety features, a prolific start to a career that lasted over thirty years. Jeannie MacPherson also acted with Biograph, but she soon moved to Universal, the studio that boasted the largest number of women directors at the time. She was asked to direct a film she had written after the original negative was accidentally destroyed and the initial director had left the studio, and her success earned her the position of both leading lady and director of one of Universal's production companies. In 1915, overworked and exhausted, she gladly went to work as a writer for Cecil B. DeMille, a close association that lasted well into the 1940s.

DeMille's brother, William, also depended on one woman for most of his films: his wife, the former actress, Clara Beranger. "The minute a director thinks he can do it all, he is beginning to write his own death warrant," Beranger told a 1929 film class at the University of Southern California. "There are a few who can do it, but the majority of directors need writers as much as writers need directors."[4]

Lewis Jacobs gives June Mathis credit for "the make up of continuity as we know it today" and for originating "the writer-director combination which was to plan the film's action before any shooting began."[5] During her most influential period, when she served for a time as head

of the Metro and Goldwyn units, her name appeared on many important productions, including *Four Horsemen of the Apocalypse* (1921),
Metro's greatest success. Mathis was involved in introducing Rudolph
Valentino to the screen (Suzanne Pleshette plays her in the 1977 film
biography, *Valentino*). She also had the dubious honor of cutting Von
Stroheim's twenty-four reels of *Greed* (already down from the original
forty) to about sixteen. In the uproar over the huge 1926 production of
Ben Hur, Mathis not only prepared the scenario (later Bess Meredyth
revised it), but she was given control over the picture, having done the
most of any Goldwyn employee to push the project along.

In 1912 Anita Loos began her writing career by copying the name of
a producer off of a film can, dashing off a movie script, and sending it
to him. She received $25 for "The New York Hat," filmed by D. W.
Griffith, and became, according to her own account, the industry's first
resident scenarist. Before sound arrived, two hundred of her scripts
had been filmed. Her first of many films for Douglas Fairbanks, *His
Picture in the Papers* (1915), introduced the use of titles for something
more than odd scene changes. While working with her husband, the
director John Emerson, she often allowed him to assume collaboration
credit when correcting her punctuation was his major contribution to
a script. She explains her motive for this in her autobiography, *Kiss
Hollywood Goodbye*, by quoting lyrics from the musical version of her
most famous work, *Gentlemen Prefer Blondes* (the novel was published in 1925 and first filmed in 1928):

> I'm really in my hey-day
> If he wants ten bucks till pay day
> 'Cause I love what I'm doing when I'm doing it for love.[6]

In the thirties, Loos's name appeared on several important MGM
films, including the Jean Harlow vehicles *Red Headed Woman* (1932),
Hold Your Man (1933) and *Riffraff* (1935), and the prestigious productions of *San Francisco* (1936) and *The Women* (1939). But primarily she served the studio as a script doctor, more an executive than
a writer.

Veteran film writers found themselves in a different role in the first
decade of sound. "Bess Meredyth, Anita Loos and I were asked our
advice on virtually every script MGM produced during the '30s,"
Frances Marion admitted in 1969.[7] "The best movies we made on the
lot were turned out by Frances Marion who wasn't a writer at all,"
Anita Loos explained. "She just sat in conferences and made up
stories."[8]

So why didn't these women move into directing or producing? Marion, for example, had done both during the silent days, but without enjoying the substantial success her writing achieved. While she claims in her autobiography that writers were mere "shadows of the substance,"[9] she wielded considerable authority and enjoyed important status at MGM, the greatest studio of the decade. She initiated projects or completed them, rather than scrambling for recognition in the middle. Why should she have taken chances by switching to another role?

Besides, a large reason why more women didn't follow Dorothy Arzner, the only woman director to survive the transfer to sound, was the developing corporate nature of the industry. Sound increased production costs, and by the thirties all but a few small studios were controlled by New York financiers. Gaining promotion or being offered a chance to direct was no longer a matter of face-to-face confrontation between old friends. And the furious rate at which films were being cranked out demanded a kind of production-line obedience. Why become just another cog in the production wheel, even a top cog, when one was successful, satisfied, and earning a very good living during a very bad depression, while remaining in the less visible crafts like writing or editing?

One is tempted to argue for a "Betsy Ross Syndrome": women serving traditionally as symbolizers rather than as front-line heroines. But such a theory would ignore the period in Hollywood. Directors had not yet achieved the stature the *politique des auteurs* would later award them. They were contract workers, subject to the controls of the studio, and the job was not that much more important than the writers'. Producers depended much more on their writers, who stood first on the production line, before the director and stars were hired. One expression of how important writers were was the practice of systematically destroying their individuality by frequently dividing the script responsibility among a large number of writers, keeping them subservient to the producers and often sacrificing the integrity of the script itself.

However, outstanding writers like Frances Marion did enjoy a great deal of prestige. Virginia Kellogg, who wrote stories for various studios in the thirties and forties, recalled visiting MGM to interview Clark Gable for her college newspaper, the UCLA *Daily Bruin*. Waiting at the gate for the proper permission to enter, Kellogg ogled all the greats arriving for work. Up drove a long, low, powder-blue Packard, a chauffeur in front and a beautiful auburn-haired woman wearing a matching powder-blue outfit in back. "Who is that gorgeous lady?" Kellogg asked, expecting the name of some rising star. "Frances Marion, the writer," the gateman informed her, and young Kellogg decided that writing was definitely a promising career.

Many of the personal and professional accounts show that a loose-knit but strong mutual support network existed among the women in Hollywood. Marion speaks of feeling "consoled" by the fact that many women "gave me real aid when I was at the crossroads. Too many women go around these days saying women in important positions don't help their own sex, but that was never my experience."[10]

Anita Loos's account differs:

> When I [worked in films] I found my male bosses adorable. I don't like women very much. I don't like their films so I pass them up. Throughout my career, women have done me more dirt than men. I just find them tiresome, if not vicious.[11]

But one gets accustomed to taking Loos's flamboyant remarks with large doses of salt. She does admit elsewhere that "the two most important executives I knew in the movies were Mary Pickford and Lillian Gish,"[12] and her various published memoirs record close associations with many women, including Norma and Constance Talmadge, Helen Hayes, and Tallulah Bankhead.

Frances Marion's personal and professional connections with various women in Hollywood seem to be more the norm. They began with her work with Lois Weber, whose funeral expenses she paid in 1939. She wrote thirteen scripts for Mary Pickford, often helping to revive Pickford's long, but not always distinguished career. These included *The Love Light* (1921), which co-starred Marion's third husband, Fred Thomson, and which Marion directed and Pickford produced. After Marie Dressler had fallen from stardom, Marion helped her, first with *The Callahans and the Murphys* (1927) and again with *Min and Bill* (1930), which earned Dressler an Oscar. *Min and Bill* has an interesting inception: Marion claimed it was adapted from *Dark Star,* a morose Scottish tale written by Lorna Moon, an unsuccessful writer who was then suffering from tuberculosis. Marion was paying for Moon's convalescence, and Moon hoped to sell the novel to repay the debt. Knowing the tale had little screen potential, and fearing her friend would die soon, Marion presented the raucous story of Min and Bill in Moon's name.

A number of other special friendships existed between women in Hollywood, and one of the most productive was between former actress Salka Viertel and Greta Garbo. Viertel, a Pole who had appeared with Max Reinhardt's company in Germany, emigrated to Hollywood at the beginning of the thirties with her husband, a director. She soon became friends with Garbo, who asked her to help rewrite *Queen Christina* (1933). Both Europeans were very lonely in southern California, and Viertel quickly became part of Garbo's tight inner circle. With two exceptions, Viertel collaborated on the scripts of every subsequent film Garbo made, including *The Painted Veil* (1934), *Anna Karenina* (1935), and *Conquest* (1937).

Despite such proofs of female bonding, however, finding solid evidence of feminist concerns in Hollywood scripts would be difficult. Frances Marion's suggestions in her manual, *How to Write and Sell Film Stories,* indicated that she, like most women writing in Hollywood, was less concerned with breaking stereotypes than with maintaining the Hollywood formulae for characterizing women.

> Women, and do not forget that the majority of movie-goers are women, like to see well-furnished interiors and modes of life among cultured people of more means than their own.
>
> *Domestic relations,* with their loves, apprehensions, struggles, anxieties and joys, offer a plot pattern that has tremendous interest to women. . . . These plots often skirt immorality, bleached a bit by the insistence that the heroine's motives are pure. They threaten a sex problem rather than portray it.[13]

Marion suggests two successful storylines in her chapter on "The Theme," two classic formats of the woman's film: "The wife who earns more than her husband loses his love," and "A woman's need for romance makes her an undependable factor in business."[14] These themes strike an ironic note, considering that Marion and other women writers supported their families and were extremely dependable businesswomen.

But few of the successful women screenwriters writing in the thirties would attempt what we would today call a feminist perspective. Even the woman's film, which enjoyed extreme popularity in the thirties and forties, could not be called a feminist genre. The monies in Hollywood were too tightly controlled by men, and few risks were taken with studio funds. Besides, women writers perhaps saw little to fight for. They were well paid, enjoyed high professional status, and easily combined glamor (an important thirties commodity) with success.

They enjoyed, as well, certain freedoms by virtue of being part of unconventional Hollywood, and they relished overturning stereotypes in their own lives. Virginia Kellogg recalled that when Marion was doing research for a prison picture, she found herself forced to drive into downtown Los Angeles without her chauffeur. A policeman stopped her to question her erratic driving, and she explained that she wasn't accustomed to driving herself. "Just another dumb lady driver," he mumbled as he let her go. She drove around the block, thinking, then returned to challenge the officer. "My brains earn me $300,000 a year; how much are yours worth?"

But Marion's was not the only trail to success for women screenwriters. While she and others were practically raised by the movies, some of these women, like Zoë Akins, didn't arrive in Hollywood until a New York writing career was well established. Akins began writing plays in school, but her first published works were articles for the St. Louis *Times*. A piece she wrote on Emma Goldman began a lifelong friendship. Akins's poetry was rejected by Willa Cather, then managing editor of the prestigious *McClure's* magazine, who advised her to write for the stage instead and encouraged a friendship through correspondence. Despite Cather's advice, in 1907 at the age of twenty-one, Akins published her first volume of poetry. But by 1916 she had turned to the stage and three years later she scored her first big hit, *Déclassée*, starring Ethel Barrymore. *Daddy's Gone A-Hunting* in 1921, her next major success, was later adapted by MGM. In the early twenties, three of Akins's plays ran on Broadway at the same time, a record not duplicated by any other playwright of the period.

The Greeks Had a Word for It (1930) finally earned Akins her ticket west, and she joined the migration of stage writers brought to Hollywood to help make pictures talk. Her first credits appeared on two films directed by Dorothy Arzner in 1930: *Sarah and Son* and *Anybody's Woman,* both featuring stage star Ruth Chatterton. The association with Arzner yielded two more films: *Working Girls* (1931) and *Christopher Strong* (1933). In 1939, considering a salary cut in order to work with the director again, Akins described Arzner to her agent, Alice Kauser: "She is easy to work with and does not intrigue or lie or get drunk; she is neither hog, cat, pig, nor prima donna, nor a tyrant."[15] Backhanded praise, but their friendship lasted many years and included collaboration on productions at the Pasadena Playhouse in the 1950s, after both had retired from Hollywood.

It is interesting to note that women scripted ten of Arzner's sixteen features. Mary C. McCall, Jr., was prepared to leave Hollywood when her four-year contract with Warner Brothers ran out, before Arzner borrowed her to work on *Craig's Wife* (1936). McCall had been brought to Hollywood at the height of her magazine fiction career, and she highly resented the treatment she initially received. But of Arzner she said,

> For the first time since I came to Hollywood I had a sense of helping to make something. I've never had a better time in my life than I had during the eight or ten weeks when that picture was being made.[16]

McCall remained in Hollywood, eventually serving as the first and thus far only woman president of the Screen Writers Guild.

Like many New York writers who came west, Akins saw Hollywood primarily as a money-making venture, and she used her free time to continue "serious" writing and to secure stars for her east coast productions. "Writing for Hollywood was not difficult," she said. "All you have to do is write six pages every day, then grab the money and run for the train."[17]

In 1935 she earned the Pulitzer Prize for Drama for *The Old Maid*, an adaptation of an Edith Wharton novel, later filmed (in 1939) with Bette Davis and Miriam Hopkins. The play is typical of Akins's work— light, romantic, full of witty dialogue, and just barely touching issues of double standards, sexual freedom, and woman's role. Although Akins was proud to have been able to create great roles for women theatrical and screen stars, only in her films for Arzner can one detect feminist tendencies, and that probably was due more to the director than to the writer.

In the late thirties, many of the individual giants who had made Hollywood so great were disappearing, in part phased out by the developing financial structure of the industry. Women writers appear to have been strongly affected by these changes, particularly by the sudden death of MGM's boy genius, Irving Thalberg, in 1939. "I felt as though the earth were giving way beneath my feet," Akins wrote to her friend, the director of *Mädchen in Uniform*, Leontine Sagan, "as I was working for him at the time and very happily." Her letter to Alice Kauser on 20 October of that year explains many of the difficulties she and other writers faced at the end of a "golden" decade.

> While I had Mr. Thalberg's protection I was reasonably sure that I was out of the political fires, and that what I wrote would reach the screen. But since he is dead, and now that panic has descended on the "Industry" as a whole, I had rather return to a room in Washington Square and walk to and from the theatre, than go through the onslaught of nerves I have endured for so many years. But one thing I must concede: after being through the terrific ordeal of getting a movie script written and before the cameras, writing what one chooses becomes a rare privilege; also the

training and the hard work increases one's technical powers and resourcefulness, and I do love California and feel better than when I came
out![18]

Bent on freeing herself from "the movie apron strings," Akins published a girls' school novel in 1940, *Forever Young*. In publicity interviews, she repeated the same theme: "I cannot tell you what a release
this novel has been. It has made me free; it has made me appreciate
the value of words."[19] Akins returned to her playwriting career, but
she kept her Pasadena home and Hollywood connections.

Another woman who moved between New York and Hollywood
careers was Frances Goodwich. She had acted on and off Broadway for
nearly twenty years before she met and married Albert Hackett (her
third husband), also an actor. While performing in a stock company in
Denver, Goodwich showed Hackett a script she had written and they
decided to rewrite it together. Their second play, *Up Pops the Devil*
(1930), was quickly purchased by Paramount (Bob Hope starred in the
1938 film, retitled *Thanks for the Memory*). Soon after that, they were
hired by producer Hunt Stromberg at MGM, and they began a long
career that combined screen and stage work.

Stromberg was one of the more quiet giants in Hollywood, and the
Hacketts benefited greatly from the association. Goodwich told *Films
in Review:*

> It was wonderful working with him. It was like the theatre. He gave you
> responsibility. You were consulted about casting and you saw all the
> rushes and you were part of the whole project.[20]

But the couple was not always so well treated in Hollywood. Their
friend and Garden of Allah neighbor, Scott Fitzgerald, used them as
models for the Tarletons in *The Last Tycoon*. "These are good writers,"
Monroe Stahr explains to a studio visitor, "and we don't have good
writers out here."

> "These Tarletons are a husband and wife team from the East—pretty
> good playwrights. They've just found out they're not alone on the story
> and it shocks them—shocks their sense of unity—that's the word they'll
> use."
> "But what does make the—the unity?"
> Stahr hesitated—his face was grim except that his eyes twinkled.
> "I'm the unity," he said.
> He saw the Tarletons. He told them he liked their work, looking at Mrs.
> Tarleton as if he could read her handwriting through the typescript. He

told them kindly that he was taking them from the picture and putting them on another, where there was less pressure, more time. As he had half expected, they begged to stay on the first picture, seeing a quicker credit, even though it was shared with others. The system was a shame, he admitted—gross, commercial, to be deplored. He had originated it—a fact that he did not mention.[21]

Eventually the Hacketts adapted to their position and came to look back on it philosophically. "We were contract writers," Goodwich re-members. "You don't get any hosannas, you don't get entertained by the producers, but you get money. You get very good, pleasant money, you know." Their steady success, their maintaining their New York careers, their strong marriage and working relationship, and their habit of jumping on the first train east at every opportunity all helped them survive whatever indignities Hollywood offered.

They worked best together by writing separately, then exchanging drafts. "We both would bat out a scene and then get together," Good-wich recalls. "I'd tell him his stinks and he'd tell me mine stinks and then we'd finally get down to a medium on which we could agree." Goodwich admits that when she once tried to collaborate with a woman writer, she found it difficult; she felt she had "to be polite all the time." Working with her husband had other benefits. Goodwich claims that, "As a woman I never felt discriminated against," but admits that that may have been in part due to Hackett's presence. Moreover, she remembers that "being a woman was a marvelous asset."

> I could go into a big conference of men, and if there was a big argument, I could say, "I represent the woman's point of view. A woman wouldn't do that." And in a man's conference like that it really carried weight. I would be listened to.[22]

Screenwriter–drama critic George Oppenheimer called the Hacketts "the most devoted and friendliest couple in a town noted neither for its monogamy nor affability."[23] And they were responsible for bringing to the screen one of its most memorable married couples—Nick and Nora Charles in *The Thin Man* (1935) and *After the Thin Man* (1936), the first two parts of a successful series based on the work of Dashiell Hammett. Director William Van Dyke, with whom they created many hits, said to them, "I don't care anything about the story; just give me five scenes between those two people." The Hacketts, knowing that the couple was based on the Hammett-Lillian Hellman relationship, triumphed, cleaning up the novel characters for the censors without sacrificing the lively, witty, sexy spirit of the originals. Years later in the 1950s, when Lillian Hellman was offered the task of adapting *The Diary of Anne Frank* to the stage, she sent it instead to the Hacketts, who earned a Pulitzer Prize and a Tony Award for their play and an Oscar nomination (their third) for the screenplay.

Working at MGM, they too were struck by Thalberg's death, particularly because Hunt Stromberg, with whom they had worked so well, was devastated by the loss. In 1939, the Hacketts suddenly left Hollywood. "We had a nice collaborative nervous breakdown," Goodwich explains.

> Albert was crying and I was crying. We were tired. And Stromberg said to us, "Now we'll have a *Thin Man* next year and a Nelson Eddy and a *Rose Marie*." It was just too much. So we stayed away until our money ran out.[24]

For the next twenty years or so, the Hacketts traveled frequently from coast to coast, scoring some of their most enduring successes. These include *It's a Wonderful Life* (1946—they claim more credit than Capra was willing to give), *Summer Holiday* (1948—a musical remake of their 1936 hit, an adaptation of Eugene O'Neill's *Ah, Wilderness*), *Easter Parade* (1948), *Father of the Bride* (1950), and *Seven Brides for Seven Brothers* (1954).

They were not the only couple working together in Hollywood in the thirties. Dorothy Parker had come west in 1931 on a short contract with MGM, but she quickly returned to New York, disgruntled by the working situation. In 1933 she married Alan Campbell, an actor much younger than herself, and they came back to Hollywood, where Campbell took up writing. He enjoyed the work and took it seriously; Parker never did. She complained vociferously but Christopher Isherwood claimed, "She complained about Hollywood the way English people do about the weather."[25] She did find pleasure in a west coast version of her beloved Algonquin round table in the form of life at The Garden of Allah, the former home of silent screen actress Alla Nazimova, which in the thirties housed, among other writers, the Hacketts and Parker's Algonquin pal, Robert Benchley. She and Benchley invested in Romanoff's Restaurant, which quickly became another Hollywood hangout.

Throughout her Hollywood career, Parker was active in political causes, helping to organize the Screen Writers Guild, helping to found the Anti-Nazi League, reporting on the Loyalist cause in Spain, marching to free Sacco and Vanzetti, raising money for the Scottsboro Boys. Later, in 1949, she was blacklisted. It was through these activities that Parker met Lillian Hellman and began a friendship that would last until Parker's death. Despite all this activity, Parker was distracted: she had used her Hollywood earnings to purchase a home in Pennsylvania where she wanted to settle down a bit and have children (having first attempted motherhood at age forty-three and having miscarried, she was frustrated in her desires).

Parker's most memorable script of the period is the 1937 *A Star Is Born*. She and her husband contributed to fifteen films in the 1930s, but only Parker's name appeared on the list of esteemed writers on the new Thalberg Building at MGM (Zoë Akins also was listed). She is said to have leaned out of her window there once and yelled, "Let me out! I'm as sane as you are!"

Tess Slesinger began her writing career alone, but she collaborated with her second husband for most of her Hollywood assignments. Her first stories were published in *The Menorah Journal*, a magazine pledged to "the study and advancement of Jewish culture and ideals."[26] The assistant editor was her first husband, Herbert Solow, a political journalist and part of an intellectual circle that included Lionel Trilling and Clifton Fadiman. The group was "cynical and aggresively hopeful," and "mildly leftish," Fadiman admitted. "I suppose for our time we were fairly bold, courageous, unconventional."[27]

After divorcing Solow, Slesinger wrote *The Unpossessed* (1934), a novel about a group of young leftists trying to start a magazine. Her writing was favorably compared to that of Mary McCarthy, Dorothy Parker, Katherine Mansfield, and Virginia Woolf, particularly the last, for what one critic dubbed Slesinger's "stream of rationalization."[28] *Time: The Present,* a collection of short stories, soon followed, and her critical success earned her a ticket to MGM in 1935 at a weekly salary of $1,000 (equal to what Scott Fitzgerald was earning at the time).

On her first assignment, *The Good Earth,* Slesinger met and soon married the picture's assistant producer, Frank Davis, who switched to writing and collaborated with her on the rest of Slesinger's scripts. Before *The Good Earth* was scheduled for release, Slesinger learned that her name had been cut from the credits and, according to Davis, she became the first writer to take her case to the fledgling Motion Picture Academy.[29] They contacted Thalberg, who eventually gave her credit. From that point on, Slesinger was involved with Hollywood politics, especially concerning the new Screen Writers Guild. She and

Davis were close to Dorothy Parker and Alan Campbell, and were involved with them in other causes, like the Anti-Nazi League and the Abraham Lincoln Brigade.

Slesinger's next assignment was the Dorothy Arzner production, *The Bride Wore Red* (1937). She and Davis worked again for Arzner on *Dance, Girl, Dance* (1940), the director's most blatantly feminist film. The day after it previewed, the couple were named in a "red inquiry" by the Los Angeles *Times*. When Slesinger died in 1945, a young victim of cancer, she left behind a one-hundred-fifty-page manuscript for a novel about Hollywood, "written from the perspective of the ordinary talented workers of the film industry in their personal, professional and political interactions."[30]

Although MGM employed more women writers than any other studio in Hollywood (they simply employed more writers), other studios benefited from the talents of successful women. Sonya Levien ruled the roost at Twentieth Century Fox in the thirties. Levien, daughter of a Russian radical who had escaped to America from Siberian exile, enjoyed a varied career. She could speak four languages by the time she was eight, took a law degree at New York University, studied stenography when the law bored her, and eventually turned to magazine writing. She traveled to England to report firsthand on the suffragette movement for *The Women's Journal*. Later, while working for *Metropolitan Magazine*, she met and married its assistant editor, Carl Hovey.

In 1921 Paramount purchased about a dozen of Levien's stories, and she soon left for Hollywood. But despite her $24,000 a year starting salary, she broke her contract after six months to return east to care for her very young son. However, in 1926 Hovey also found work in Hollywood, as an executive for Cecil B. DeMille, and the family moved west. Levien began to work at Fox, where she remained until 1938. Her biggest hits were both released in 1933, *State Fair* and *Cavalcade*, and her career lasted long into the 1950s.

Asked to discourse on "The Screen Writer" for a 1934 volume on *Careers for Women*, Levien described the advantages and disadvantages of her work.

> The reward for stoicism, for courage, for tremendous persistence under difficulties and under pressure, comes when the picture is finished and is a success. If it turns out to be good you have the excitement of winning a battle—and money in your pocket—or, if it turns out badly, you still have the money. There is nothing in the screen-writing profession for a woman who wants a quiet, peaceful life or for a writer who is ambitious for literary fame.[31]

"A woman has as good a chance as a man to become a successful screen writer," Levien explained. "Her sex creates no awkwardness or difficulty. She has always been a familiar figure in the screen ranks."

Discerning a pattern of distinctly feminist concerns in the styles or themes of screenplays by women writers in the 1930s is almost impossible and would be inflicting fifty years' worth of consciousness-raising on products originally intended to last only as long as dreams do. Women did seem to write an inordinate number of films about women's lives, but this was not necessarily by choice; often they were hired with the excuse that they could best represent "the women's point of view," as dictated by the almost exclusively male producers and studio heads. Women may not have been much responsible for the more masculine genres, but only because they simply were not assigned to write them. And the strong female characters we like to recall from thirties films are as often products of a man's pen as of a woman's.

What is important in looking at the careers of these women is establishing that strong women *did* work in Hollywood, contrary to film histories that relegate women to positions in front of the camera or behind a sewing machine or make-up mirror or typewriter. Women survived the "terrific ordeal," as Zoë Akins called it, as well as men. Like their male colleagues, they were often most successful when they could develop a special relationship with someone in another important production role, like a director, producer, or star. Film is, above all, a collaborative art.

Frequently, their work severely tried their egos and their sense of artistic integrity. The pressures for success were great and these pressures increased as films demanded larger financial investments. The competition was stiff. But many women, some remarkable, some more ordinary workers, filled the screenwriting ranks. Some were content to be successful professionally; some used their positions and new-made wealth to become involved politically. While women in their films may have been perpetuating sometimes degrading stereotypes, the lives of women screenwriters challenged those images. The great variety of women working in Hollywood in the 1930s and the range of their accomplishments invite a much longer study.

Notes

1. Andrew Sarris, "Notes on the Auteur Theory in 1962," *Film Culture* 27 (Winter 1962–63); and *The American Cinema* (New York: E. P. Dutton & Co., 1968). The *politique des auteurs* as originally defined by Francois Truffaut

and others in *Cahiers du Cinéma* in the 1950s, presumes that the director is in total artistic control over each film. Every work, therefore, can be judged by how well it conforms to the director's already revealed patterns.

2. Corliss's various articles were compiled in his *Talking Pictures: Screenwriters in the American Cinema* (New York: Penguin Books, 1974). Of the thirty-eight writers he discussed, only two are women and both collaborated with their husbands: Betty Comden and Ruth Gordon (Gordon's name appears only in parenthesis).

3. This information came from an interview with Frances Marion's son, Professor Fred Thomson. Other information in the text that will not be footnoted, including some quotations, was gathered from interviews with Virginia Kellogg Mortensen (now deceased), Mary McCall, Jr., Francis Goodwich and Albert Hackett, and Howard Strickling (former head of publicity at MGM and now deceased). The author wishes to express her gratitude for their time and energy.

4. From a typescript in the William DeMille Collection at the University of Southern California.

5. Lewis Jacobs, *The Rise of the American Film: A Critical History* (New York: Teachers College Press, 1967), 328.

6. Anita Loos, *Kiss Hollywood Goodbye* (New York: Viking Press, 1974), 13.

7. Dewitt Bodeen, "Frances Marion," *Films in Review* 20 (1969): 138.

8. Glenn O'Brien and Lillian Gerard, "Anita Loos: Gentlemen Prefer Genius," *Inter/View,* 23 (July 1972): 22.

9. Frances Marion, *Off With Their Heads! A Serio-Comic Tale of Hollywood* (New York: MacMillan, 1972), 27.

10. Bodeen, "Frances Marion," 141–42.

11. Anita Loos, "Women on Women in Films," *Take One,* 3 (November-December 1970): 11.

12. O'Brien and Gerard, "Anita Loos," 26.

13. Frances Marion, *How to Write and Sell Film Stories* (New York: Covici Friede, 1937), 62, 56.

14. Marion, *How to Write,* 105.

15. Letter dated 12 September 1939, in the Akins collection at the Huntington Library. Other Akins letters cited in the text are also from this collection.

16. Mary C. McCall, "Hollywood Close-up," *Review of Reviews* (n.d.), 44.

17. Obituary, *Time,* 10 November 1958.

18. Akins letter to Alice Kanser, 20 October 1939, Akins collection at the Huntington Library.

19. "Zoë Akins Turns Out a Novel, Her First, And Forswears 'Bondage of Hollywood,'" *New York World Telegraph,* undated clipping in Huntington Library collection.

20. Ronald Bowers, "Frances Goodwich and Albert Hackett," *Films in Review,* 28 (1977): 464.

21. (New York: Charles Scribner's Sons, 1941), 57–58.

22. Bowers, "Frances Goodwich."

23. Ibid.

24. Ibid.

25. Lisa Mitchell, "Dorothy Parker as the Lady of With in a Life of Sorrow," *Los Angeles Times,* undated clipping in the Parker file, University of California, Los Angeles.

26. Quoted by Shirley Biagi, "Forgive Me for Dying," *Antioch Review,* 35 (Spring-Summer 1977): 225.

27. Biagi, "Forgive Me," 225.

28. Ibid., 227.

29. Ibid., 233.

30. Janet Sharistanian, "Tess Slesinger's Hollywood Sketches," *Michigan Quarterly Review,* 18 (Summer 1979): 433.

31. Sonya Levien, "The Screen Writer," in *Careers for Women,* ed. Catherine Filene (Boston: Houghton Mifflin, 1934), 436.

10

"The Lady Doth Protest Too Much, Methinks": Jane Fonda, Feminism, and Hollywood

BARBARA SEIDMAN
Linfield College

In the last decade, feminist film scholars have engaged in an energetic debate over the nature of and means toward a cinema that honestly escapes androcentric biases by articulating an authentic female imaginative voice. Sociological analyses of how the mainstream film industry has expressed and shaped repressive cultural myths concerning women have come under attack from Marxist and semiologist critics, who challenge "realist" equations between filmic images and the world, insist upon the importance of the material conditions under which films are produced, and identify the dynamic interplay between film and audience as the true locus of ideological formulation. Beneath these controversies, however, lies a shared conviction that traditional filmmaking activities, both before and behind the camera, have reductively objectified female experience, in the process ignoring the knowledge women possess of their own lives. It is this "patriarchal ideology," heavily bourgeois in orientation and rendered "invisible" by the naturalistic illusion of the medium, which feminist critics seek to expose or deconstruct and feminist filmmakers hope to supplant. Their antagonist in both endeavors is termed "dominant cinema," which Annette Kuhn summarizes as

> the institutional frameworks surrounding the production, distribution and exhibition of films for world-wide mass markets and also as the distinctive characteristics of the films themselves—what they look like and the kinds of readings they construct. Hollywood is usually considered to be the limiting case, the ideal-type, of dominant cinema. . . .[1]

While Kuhn's reference here is to the Hollywood of the pre-sixties studio era, the economic realignment that has transformed the American film industry since that time has allowed mainstream filmmaking in the United States to remain a hierarchical capitalist activity, dominated by male directors and technicians and dedicated to box office profits. Such conditions do not promise much opportunity for serious assaults within the industry upon the dominant ideological conceptualization of the female, and yet in the very lap of Hollywood sits one of America's most popular feminist icons, Jane Fonda, a woman whose life even more than her films has dramatically personalized the middle-class woman's discovery of her entrapment within "the feminine mystique." In the course of her career, she not only has denounced the fetishization of woman's image to which she was an unwitting accomplice as a young actress, but she has metamorphosed in only a decade from being the despised "Hanoi Jane" to being one of the nation's most admired women,[2] regularly featured on the covers of women's magazines as the reasoned embodiment of the modern female sensibility. Moreover, she commands the means of film production and a power few women in the industry (nor even her famous father) have ever known, managing her public popularity so as to finance an independent production company that realizes projects expressing her reformist politics. On the surface, then, Fonda's success seems to contradict the feminist critic's assertion that the pressures of the dominant cinema silence the female, for it is difficult to imagine a more voluble champion of liberated consciousness. In inter-

view after interview, as well as in her enormously successful exercise
books, Fonda has explained not only the roots of her own feminist
awakening, but her avowed commitment to reshaping a society congruent with her feminism:

> Sometimes one has the impression that the women's movement is saying,
> "Move over, We want in," and that when women get power, the problems
> will be over. I don't think that's true. . . . [T]he mass of women would be
> in just the same situation as they're in now. I think you need a whole
> restructuring of who has power and what it is being used for.[3]

Yet those who have followed Fonda's career to date recognize that in
uttering such statements in the pages of *Time, Redbook,* and even *Ms.,*
she has left behind what she herself labels the "shrill" voice of her
radical "phase" and she speaks with the confident authority of the
Hollywood insider she has become, professing unabashedly her interest in making movies that entertain and make money while they
educate. Fonda's reconciliation with the American film establishment
has served each partner well: traditional Hollywood institutions like
stardom and "the woman's film" have enabled Fonda to assume a
reassuring familiarity with which to woo back audiences, and her
always newsworthy presence within mainstream productions testifies
to the notion that the new Hollywood has become duly sensitized to
women's unchanging perspectives. In other words, Fonda's efforts as a
feminist filmmaker exist very much within the context of the dominant cinema, and as such they are compromised against being full
frontal assaults upon the illusory depictions of women in the mass
media. Kuhn's two avenues of feminist film endeavor—deconstruction
of established modes of female representation, and creation of a sin-
gularly feminine cinematic style—find only the faintest echoes in
Fonda's work of the last decade, touted though some of it has been in
the press. As Tracy Young has pointed out, "it is [the values of the well-
intentioned middle class] she both celebrates and validates all over
again."[4] Accordingly, in becoming a feminist star, Fonda has necessarily become less than a feminist, remaining safely within the bourgeois comfort zone even when making admirable forays like *The
Dollmaker.* The complex accommodation Fonda has made to reconcile
her determined continuation as a Hollywood filmmaker with her vocal
allegiance to feminism will be the focus of this essay.

The Paradoxical Evolution of a Feminist "Star"

While it is finally her films that should merit the concentrated
scrutiny of feminist critics, one cannot divorce Fonda's work com-

pletely from the context of her life, particularly since her very public odyssey from Hollywood starlet to international sex kitten to feminist political activist has been mirrored in the film projects she has chosen at each stage. Fonda's prominence in the nation's popular consciousness demonstrates the blurring between life and art that Richard Schickel has associated with the phenomenon of American celebrity: her individual films have been perceived "as incidents in a larger, and more compelling drama—the drama of the star's life and career, the shaping and reshaping of the image of him or her that we carry in our minds."[5]

More important for this discussion is the fact that the public drama of Jane Fonda's life seems to offer a "script" resonant with feminist lessons. Fonda's decisions have from the first reflected her sensitivity to relationships between gender and power in American society; the seemingly contradictory phases of her life reveal her differing responses to its consequences. Her youthful ambitions to compete within the male sphere and for male approbation were born out of her early conclusions concerning female helplessness, just as her later emphasis upon affiliation with women sprang from her increasingly politicized view of power arrangements. Fonda's first and most potent lessons in sexual politics were learned through her parents, whose catastrophic marriage ended in Frances Seymour Brokaw's suicide in a mental hospital after Henry Fonda suggested a divorce. Fonda has repeatedly acknowledged that her mother's death taught her "that women were not survivors. . . . [I]f you wanted to be strong and to survive, you had to align yourself with a man or be a tomboy or whatever. That was where the energy was."[6] The impotent self-destructive rage Frances turned upon herself reinforced Jane's childhood conviction that the real locus of authority and power within her family was her father, an emotionally aloof man whose affection and respect she hungrily pursued right up until his death in 1982. At the beginning of her career, she noted, "I've spent half of my young life wanting to be a boy because I wanted to be like my father."[7]

Such unbridled identification with Henry reflected more than a daughter's poignant yearning for fatherly approval; it also hinted at the avenues through which a markedly ambitious female might envision realizing her talents, in a culture where women's energies were more often expressed in the twisted directions taken by her mother. Fonda's several biographers share the opinion of her childhood friend Brooke Hayward that "I've never seen ambition as naked as Jane's."[8] It is then surprising that, for all her publicly proclaimed ambivalence toward her father over the years, Jane kept his name when she embarked on her own career and accepted the opportunities his connections afforded her to secure her first film projects (for example, Joshua Logan, an old friend of Henry's, provided her first major film role *Tall Story,* released in 1960). Not that Jane relied on her family name in lieu of her own efforts to win acknowledgment of her gifts. She enrolled as a student in Lee Strasberg's prestigious Actors' Studio, relocating to New York and establishing herself in the theater to prove her artistic seriousness.

The lines of intersection and contradiction became quite complex at this point in the evolution of Fonda's public image, for while she did enter her father's profession, she challenged his notion that, in acting, "Less is more": Fonda senior scorned acting "instruction" generally and rejected the introspective self-exposure of "the Method" in particular. Perhaps an even more striking paradox lies in the fact that to move beyond her father's authority, Jane apprenticed herself to Strasberg, a man with an equally domineering psychological presence. Fonda's forceful career ascent has since been marked by affiliations with strong-willed males, who have undertaken to guide her decisions and carefully shape her image. Strasberg was succeeded by Andreas Voutsinas, another "Method" disciple, who coached Fonda through several film and stage productions, in the process becoming her lover—one to whom Henry was outspokenly opposed in the first of their public debates over private matters. In the late sixties, French director Roger Vadim transformed Fonda into "Barbarella," an American version of the international sex symbol he had first created with Brigitte Bardot. Even in her radically feminist period during the seventies, Fonda found a perfect mentor in New Left leader Tom Hayden, who arranged her infamous trips to Hanoi, married her, and eventually redirected her politics into pragmatic avenues more conducive to their respective career ambitions. Revealingly, all of these men figure far more prominently in Fonda's interviews than do women friends; little evidence exists that any woman has exerted a comparable degree of influence over her. It is Vadim and Hayden whom Fonda has credited with giving her life its distinctive emphases. She once praised Vadim for providing "a way to live, the European way. He gave me a life in which there can be no secrets between men and women."[9] She now just as enthusiastically declares of her second husband, "[Y]ou've got to have visionaries and saints. [Tom Hayden], I think, is an example of one; Martin Luther King, Cesar Chavex, Malcolm X and others."[10]

Fonda's affinity for men who inspire the same kind of awed respect she has accorded her father should not mask the fact that in each case she has chosen a man just as driven toward success as she is. Despite the venerating tone, her romantic partnerships have furthered her professional ambitions rather than eclipsed or seriously competed with them. It is in the light of this unyielding determination to extend her creative opportunities that one must view her response to Hollywood upon her arrival at Warner Brothers in 1959. Fonda has explained how studio head Jack Warner reductively evaluated her potential in terms of a sterile definition of manufactured glamor: "She's got a good future if you dye her hair blonde, break her jaw and reshape it, and get her some silicone shots or falsies."[11] While she initially cooperated with the notion of coy "all-American" sexuality so effectively that she earned the title "Miss Army Recruitment of 1962," she soon began to challenge the mindlessness of her starlet image by applying Method techniques to her performances, thereby "getting behind a mask and revealing things that I, as an uptight, middle-class woman, had been told I should not show."[12] Accordingly, Fonda deliberately cultivated a sexually uninhibited and psychologically complex public persona to distinguish herself from saccharine ingenues like Sandra Dee and simple-minded bombshells like Marilyn Monroe (in some apprehensions of her). To enrich the insights she brought to her acting, she underwent psychoanalysis and became increasingly honest and unconventional in her views, scandalizing Hedda Hopper by announcing at twenty-three that "I think marriage is going to go out, become obsolete. I don't think it's natural for two people to swear to be together for the rest of their lives."[13] The feminist declarations Fonda would make a decade later, then, did not emerge from a vacuum; her determination as a young woman to flout the constricting expectations of bourgeois respectability and "ladylike" decorum had already established the rebellious and outspoken public image whose nuances and targets Fonda has simply redefined over the years as her preoccupations have shifted.

Her acknowledged inspiration for the bold, independent sexuality she sought to convey in her films was French actress Brigitte Bardot, whose contribution to sexual equality had already been praised by no less an authority than Simone de Beauvoir.[14] Contemporary film feminists may certainly argue that Bardot merely updated and expanded the reductive uses of women within a voyeuristic cinema; few actresses have been so completely subsumed by the phenomenon Laura Mulvey has identified as "fetishistic scopophilia," or "the cult of the female star," whereby pleasure results from the "exhibitionist role" women play in film, "simultaneously looked at and displayed, with their appearance coded for strong visual and erotic impact. . . . Woman displayed as sexual object is the leitmotif of erotic spectacle. . . . [S]he holds the look, plays to, and signifies male desire."[15] But while Fonda today admits the validity of the feminist criticisms that have been leveled at Bardot, she continues to assert that her own admiration sprang from the sexual honesty Bardot insisted upon in her depictions of women:

> [In Bardot's films] the women were always strong. They were always the central characters, always the winner. She may have been presented as a beautiful object, but Brigitte Bardot ruled the roost. She kicked out any man she was tired of and invited in any man she wanted. She lived like a man in Vadim's [And God Created Woman]. . . .[I]t was a very liberating experience for a lot of women to watch her on the screen.[16]

The echo of Jane's childhood attraction to the more powerful life of boys reverberates in that defense. So does Fonda's own susceptibility to cinematic mythologizing that translates the female into a "natural" icon outside time and history—the embodiment of the mysterious, erotic Other. There is in fact very little imaginative distance separating Fonda's respect for Bardot and her current marketing of an exercise regime that makes woman's body a totem for personal power and independence.

As many an American film critic has done since, the young Fonda revered those iconoclastic European cineastes who transcended the fraudulent notions of female sexuality under which she chafed in Hollywood. When Fonda eagerly accepted an invitation in 1963 to go to France and make Joy House with director René Clement, the French press just as eagerly bestowed upon her the role she coveted as the symbol of sexual liberation for the new decade, describing her as "A super BB, a cyclone of femininity, a marvelous baby doll," a woman "sultry and dangerous, like a caged animal."[17] Cahiers du Cinéma posted her of its cover. Fonda's growing notoriety as a sexual adventurer commanded the attention of Roger Vadim, master of French erotic cinema, who had been the force behind Bardot's stardom and who had similarly directed the careers of Annette Stroyberg and Catherine Deneuve. Although initially she was intimidated by his offers to work together, Fonda's ambition and her attraction to Vadim led her to give herself over by 1965 to enacting his vision of sexual liberation, both onscreen and off.

This association began the period of Fonda's career most at odds with her subsequent feminism, since it was under Vadim's tutelage that she allowed herself to become fetishized beyond anything she'd experienced in the "unliberated" Hollywood she'd disdainfully fled (the popularity of Fonda pin-ups dating from this period can still be noted in movie memorabilia shops). The medium's iconizing power, handled with deft manipulation by Vadim, transcended Fonda's own conviction that she was at last in control of her cinematic image and its message, and she found herself in the untenable position of denying the evidence of the screen and its pop culture manifestations, asserting "I'm no sex siren just because I believe in approaching sex and the human body with honesty."[18] Ironically, in pursuing artistic and personal freedom, Fonda had allied herself with a director already notorious for subordinating actresses of very different types to his own distinctive vision of the erotic feminine. Critic Clair Johnston could have told Fonda that

> sexist ideology is no less present in the European art-cinema because stereotyping appears less obvious; it is in the nature of myth to drain the sign . . . of its meaning and superimpose another which thus appears natural: in fact, a strong argument could be made for the art film inviting a greater invasion from myth. . . .
>
> Within a sexist ideology and a male-dominated cinema, woman is presented as what she represents for man.[19]

Moreover, Vadim's participation in French New Wave theorizing further ensured Fonda's subordination to the notion of the director as *auteur,* wielding absolute control over his "creation."

With Fonda a willing accomplice, Vadim entered a new phase of his cinematic exploration of the erotic. His "liberating" sexual vision, which assumed increasingly inflated proportions in such films as *Circle of Love* (1965), and *The Game Is Over* (1966), became unalloyed camp in the best-known Vadim-Fonda collaboration, *Barbarella* (1968). In many ways a classic example of free-wheeling, tongue-in-cheek sixties filmmaking, the movie's playful sexuality reflects the decade's youthful irreverence toward the establishment. Vadim, together with Terry Southern, adapted the script from a semi-pornographic European cartoon strip of the same name, using its science fiction narrative to satirize the repressive bourgeois conventions of contemporary society. But with Dino de Laurentiis pouring millions into the film's production in hopes of achieving an international hit, Vadim's professed goal was subsumed within overwrought scenes designed primarily to titillate viewers through fantasies of adults behaving with childishly uncomplicated abandon. Whatever new voice proclaimed sexual freedom therein did not speak for the silenced impulses of female eroticism. Although Vadim described Barbarella as "a kind of sexual Alice in Wonderland of the future," her adventures expressed a blatantly male interpretation of women's increasing sexual freedom as total sexual compliance; the unique dynamics of female desire itself were ignored in favor of jarring sexist clichés.

The iconography of the film neatly demonstrates the multiple levels of the male gaze as Mulvey has defined it. The pro-filmic gaze of the camera captures every seductive movement of the leggy redhead, whose status as the director's wife further heightens the voyeuristic pleasure of observing Barbarella's casual sexual couplings. Her numerous lovers in turn fix their own excited gazes upon her, reinforcing the viewer's fantasized identification with the men who not only achieve possession of her but succeed in teaching her to prefer the ecstasies of "old-fashioned" phallic penetration to the futuristic method of taking a pill. Enclosing the whole viewing experience is the gaze of the spectator, established as indisputably male from the first, as Barbarella does a zero-gravity striptease while floating over the opening credits. Her outlandish costumes, all designed to emphasize her femaleness by reinforcing the sexual difference she epitomized,

Barbarella, Paramount Pictures Corporation
Courtesy of Museum of Modern Art/Film Stills Archive

equate gender and sexuality so completely that Barbarella becomes a cannily masked symbol of the patriarchal desire to control female sexual liberty by subverting it to the service of male gratification. Female eroticism is not in itself a positive force in the film, as the witch-like lesbian ruler of the evil kingdom demonstrates. Nor, for all the claims regarding Barbarella's supposed adventuresomeness, does she show herself to be in command of the various crises into which she falls. When she proves totally mystified by the mechanical failures of her spaceship, she relies on a fur-clad Hercules to help her. She is sent on her mission by a male president who beams himself onto her two-way video screen (finding her naked in the privacy of her spacecraft), and she is later rescued from the destruction of the evil kingdom by the innocent strength of a blind but virile young angel, who flies away with her in tow. Her capacity for heroic action lies entirely in her ability to deliver such intense sexual satisfaction that she even short-circuits a pleasure machine intended to kill her with ecstasy: this is hardly an escape from the cinema's trivializing objectification of women. Iron-ically, Barbarella demonstrates none of the aggressively individualistic independence for which Fonda had admired Bardot's performances in Vadim films; rather, Barbarella remains a wide-eyed ingenue, unasser-tive and sweetly agreeable. It is no wonder that Marjorie Rosen has castigated this work as a depersonalized and narcissistic cartoon that demeans the actors associated with it.[20]

It is worth noting, however, that even while Fonda collaborated with her husband's cinematic libertinism,she did not completely renounce Hollywood, despite her mocking evaluation of it to the press. Instead, she gingerly balanced two seemingly opposed filmmaking agendas with a skill that has become a trademark of her career. Her iconoclastic sexuality, enhanced by her French ventures, proved well-suited to furthering Hollywood's efforts at reflecting the more free-wheeling attitudes of sixties society, and concurrent with her work for Vadim she made *Cat Ballou* (1965), *Any Wednesday* (1966), and *Barefoot in the Park* (1967), all commercial successes that helped to establish the characteristic comic ingenuousness that Vadim exploited for his own satiric ends in *Barbarella*. Pauline Kael has argued that it was Fonda's already-formed persona, with its distinctly American wit, energy, and innocence, which saved her from being overwhelmed by Vadim's imaginative excesses and which in fact provided its own subtly droll commentary upon the Frenchman's prurience. Even before her pol-iticization, Fonda had discovered how her stardom could be made to take on a self-reflexive level of meaning all its own in her films, a lesson she had been learning from the outset of her career, as Henry

Fonda's daughter. With Vadim, she found a new power in manipulating that public persona so as to comment on the cultural scene and thereby flaunt its hypocrisies. It is a strategy she has continued to explore through numerous personal transformations since.

Molly Haskell has asserted that by educating Jane Fonda in the fuller possibilities of her screen persona, Vadim's "liberating . . . voyeur's appreciation" made Fonda's eventual break from him in pursuit of greater creative independence inevitable.[21] Both Fonda and Vadim have indicated, however, that her evolution was hardly so felicitous or painless at the time, for the woman who had made *Barbarella* felt anything but triumphant self-realization by the end of the decade. In exploring sexual liberation as the expression of her own rebellious energies, Fonda discovered it was a dead end and she herself was reduced to a fantasized, insubstantial erotic image, both in the films she did with Vadim and those she made in America. Of her years with Vadim she admits, "I was so used to being considered a sex symbol that I began to like it. I didn't expect people to treat me as a person who thinks."[22] In viewing *Barbarella* today, she sees "my own alienation [coming] at me,"[23] the hollowness of the characterization justifying her fears that, in contrast to her brother Peter, whose film *Easy Rider* had exposed some vital truths of the cultural and political climate, she was becoming "totally irrelevant, both as a human being and an actress."[24] Interestingly, Betty Friedan's *The Feminine Mystique,* published only a few years earlier, in chronicling the malaise of a generation of American women, aptly diagnosed the sources of Fonda's own failed experiment with Vadim:

> In the past fifteen years, the sexual frontier has been forced to expand perhaps beyond the limits of possibility, to fill the time available, to fill the vacuum created by the denial of larger goals and purposes for American women. . . . [S]everal generations of able American women have been successfully reduced to sex creations, sex-seekers. But something has evidently gone wrong.
>
> Instead of fulfilling the promise of infinite orgastic bliss, sex . . . is becoming a strangely joyless national compulsion, if not a contemptuous mockery.[25]

Despite her new French milieu, her sensual husband, and her exotic film career, Fonda discovered herself imprisoned within her libertinism.

The event that redefined Fonda's perceptions of her gender identity and began to release her from Vadim's limiting definitions was motherhood. Conceiving a child at thirty, she realized that

Pregnancy stamped me irrevocably as a woman. It was the very thing I had always been afraid of. . . . Then everything changed. . . . I felt a tremendous bond with the subterranean forces of womanhood. . . . I have not felt threatened by being a woman since then. And my coming to peace with being a woman was made even stronger by the fact that the child was a girl.[26]

In another of the almost too neat feminist paradigms that seem to structure Fonda's biography, it was maternity, the female rite of passage, that accelerated her increasingly voluble critique of American society. Giving birth in the political climate of the late sixties wakened her consciousness in ways news headlines had failed to do, for she now personally understood "that we do not give life to a human being only to have it killed by B–52 bombs, or have it jailed by fascists, or to have it destroyed by social injustice."[27] This heightened sense of social responsibility made the self-absorbed sexist hedonism of Vadim increasingly repugnant to her and she sheared away her Barbarella locks, explaining that she felt "a victim of that hair."[28] Fonda also found herself garnering a new respect from her associates in the anti–Vietnam War movement: a respect that shocked her into realizing how completely she had come to regard herself, under Hollywood's and Vadim's tutelage, as a beautiful, irresponsible "doll." Through her expanding engagement with New Left political philosophy, she heard scathing condemnations of bourgeois society that implicated Vadim himself as a panderer; her estrangement from the roles of wife and sex kitten brought their marriage to an end.

Fonda's conversion was not an unalloyed triumph for the feminist movement, however, for while she became a highly visible spokesperson against the devaluation suffered by women in the media and entertainment industries, she employed a rhetoric that oversimplified the issues and continued to exploit her star image by placing herself and her experiences always at the center of her analysis. Celebrity continued to be the name of the game, as the press handled her pronouncements as part of the hype characterizing the so-called New Hollywood; her controversial opinions were regularly reported on the entertainment pages, even by *The New York Times*. Moreover, her past history of trendy and exhibitionist rebellion undermined her credibility and hence her cause, as critics cynically noted that she now spoke as vehemently against sexist trivialization of the female as she had once flaunted sexual license as a weapon of liberation.

In a 1971 *Times* manifesto entitled "I Want to Work with Women," Fonda demonstrated the problem she would continue to present in her role as feminist leader. The well-intentioned piece reflects genuine courage in articulating beliefs still regarded at that time as extreme and separatist by the very public on whom her livelihood depended; on the other hand, she added nothing new to the public dialogue on the issues except her notoriety, which by that date, well into the antiwar movement, was the real basis for any feature article devoted to her views. Ironically, despite her radical image, what she was about in that essay was the popularization of feminist politics: however programmatic her ideas might have sounded, they were essentially affirmative and comforting to those who worried about the changes she implied: Yes, "Our lives are defined by men—the men we live with, or the men we love, or the men we're married to, or the men we work for—and, indirectly, through television, film, radio and other media, which are controlled by men." But by means of a societal struggle to realize in public life those virtues traditionally associated with women—compassion, emotional honesty, instinctual empathy—"the world will truly be a much better place."[29] It is with exactly this message, uncomplicated and confident, that Fonda has steadily won her current position as the Hollywood feminist with whom American women can most easily identify. And she achieved that stature not through her dialectical skills but through her willingness to place herself centerstage, living out the feminist drama in a manner akin to popular melodrama, playing to the emotions and not the intellect. She concluded the *Times* piece by announcing her own course: "I began to realize that this particular revolution is not only [other women's] revolution, it's my revolution too. I mean, if I don't fight it, nobody else is going to." In this context one cannot overlook Jean-Luc Godard's contemporaneous 1972 assessment of her in a brief film he made on Fonda's antiwar activism, *Letter to Jane*. Godard and screenwriter Jean-Pierre Gorin analyze the famous photograph of a distraught Fonda talking to North Vietnamese victims of U.S. bombings and conclude that her bourgeois preoccupation with personality and celebrity lead her to turn politically significant behavior into a self-serving performance, devoid of authentic intellectual or emotional resonance. While Fonda reacted with outrage to the film, the director's insights into her limitations as an activist have been echoed repeatedly by others within the various movements with which she aligned herself during the seventies, and such insights or accusations offer another important biographical dimension of any evaluation of Fonda's impact on feminist politics over the last two decades.[30]

This is not to say that Fonda's pronouncements did not intensify as she responded to the resentment her feminism sparked in the unenlightened public and in her comrades-in-arms alike. During her time with the FTA (Free the Army) tour, she aligned herself with co-workers Nancy Dowd and Francine Parker to purge sexism from the troupe's performances, and she promptly discovered the paralyzing hostility such efforts frequently aroused among her male colleagues in the New Left. Fonda had already concluded that much of the American public's reaction to her activism was itself sexist, the result of angry disbelief that a pin-up fantasy could shake off her trivialization to speak so pointedly against their deepest-held values. Nor was she still delivering the same frothy entertainment as a film actress, for in keeping with the political awakening she experienced following her daughter's birth, she had radically altered the direction of her acting career, replacing Barbarella's vacuous sexiness with the grim desperation of the cynical, suicidal Gloria in *They Shoot Horses, Don't They?* (1969) and the aggressively distrustful Bree Daniels in *Klute* (1971). These films not incidentally won Fonda a new level of critical respect for her abilities as a dramatic actress. Clearly, Fonda was determined to revolutionize every facet of her life in order to make all her efforts, personal and professional, congruent with her growing awareness of the political realities of women's condition, and the two films that most loudly signaled that agenda to American audiences paradoxically made her a star of greater magnitude than she had even been before. At the same time that her politics themselves were alienating her from the bosom of Hollywood, she was nominated for Academy Awards for both roles and received the Oscar for *Klute,* a film that illustrates how such inconsistencies were possible in Fonda's career by highlighting the unresolved contradictions in her feminist understanding. The film's enthusiastic reception by the same industry that shunned Fonda personally dramatized the ironic truth that, however outspoken she may have seemed, she has always selected film vehicles in a way that reveals the fact that she is very much a child of her time, not in the intellectual vanguard, but conveniently and entertainingly attuned to the same energies that are altering the sensibilities of her audience.

It is difficult to view *Klute* today as fundamentally different from the subsequent proliferation of films that subjected women to hostile brutalization, both physical and psychological. At the time of its release, however, it was regarded as a breakthrough in Hollywood's depiction of contemporary women. Revealingly, the sophisticated Bree Daniels (who does not give *her* name to the film) pursues a career as a top call girl: her aggressive and ambitious temperament is channeled into activities that allow her to control the stage for an hour with each new client. She exploits her own body and retains an emotional de-

tachment from her duties that would be the envy of any young professional. Moreover, she is an actress's dream creation, as quirky and
inconsistent and complex a character as Fonda has every played. In
defending the film, critic Diane Giddis has argued that "in her tormented journey [Bree] succeeds in embodying one of the greatest of
contemporary female concerns: the conflict between the claims of love
and the claims of autonomy."[31] Very simply, for Bree, sex means
power, while love brings helpless dependence and vulnerability. Fonda
herself partially justifies the film on political as well as aesthetic
grounds, because it shows prostitution to be the sordid logical result of
repressive bourgeois morality and capitalistic greed: "the inevitable
product of a society that places ultimate importance on money, posses-
sions and competition."[32]

Director Alan Pakula encouraged Fonda to explore Bree's character
as thoroughly as her Method training would allow, and many important scenes, including those with the psychiatrist, resulted from inspired improvisation on the set. What resulted so powerfully from
those interludes with her therapist was the emergence of Bree's own
voice—a voice at once the character's and Fonda's, no doubt for the
first time in her career. Bree's angry posture toward a hypocritical and
unreceptive culture mirrored Fonda's own situation in those turbulent
years when she was so desperately pursuing alternative definitions of
herself as woman; appropriately, Bree aspires to become an actress too,
but is subjected to repeated rejections and humiliating critiques. Here
Fonda explored female desire of a very different kind from the mind-
less capitulations of the sex toys she was used to playing. Moreover,
the desire she articulated was shockingly honest and unfeminized:
Bree wanted control, success, power, and it was those admissions
about the motivating core of an ambitious woman that alerted filmgoers to the fact that here was something new in Hollywood's depiction
of the female. But if Bree's voice was startlingly feminist in its challenges to accepted notions of women's desire, it was met in the context
of the film with a decidedly antifeminist backlash. For the film is
finally a warning about the appalling abuses unleashed by female
sexual liberation. The camera eye is male, prying into Bree's privacy
and making her suffer for her flagrant disregard of the role she is
expected to play. Instead of an exhilarating model of freedom, she is
shown overwhelmed by a bitchy hunger for manipulation and lost in
debilitating psychic isolation.

Over the credits we first hear Bree's voice coaxingly assuring a john
that "I'll do anything you ask. . . . Nothing is wrong; nothing is ever
wrong." Through the voyeuristic gaze of Cable and even Klute, the

amateur detective trying to solve the case, the viewer has been made witness to Bree's "tricks" with numerous men and has seen her threatening ability to emasculate. Such power must be brought under control, and the film employs several strategies to do so. One is the most obvious—Cable's attempt to kill her. He condemns her and her kind as "too lazy and warped to do anything meaningful with your lives other than prey on the sexual fantasies of others," and his remarks, albeit the ravings of a madman, are eerily supported by the dramatic emotions aroused in many spectators by the film. In addition to Cable, however, the subplot involving other call girls, whose hellish descent into addiction and death Bree is gruesomely made to watch, echoes this punishment theme. Finally, Bree is "recuperated" into the mainstream that Klute represents. The common psychological dynamic of the women's film described by Teresa De Lauretis applies here as well, for even when a film

> actually sets in play the terms of female desire, dominant cinema works for Oedipus. . . . Alas, it is still for him that women must be seduced into femininity and be remade again and again as woman. Thus when a film accidentally or unwisely puts in play the terms of a divided or double desire . . . it must display that desire as impossible or duplicitous . . . finally contradictory . . . and then proceed to resolve the contradiction . . . by either the massive destruction or the territorialization of women.[33]

Klute takes the skeptical but willing Bree away from the urban jungle altogether at the end of the film. Her empty apartment suggests an obliteration of her past, and her identity, as she gamely tries out a new life in a woefully inappropriate setting with the man who has rescued her by teaching her womanly love and vulnerability. Joan Mellen has been even more pointed in identifying the film as reactionary:

> Hollywood has long delighted in exposing the new woman as sexually confused, self-destructive . . . and masochistically at home in relationships where she can preserve "control" by renouncing feeling.
>   . . . Pakula finally proposes only three alternatives for the sexually alive woman: call girl, lonely recluse, or dependent wife.[34]

But the avowed feminist who could regard *Klute* as a liberating statement about women was not so far removed from the sexual rebel who had earlier proclaimed *Barbarella* an attack on bourgeois prurience: Fonda's talents lie in her dramatic abilities, not in her skills with analytic deconstruction, and her career since becoming a women's advocate has allowed her to wrestle her inner confusions about her gender identity into the consoling reassurance of a happy ending, both on- and offscreen. In the years following *Klute*'s release, her stardom was sustained and enhanced by her visibility on the nightly news rather than in successful films; the drama she was enacting came from the theater of the real, as she played out a nation's neurotic self-loathing and confusion about Vietnam and shaded that conflict with the anxieties of the newborn feminist struggling to remain reassuringly heterosexual while still basking in the joys of sisterhood. The absolute publicness of her assessment of each new idea marked her simultaneously as an endearing naif and an addicted celebrity hound, and it cemented her star status perhaps more solidly than any succession of *Klutes* might have done. Whether or not they knew it, Americans delighted in Fonda's willingness to act out their own complex reactions to the changing social order, and in no context did she better reflect the contradictions of her society than in her engagement with "the women's issue."

On one hand Fonda championed the possibility of all-women production crews in the arts, such as the group with whom she made the 1971 special, "Fascinating Woman," part of the PBS series, *The Great American Dream Machine*. An overtly feminist enterprise, the program allowed Fonda to play six different characters ranging from a Playboy bunny to a housewife, each dramatizing oppressively narrow American definitions of the modern female. Her enthusiasm for the creative freedom she experienced during this project, when suddenly all the words and images were shaped by female, not male, imaginations, implied that a true epiphany had occurred in her career. But Fonda has undertaken no production like it since that time. Moreover, the dynamics of her private life contradicted any suggestion of redirected loyalties, for she remained deeply dependent upon the presence of strong men to guide her actions. For awhile, Donald Sutherland, her co-star in *Klute* and a fellow antiwar activist participating in the FTA tours, became her constant companion. Before long, Tom Hayden, of the SDS, Days of Rage and Chicago Seven Conspiracy Trial, assumed the central emotional role in her life.

Fonda insists that Hayden embodied the new kind of egalitarian male she had begun to conclude did not exist amid the flamboyant rhetoric of the New Left. Early in their relationship she had been profoundly moved by the feminist dimension of a slide show he'd put together on the corrupting influence of American culture on Vietnamese life; his presentation included pictures of Asian women who had surgically westernized their appearance to appeal to U.S. servicemen. While in Hayden she might have glimpsed the theoretical possibility of a harmonious ideological merger of her pacifism and her feminism, in fact, more typically, she translated the political into the personal by idealizing him as the perfect New Left lover—a man who amazed her by showing he could "be sensitive to the self-destructiveness" of the war on women's as well as men's psyches. Their subsequent affair counteracted the despair into which she had fallen, in part because of the suspicions harbored against her by many of her comrades in the movement, and in part because of the very real government harassment to which she was subjected. With Hayden, Fonda underwent a transformation uncannily like that of Bree Daniels, moving from self-absorption to isolation to love and security with a protective and nurturing male. And like Bree, her hostile paranoia ebbed as she aligned herself with a man who could intercept and order the complex and contradictory responses she was eliciting from the American public at large and the antiwar movement in particular. Hayden had already demonstrated himself to be as shrewdly and aggressively ambitious as Fonda herself was, and they provided one another with a much-coveted legitimacy: his credentials in radical politics gave Fonda respectability in those circles where she was often scorned as a bourgeois lightweight, and her celebrity provided Hayden with media visibility to bolster his weakening ability to command public attention. His effect on Fonda's still-evolving feminism was equally significant. In providing her with the stable and satisfying emotional life she craved, he, as Vadim had once done, provided the unlikely impetus for her move away from her radical denunciations of marriage and monogamy, and the nuclear family, and toward views more congruent with her personal needs for familial security. Upon visiting North Vietnam through Hayden's machinations, she was attracted to the blend of traditional and feminist sentiment with which that nation's women responded to the devastation of the war. Chanting, "Nixon, we will fight you with all the joys of a woman in childbirth," they introduced Fonda to the idea of bearing a child as a gesture of revolutionary optimism—an idea she promptly suggested to Hayden on her return. In 1973, some months after Fonda became pregnant, they were married, defending the decision as a pragmatic step to protect their activities on behalf of the North Vietnamese—but they also admittedly welcomed the opportunity to "cement" their relationship. Here, as in the sixties, Fonda's behavior modulated from iconoclastic sensationalism to societal normality within a few years. Her awe for Hayden's political theories led her to subordinate her feminist causes to his "larger" vision of societal reform to such a degree that in 1975 she could argue, without a hint of self-irony:

Some people think marriage should be abolished. Who knows? I believe
that you can't build a mass movement around the questions of sex and
marriage. I've been in a revolutionary society where marriage is very
much an institution. It did not appear to be particularly oppressive for
women. . . .[35]

Such a statement, midway through the seventies, signaled the tran-
sitions characterizing the couple's entire political agenda with the end
of the Vietnam War. Not yet as temperate as they would become, the
Haydens were demonstrating nonetheless that they were mellowing,
for reasons more complex than a blissful new marriage or the onset of
middle age. Hayden shrewdly recognized that with the dissolution of
the antiwar movement, political activism would become less aggressive and more grass-roots in its orientation; it was thus necessary
to develop a broader, more appealingly inclusive reformist agenda if
the New Left was to retain its constituency and continue to agitate for
social reform. Consequently, in 1975, he founded the Campaign for
Economic Democracy (CED), replacing the more controversial Indo-
china Peace Campaign (IPC), which Fonda and Hayden had organized
to muster popular support of the North Vietnamese (IPC eventually
became the basis for Fonda's new film production company). CED's
program, the platform upon which Hayden was finally elected to the
California state legislature in 1982, urges the citizenry to take the
initiative to safeguard the environment, secure the rights of minorities,
and deal with the social abuses of multinational corporations.

In consolidating his new approach to the American electorate, Hayden recognized Fonda's stardom as an asset rather than as the liability
it had presented to the leaders of the antiwar movement, and together
they set out to rehabilitate the image of Hanoi Jane by moving her
slowly back into the mainstream of the Hollywood film industry, itself a
new animal as a result of the sixties. The goals of that reconciliation
included the desire to win Fonda more satisfying film work in projects
best suited to her Hollywood-bred acting style and talents. Winning
back the hearts and minds of Hollywood executives was itself no easy
task, given her pointed denunciations of the American film industry
years earlier and her ventures into alternative filmmaking with the
antiwar documentaries *FTA* (1972) and *Introduction to the Enemy*
(1974), the counterculture *Steelyard Blues* (1972), and Godard's revolutionary treatise *Tout Va Bien* (1972). Between 1972 and 1976 she
had completed only one mainstream effort, *A Doll's House*, released to
television rather than to movie theaters and again made outside Hollywood itself. Fonda would have to prove herself a viable film property

again if she was to reenter the Hollywood fold, and she would have to redress the notions of her held by the public in order to do so. But why would such a dedicated revolutionary and feminist want to return to the debased practices of the American film industry at all? Quite simply, as Hayden deftly explained, because her new political vision was not necessarily at odds with her past but could actually be supported and disseminated by her popular star appeal and her money-making abilities. It is Hayden Fonda credits with having revived and redirected her career: "[W]e'd talk about films in a way I'd never thought about. He had more respect for films than I did. So I thought, through some strange quirk in my life I've become a movie star. Now I've become a political activist. Why not try to blend the two?"[36] And Hayden has just as frankly admitted, "It's important that Jane be restored to legitimacy now, when she's active, and not in the 21st century."[37]

Fonda has not only regained her niche in Hollywood, but she has become one of its most respected icons, by the mid-eighties. She has been accorded a second Oscar (for *Coming Home* (1978)) and has become a leading box office attraction, based on such popular films as *The China Syndrome* (1979), *Electric Horseman* (1979), *9 to 5* (1980), *On Golden Pond* (1981), and *Agnes of God* (1985). Her exercise manuals and videos are runaway bestsellers, she has successfully entered television production with *The Dollmaker,* and she regularly appears as a host for such self-congratulatory establishment endeavors as the 1983 Democratic telethon and the 1986 Academy Awards ceremony. Fonda's family life with Hayden, now an elected public official, has become so enviably idyllic by middle-class standards that it merits repeated coverage in the pages of *Redbook, People,* and *Ladies Home Journal:* whatever public threat was once perceived in Fonda's political agenda has all but vanished, even as her face and opinions seem to have become ubiquitous. What has this recuperation into the mainstream meant for Fonda's use of film as a feminist tool, however? Now that she has regained stardom, has she put that public voice to work to expand her society's understanding of feminist issues? Or is the stardom itself a measure of how carefully she has avoided any filmic confrontation of feminism's complex and uncompromising insights into the lives of modern women? Analysis of the films that have resulted from Fonda's reconciliation with the American film industry and the renovation of her star image suggest that Fonda's talent as a filmmaker rests upon her skillful manipulation of established Hollywood forms like the women's film, in order to explore and render "safe" those consequences of the women's movement that have already begun to be felt by the popular consciousness. It is this dynamic that will be the subject of the remainder of this essay.

Fonda as a Feminist Filmmaker

In judging Fonda's career as a feminist filmmaker since the early seventies, it is first necessary to clarify what one means by "feminist filmmaking." It is not enough that in her personal life Fonda addresses feminist issues like equal pay, for one expects such a spokesperson to put forward creative efforts that meaningfully challenge the traditional or dominant ideology responsible for the current condition of women's lives. She might perhaps even explore alternatives. How a film artist might go about questioning gender stereotypes and deconstructing patriarchal power structures is a hotly debated topic in feminist critical discourse, with some analysts arguing against the possibility than any truly subversive feminist vision might emerge from within the established film industries, some analysts doubting the ability of entertainment media to function effectively as stimuli for revolutionizing assumptions about gender, and still others asserting that it is only through the recognized tools of popular entertainment culture that real inroads can be made to change mass consciousness. Teresa De Lauretis, extending the views of other feminist theorists, perceives the likelihood that women's cinema will "respond to the plea for 'a new language of desire . . . in order to represent not just the power of female desire but its duplicity and ambivalence. . . . The real task is to enact the contradictions of female desire, and of women as social subjects, in the terms of narrative."[38]

It is against such expectations that Fonda's film efforts of the last decade must be weighed, for, as feminist critics regularly point out, the production of positive images of women for the screen is no longer sufficient as a means of countering the well-entrenched strategies for silencing an authentic female voice in cinema. Fonda's privileged position in the very lap of the dominant industry bodes ill in its nature for her being able to contribute to any substantive feminist reorientation of the dynamics of the cinematic apparatus itself, as it constructs meaning around the female image, and her undisguised reliance upon industry staples such as her stardom and familiar Hollywood narrative structures testifies to her preference for predictability and profitability over any serious redirection of the medium. Finally, I will argue that the female voice Fonda raises in her films is all too clearly a voice that speaks through essentially male structures and conceptualizes female experience the way women have been taught to imagine themselves. Neither the angle of vision nor the discourse through which it is conveyed offers any honest alternative to "business as usual" in the Hollywood system.

Fonda has been moving steadily toward such mainstream security ever since she began to revitalize her career in the mid-seventies. Her decision in 1975 to found her own production company grew out of her political convictions in tandem with her increasing need to exercise full personal control over her projects (some FTA colleagues had complained that Fonda's grandstanding ego, and not her feminism, really lay behind the hostilities that destroyed the troupe). Her experience in making *A Doll's House* in 1973 with Joseph Losey confirmed her determination to escape the hegemony of male authority on the set, since she and Losey squared off repeatedly over her interpretation of Nora. Even more telling was the production crew's homophobic rejection of her efforts to deepen Nora's relationship with Christine. But while Fonda cites this experience as the goad behind her decision to seek out the means of cinematic production for herself, she has not in any way pursued other logical extensions of her complaint: despite her celebratory response to working with an all-woman crew in the early seventies, she has not implemented even a skeletal version of such an organization herself. Fonda's power alignments have remained staunchly with men in all facets of her life, and so it was with Bruce Gilbert, whom she met through his job at a daycare center, that she established IPC as a film production unit. Nor in the eleven years since its inception has IPC employed a woman director or sent out the word, as Ellen Burstyn did in making *Alice Doesn't Live Here Anymore* (1975), that the crew for any given project would be predominantly female. Fonda may have founded IPC with the idealistic argument that "if I was going to work, and if there were going to be movies that I thought were important, and if I wanted to remain in the context of the mass media, I was going to have to produce them myself,"[39] but the damning reality for feminists is that she has done little or nothing to break down the sexist divisions within Hollywood that persist in keeping women out of key positions behind the camera. One can easily conclude that the real goal of the power she has sought within the industry is personal rather than selflessly feminist, for her own preoccupations about women's roles in the media are painfully self-centered and outdated, shaped by her conditioned Hollywood notions about women as actresses and men as technical authority figures. She tacitly acquiesced to the prejudices of the industry when she explained in 1975:

> There's real reluctance to finance a major film . . . with a woman direct-
> ing because producers believe women are not good at handling large
> numbers of people. . . . I've never tried to direct and I don't know many
> women personally who have tried to direct feature films. . . . I know
> [financiers] would not trust a woman to handle a crew of men and bring
> in a product that is salable.[40]

Since acquiring the means to make such decisions herself, Fonda has
evinced no sisterly trust of her own. Similarly, when working with
women scenarists, she has invariably hired men to do the rewrites, a
situation that exploded into open hostility with former FTA member
Nancy Dowd, author of the original story for *Coming Home,* who took
Fonda to arbitration over the handling of her material.

Fonda pointedly rejects the argument that audiences avoid films
with serious content and she challenges the assumption that because
popular entertainment stimulates the emotions rather than the intellect, it cannot effect real political change. These convictions lie behind
her refusal to make what she calls "cynical" films or "downers" which
leave viewers despondent about ways of dealing with social injustice:

> I prefer films or any kind of cultural expression that strengthens rather
> than weakens people. . . . Perhaps the best we can do now is create in the
> audience a sense of hopeful frustration. Perhaps they should leave the
> theatre with a sense of wanting to move and a feeling that there is good
> reason to move.[41]

These pronouncements, while indebted to such disparate sources as
Fonda's contacts with the North Vietnamese cinema and her work
with the equally nonmainstream Godard, have paradoxically provided
her with a winning capitalist formula for a broadly appealing and
peculiarly home-grown American social realism. As Farber and Green
acknowledge, her "sure commercial touch," forged in the early years of
her film career, was rekindled by 1975 with her adoption of "a conventional middle-of-the-road approach to controversial subjects. Despite her reputation as a firebrand, Jane seldom risked including
anything in her films that might alienate the mass audience."[42] Hers
is a theory of filmmaking that encourages audiences to come to a film
by cultivating a high degree of familiarity in its narrative and characterizations, then gently tugging at their sense of fairness and decency;
it is not an ingenious confrontation of an ideology so deeply en-
trenched that it has become all-but-invisible to the average moviegoer.
Her films consequently do not upset viewers by insisting upon radical
new social structures, but instead they dramatize the reassuring mid-

dle-class premise that good people, when better informed about the issues at hand, will necessarily initiate the proper reforms: conveniently, a premise upon which Hayden's CED also operates.

Not coincidentally, films that effectively achieve the illusion of easing pressing cultural tensions in nonthreatening ways also attain greater commercial success than more disturbing, unresolved depictions of American life, and Fonda is unabashed in declaring that her primary goal in cinema is to bankroll the political agenda and organization spearheaded by her husband: "We have to find ways to raise millions of dollars if [CED] is going to win."[43] In order to fulfill her societal and financial ambitions, then, Fonda pointedly strives "to reach as many people as possible. The bottom line is, is it good entertainment? I'm not interested in lecturing people or hitting them on the head with a deep message."[44] IPC's projects to date have for the most part met these criteria: *Coming Home* (1978), *The China Syndrome* (1979), *Nine to Five* (1980), and *On Golden Pond* (1981) have each garnered considerable profit, and *The Dollmaker* was showcased as a major ABC television movie; only *Rollover* (1981) has been a financial and popular disappointment.

Inevitably Fonda's rededication to making films that are first and foremost "good entertainment" has altered the feminist content of her films as well as the socialist vision she once advocated. She now chooses to portray "ordinary" women who undergo limited, recognizable awakenings:

> I don't want to play liberated women, roles where people say, "Oh, that's Jane Fonda, that's the way she perceives herself." I would much rather play the antithesis of what I feel—a pro-war or apolitical kind of woman existing in a situation most average people live in, helping to clarify the situation for other women.[45]

As a result she creates screen characters who reflect rather than accelerate the level of feminist awareness in her viewers, and she has become so successful in doing so that she has consolidated more power within Hollywood than most other women associated with the industry. Her diction reveals the priorities of a businesswoman rather than of a serious feminist when she asserts, "[I]n order for an industry that is profit-oriented and financially precarious to begin churning out serious new women's films, new bankable stereotypes will have to be discovered."[46]

To be fair, the "new bankable stereotypes" Fonda has successfully brought to the screen in the last decade do possess feminist attributes.

Many are ambitious women with careers that take them into the centers of power in contemporary life. While portraying a playwright, a reporter, a ranch owner, and a corporate executive, she has infused each with a marked aggressiveness in the performance of her job: Lillian Hellman in *Julia* remains stubbornly dedicated to her craft; Kimberly Wells (*The China Syndrome*) and Hallie Martin (*The Electric Horseman*) pursue their stories despite severe harassment; and Ella Connors (*Comes a Horseman*), in the tradition of the Western hero, tackles the oil companies that are obliterating her independent rancher's existence. Nor has Fonda depicted only women who work in glamorous settings. In *Fun With Dick and Jane, Coming Home,* and *Nine to Five,* she portrays housewives whose insulation from social reality suddenly ends, forcing them to discover the real machinations of the wide world outside their homes. Their experiences lead each of them to reevaluate their middle-class assumptions and reorient their personalities in acts of genuine female empowerment.

As critics have acknowledged since Rosen and Haskell's studies of the female stereotypes that have dominated movies, an important first step toward a feminist cinema involves putting such positive depictions of women on the screen. But identifying "new stereotypes," as Fonda terms it, short-circuits the full agenda, for it implies that characterization is all, ideological representation nonexistent: find more affirmative models of womanhood, the logic goes, and the questions of sexist imaging or societal injustice within the construction of the female image will take care of themselves, as though a strong female personality operates in a vacuum, unimpeded by the very forces that have kept such figures off the screen in the first place. Equally troubling in Fonda's theory is her comfortable acceptance of the existence of new "types," whose recognizability and predictability provide an easy shorthand with which to compose satisfying mass entertainment: the impetus shaping such notions is her quest for the broadest-based vehicle for liberal and semiliberal audiences she can muster, and it involves nothing so challenging as a real breakdown of monolithic assumptions about female experience to reveal its actual multiplicity. Stars by definition are themselves "types," and so Fonda's formula is neatly congruent with her own career proclivities.

Her understanding of successful Hollywood filmmaking strategies extends beyond this formularizing of the contemporary woman, however. It is in Fonda's effective exploitation of her star image that she willingly cooperates with one of dominant cinema's most effective means of subduing the female within the spectacle of the screen, idealizing her into a fetishized image supported by costuming, camera

work, make-up, lighting, settings, and the entire public relations apparatus.[47] While Fonda does control the ends served by her image
through the films she elects to make, she has by no means renounced
the associations with voyeuristic glamor that underlie female celebrity
in the entertainment industry. She announced flat out when deciding
to make *Fun With Dick and Jane,* her 1976 comeback film, that she
wanted to prove she could be "funny and pretty again," tacitly con-
ceding that her period as a political "hag" was over. More recently, in
discussing the international financial intrigues that shape the plot of
Rollover, she enthused for a *Playgirl* interviewer, "It's a very stylish,
classy, complicated movie about sex and money and the people whose
worlds are high-up and air-conditioned."[48] Her hugely popular exercise books, tapes, and salons further demonstrate her preoccupation
with the spectacle of the female body, so perfectly toned and propor-
tioned in her case that her announced intention of proving that
healthy sexiness is possible after forty (and now well toward fifty) in
fact merely extends the years over which her sisters can recriminate
themselves for less accommodating and luscious physiques and less
discipline to make "the work-out" the central passion of their lives.
When a bikini-clad Fonda preened before the cameras in *California
Suite* and *On Golden Pond,* she participated in her own continuing
fetishization, narcissistically proclaiming her sexual glamor, just as
much the victim of patriarchal notions of female value as in her
preliberated days with Vadim.

Stardom encompasses more than physical allure, however, and
Fonda has shown herself equally adept in exploiting public fascination
with the self-reflexive interplay between individual role and star persona. It is highly disingenuous for Fonda to protest that she doesn't
want her private politics to predetermine the responses to the characters she plays, for playing against type is a tried and true Hollywood
technique. Louis B. Mayer could not more astutely heighten public
interest than does a project wherein the notorious Hanoi Jane portrays
a naive military housewife awakened to the personal and political
horrors of the Vietnam War, or a mousy secretary discovering the
sexism of the working world. However Fonda herself may resist the
truth, her husband has bluntly concluded, "She's never gonna play
anything but Jane Fonda in a film. . . . She's a more important
character than any character she'll ever play."[49]

In addition to this sophisticated manipulation of her star identity,
Fonda has recast established Hollywood film formulas to contain the
new female stereotypes she has created. These familiar narrative and
genre structures reassure audiences by means of recuperative end-

ings, even when they do explore ruptures in societal constructions concerning women. *Fun With Dick and Jane* offers a case in point, for it allowed Fonda to prove her mainstream viability by returning to a form with which she had achieved the successes of her early career: the domestic comedy. The movie raises such issues as feminist liberation and economic reform, but subjects them to gentle satire that mocks the protagonists of the film as much as the system they set out to dismantle. When Fonda's housewife loses her secure middle-class existence once her husband loses his job, she is sufficiently outraged to mastermind the couple's new career as robbers who gradually move from robbing neighborhood merchants to robbing the very corporations that have bankrupted them. Sexual stereotypes also collapse as Jane takes the lead in planning their capers, while Dick becomes increasingly indecisive and incompetent. But whatever hint of revolutionary anger resides in their actions is sanitized by the television sitcom treatment it is accorded. Rather than political reeducation, the film provides therapeutic fantasy retaliation against a system whose real failure is not seen as its inherent structural inequities and exploitation but its selection of such an upwardly mobile family to shortchange. The film's suggestions of ethnic and class solidarity play today as the crudest stereotyping. As one critic notes, this "curiously mixed-up film" attempts "to burlesque American materialism" but ends up "happily endorsing any means—including larceny—necessary to stay 'in the money'."[50]

Electric Horseman (1979) offered another cautious merger between romantic comedy and social commentary, teaming Fonda with Robert Redford, her co-star a decade earlier in *Barefoot in the Park*. In it, aggressive reporter Hallie Martin discovers the humanizing power of falling in love with her subject, a burnt-out rodeo star whose spiritual restoration is achieved by rescuing a magnificent show horse from the same corporate owners who are callously exploiting both of them for their commercial value. Here the sentiments are more coherently set forth than in the earlier film, but the star packaging and glib resolution are all too familiar: the freeing of the horse and the lovemaking of the principals assure audiences of a comforting emotional equilibrium that needs to be pondered no further than the doors of the theater— certainly not in the daily worlds of the viewers themselves. As would be the case in *The China Syndrome* and *9 to 5*, the heroes and villains are so broadly delineated that political reeducation is unnecessary: everyone recognizes a scoundrel when he conveniently paints himself as such.

Fonda has received the most attention as a Hollywood feminist for her contributions to "the New Women's film," in which as Annette Kuhn explains, "the central characters are women, and often women who are not attractive or glamorous in the conventional sense. Narratives, moreover, are frequently organized around the process of a woman's self-discovery and growing independence. . . ."[51] These recent works reiterate the pattern Andrea Walsh has identified as the core plot of the classical Hollywood women's film of the studio era, for they too "are constructed around dilemmas of moral choice focusing on themes of interpersonal connection and the fear of separation from loved ones."[52] The resurgence in popularity of such films reflects the fact that since the sixties, the women's movement has created its own subgroup within the spectrum of distinct audiences characterizing the contemporary entertainment market. That these films are being made also provides some evidence that the woman's voice is being granted expression within the dominant industry. But a number of feminist critics have recently warned against hoping for too much from this phenomenon.

De Lauretis' argument that the woman's film typically recovers its deviant females from the unfeminine options the film may have let them explore has already been cited. Mulvey acknowledges that melodrama, which lies at the core of the woman's film, especially appeals to female audiences because it probes "pent-up emotions, bitterness and disillusion well-known to women," but in providing that release, it finally betrays its fans by denying a resolution that is favorable to women.[53] Rather, as Mary Ann Doane argues, the satisfaction to be derived from such fare lies either in the viewer's masochistically identifying with the passively irreconcilable sufferings of the heroine, narcissistically merging with the female spectacle on the screen, or achieving a transvestite empathy with the active male figure in the text.[54] Kuhn focuses her skepticism on the open-ended ambiguity that regularly allows the contemporary woman's film to skirt any clear-cut resolution of the dilemmas it exposes in its female characters' lives: "it reworks rather than destroys the textual operations of dominant cinema" and "permits readings to be made which accord more or less with spectators' prior stances on feminist issues. . . . Whatever positive identifications it offers to those who choose to make them, new women's cinema cannot in the final instance deal in any direct way with the questions which feminism poses for cinematic representation."[55]

These theoretical qualifications to labeling the woman's film a feminist text find ample support in an analysis of Fonda's works in the genre, the most significant of which are *Coming Home* (1978), *Julia*

(1977), and *The Dollmaker* (1983). Each is a film concerned with female crisis, growth, and survival, but each backs away from the full implications of the dramatic ruptures it reveals in its protagonists' stories, so that none finally breaks loose from conventional resolutions in order to enter into what might be called a feminist dialectic.

Coming Home, Fonda's much-awaited treatment of the Vietnam War, is perhaps the least deserving of the three of the title "woman's film," since its principal female character, Sally Hyde, dominates very little of the film: the dramatic center is held by Luke Martin (Jon Voight), the paraplegic veteran whose transformation from embittered patient to healing activist is effected through Sally's tender affection and the example of her own personal changes. Luke's centrality evolves into a tug of war with Sally's returning Marine husband in the last quarter of the narrative, concluding when the two men's ability to come to grips with war and the changes it has made in their lives is

Coming Home, United Artists Corporation
Courtesy of Museum of Modern Art/Film Stills Archive

tellingly juxtaposed: Luke addresses a high school assembly on the pointlessness of the Vietnam conflict, and Bob Hyde commits suicide. Sally has been at the supermarket during this sequence and leaves by way of a door marked "no exit," an unsubtle suggestion that Hyde's death is not the easy resolution to her conflicting loyalties that it may seem (or is the sign an oblique commentary on the blindness of Americans generally to the escalating Indochinese nightmare?). Nonetheless, one has little doubt that Sally and Luke will console one another in their mutual grief and together pioneer an enlightened heterosexual relationship.

Although Sally provides the connective tissue holding the story together, her voice can never really compete with the greater melodramatic weight of the men's circumstances, much less with the abrasive sixties soundtrack that precludes any thoughtful contemplation of the characters' situation. Ironically, the marginalization of Sally's moral choices within the larger drama of *Coming Home* was not recognized by those of Fonda's critics who resented her focus upon a trio of American participants in the Vietnam War rather than upon the Vietnamese themselves. Fonda's antiwar activities had led many to expect that latter focus, and they loudly voiced their outrage at her elevation of the angst of a housewife to epic importance in assessing the scars of the war era. The sexism of such complaints is obvious, born of the stereotypic notion that war and its consequences are men's concerns and can be explored adequately on the screen only through battlefield violence. But Fonda's rendering of Sally's awakening complicates any feminist defense, for, as Pauline Kael has pointed out, by couching Sally's development in the cliché-ridden terms of sexual orgasm, Fonda contributed to the continuing political trivialization of women on film. Instead of exploring a new perspective on her protagonist's evolving consciousness, Fonda's movie harks back to the patriotic homefront films of World War II. Determined that IPC's first important project would avoid the declamatory rhetoric of her activist period, she perfected her formula for creating recognizably "ordinary" heroines and denied Sally's discoveries the significance of becoming historically typical so as to make the individual the sole locus of struggle and change.

Nancy Dowd's original story would have necessitated much more innovative filmmaking to capture its subtleties of character and plot. No love affair existed in Dowd's "Buffalo Ghost," and the friendship between Sally and Vi provided an important arena for Sally's politicization around feminist as well as antiwar issues. Fonda hired Waldo Salt to rewrite the story in more conventional terms, turning it in the process, according to Dowd, into "a male supremacist film: men choose between ideas, and women choose between men." The dispute severed what remained of Fonda's connection with her feminist comrades from the early part of the decade. By sparing Sally the radical personal choices Fonda herself had faced in becoming politically aware, Fonda unquestionably sold out her own knowledge of the painful complexities and inner struggles involved in such growth. She has hollowly asserted that "All we wanted to do in the movie is to show this woman moving from point A to point B. . . . It would have been phony to have her undergo some great liberal conversion."[56] Unconvinced, Molly Haskell has called Sally a "Barbie doll" and concluded, "With such disregard for its characters as individuals how can the film's ultimate message of regeneration be anything but false?"[57]

Julia has been far less disappointing for those expecting strong women's films from Fonda. It appeared almost as if in direct response to complaints like Lee Israel's of the New Hollywood proclivity for presenting contemporary women as under-twenty-five-years-old, indifferent to politics and society, oblivious to intellectual pursuits, and incapable of bonding with one another.[58] Moreover, it was the script's depiction of female friendship that Fonda expressly cited as the basis for her enthusiasm about the project and that has in turn explained its general popularity among women viewers. Not an IPC enterprise, *Julia* is derived from Lillian Hellman's memoir *Pentimento;* the screen treatment, written by Alvin Sargent, achieves a penetrating female subjectivity far exceeding anything Fonda has done with her own production company, except *The Dollmaker* (not coincidentally, both films grew out of female-authored texts). At the center of the narrative is the voice and consciousness of an ambitious woman, recollecting in old age the critical challenges that galvanized her to action on the world stage in a variety of contexts. More than the actions themselves, however, she contemplates the individuals who spurred her to extend herself in crucial ways: as in the traditional woman's film, *Julia* is concerned more with relationships than with deeds, even though the major women characters distinguish themselves by their courage. The primary emotion articulated through Fonda's voice-over as Lillian is one of loss, as she broods over memories involving her devotion to Julia and to Dashiell Hammett, now both long since dead. The structure of the film unfolds in flashbacks, some to her childhood and adolescence, some to her early writing career and to the successes attendant upon the completion of *The Children's Hour,* some to her clandestine smuggling of money into Nazi Germany at Julia's request. In this regard, the work supports Tania Modleski's claim that

much melodrama gives the impression of a ceaseless returning to a prior
state. . . . [E]ach time you reach a destination you discover that it is the
place you never really left. . . . In melodrama, the important moments of
the narrative are often felt as eruptions of involuntary memory, to the
point where sometimes the *only* major events are repetitions of former
ones. . . . these modalities being stereotypically linked with female subjectivity in general (with the "cycles, gestation, the eternal recurrence of
a biological rhythm which conforms to that of nature").[59]

Both the narrative and the mood of *Julia* convey the rhythms of
subjective time: the film begins and ends with shots of the aged Lilly
in a rowboat, fishing in half-light on a still pond, and at the outset the
voice-over explains, "I'm old now and want to remember what was
there for me once, what is there for me now." As Hellman examines
her memories, she places herself and Julia at the emotional center of
the drama; its critical moments involve the women engaged in active
decisions and struggles; Hammett's male voice assumes the atypical
role of chorus to those climaxes. Lillian herself emerges as a complex
character, at once strong, gritty, and tough, yet painfully insecure,
timid, and given to idol-worship. Fonda's performance surpasses anything she had done since *Klute,* and much that she has done since that
time, for she captured the thorniness of the adult female psyche, with
its conflicting aspirations, anger, and self-doubt, its competing hun-
gers for self-definition and the safety of familiar roles. Lillian firmly
remains the protagonist of the film: Julia and Hammett command her
imagination because of their abilities to challenge her out of the
anxieties that constrict her ambition. Neither is totally accessible to
her, however, not only because of their unwavering personal convictions concerning the values and modes of action that define their lives,
but also because of the very subjectivity of individual experience,
which the narrative emphasizes as the distorting mirror of all reality—
a subjectivity compounded by the inevitable alterations of time, memory, and loss. The recuperative impulses in the film are contained far
more successfully than in any other of Fonda's films in this genre,
because the ending defies easy reassurances to viewers about Lillian's
having achieved a satisfactory compromise with life. Rather, the lonely
woman fishing in the frame story is coming face to face with how little
one can fathom and how inadequate human beings are to protect and
care satisfactorily even for those they love. Lilly's failure to recover
Julia's daughter stands alongside her failure to overcome the bit-
tersweet disappointments of her decades-long relationship with Hammett. Nor does the film lapse into the triteness of suggesting that these

losses rest on a simple dichotomy of woman as careerist versus homemaker. The dilemma facing Hellman and the viewer is far more
profoundly universal and irreconcilable than that. While *Julia* does
exploit the willingness of its audience to give itself over to unrestrained
melancholy, its protagonist is no passive sufferer but has gone out to
engage the chaos of modern existence with a toughness that invites
admiration instead of masochistic identification. Moreover, Lilly is a
survivor—her voice itself attests to that. Alone, she must now make
sense of her life and go on, however angry and perplexed she remains.

Where, then, is the problem with this film? Does it refute the
charges that Fonda has never quite achieved a fully realized feminist
cinema? Unfortunately, no. While *Julia* is a more notable achievement
than most of Fonda's movies about women's struggles, it is still very
much a product of dominant cinema and subordinates its most compelling energies to the exigencies of the market. Kuhn has pointed out
that the film becomes a woman's film by inverting an established form
of the sixties and seventies, the male buddy film: its plot dynamics,
then, draw upon recognized patterns already successful with contemporary audiences. Even more telling is the film's prominent two-tiered
star apparatus. The primary characters of the film are well-established
historical personalities of the century, and they are portrayed by
equally well-established and controversial actors: nothing is "ordinary"
about either level of the film's diegesis, and so the production of the
text's meaning is as much (or more) a function of the viewer's response
to those factors as it is to the question of female friendship or personal
growth.[60] The possibility of the film's achieving an effective univer-
salizing insight into female experience is severely compromised because the movie keeps reiterating the uniqueness of its characters on
every plane of imaginative interaction with the text.

The treatment of women's relationships has also elicited considerable complaint from feminist critics, who interpret director Fred Zin-
neman's sentimental portrayal of the "crush" between Julia and Lilly
as a means of insulating the audience within Hallmark card soft-focus
prettiness so as to evade the more complex psychological dimensions
of women loving one another. Such shallowness of depiction trivializes
the subject, and Haskell complained that "one word of grown-up
dialogue, one exchange between Jane Fonda and Vanessa Redgrave as
conversing adults, would have been worth the thousand pictures in
bucolic settings designed to show the wordless harmony of their
friendship."[61] Kuhn faults the open-ended sequence where Lilly flat-
tens the drunk who claims, "the whole world knows about you and
Julia," as allowing viewers a safe retreat into their own preconceptions

about female friendship: ironically, while the film is celebrated for exploring the bonds between women, it encourages a multiplicity of contradictory interpretations, none of which necessarily demands a reevaluation of prior notions and some of which permit a rejection of lesbianism altogether.

Some of the most biting feminist criticism of the film attacks the nostalgic abstraction surrounding Julia herself. An essence instead of a fully realized human being, Julia eventually disappears from the narrative, which in fact she seldom occupies for more than a few minutes at a stretch anyway. By relegating her to martyrdom, the film ignores the challenge of integrating this renegade female or her distinctive friendship with another woman into any coherent and continuing social fabric. Viewers avoid having to apply her example to themselves, since even the noble Lillian can follow Julia just so far. It might even be argued, as Kuhn suggests, that Hammett's presence, situated in a less relativized framework than Lilly's childhood memories of Julia, further undermines the viability of the female bond, with its dreamlike unreality, as a mode of meaningful human interaction, when contrasted with the realistic imperative embodied in the film's heterosexual jousting. Pauline Kael's remark that she would have preferred a movie on Hellman that examined "why a woman of such strength and, in many ways, of such ruthless honesty, should have deferred to the judgment of a man of lesser gifts than her own" demonstrates that even sophisticated viewers found the internal dynamics of the narrative associated with the tensions in the conventional Hollywood pairing of male and female.[62] Finally, then, as Margaret Drabble has concluded, despite Fonda's good intentions and the fine acting the film showcases, *Julia* may be "exactly the kind of film one ought to fear—one that seems to be making the right points but in the end is prevented from doing so by its commercial form." When feminism is thus coopted by the fashionable, "it will become increasingly difficult to make a serious feminist film, as the average viewer cannot distinguish gloss from originality."[63]

Only *The Dollmaker*, among Fonda's post-*Julia* films, has escaped the glossy superficiality Drabble identified in her filmmaking. Perhaps the Fonda enterprise best deserving of the label "woman's film," this adaptation of Harriet Arnouw's novel had been a preoccupation with Fonda dating from the mid-seventies. She finally decided to produce it through an alliance of IPC with ABC Television Theatre, so as to engage as many viewers as possible with the work—in itself a rather optimistic perception of television audiences, given the unrelenting grimness of Arnouw's story about Gerty Nevels and her family as they migrate from Appalachia to Detroit during World War II. The production values of the movie thoroughly eschew the glamor usually associated with Fonda's projects. Fonda herself gained thirty pounds and rejected makeup to soften her appearance; she selected a cast notable for its absence of star names (Geraldine Page alone, playing her mother, fit that category of celebrity). Filmed on location, the movie's soundtrack also boasted authentic regional music. Like *Julia*, *The Dollmaker* offered Fonda a text authored by a woman and centered on a female consciousness; in the script, Gerty remains the filter through which all the events of the story must pass and be assessed. Because Gerty's crises illustrate feminist themes, Fonda saw them as a powerful means to address the complex sexist dynamics that cripple the lives of ordinary women. Gerty's ambition that the family have its own farm, and her struggles to achieve that end, are thwarted by the massive impact of the world war and by her husband's authoritarian decision that they go north instead to take advantage of the booming war economy of Detroit. Those values associated with Gerty—the land, the rural community, and the family—are all upended by Clovis's self-centered determination to involve himself in the war in some fashion, an impulse that lands his family in a debased urban labor camp among strangers.

As a consequence of their displacement, Gerty eventually loses two children: their oldest boy runs away and back to her parents in Kentucky, and their youngest daughter is killed in a trainyard accident. Cassie's death follows her father's harsh insistence that she renounce her childish preoccupation with an imaginary friend; in her subsequent disorientation, she seeks out more distant hiding places to play with "Callie Lou" and is run over on the railroad tracks as her distraught mother helplessly watches. The child is an alter ego for Gerty, who shares Cassie's imaginative streak and feels equally constricted by the harsh conformist realities of the proletarian slum into which Clovis has thrust them. Gerty is an artist: without training she has become a woodcarver and uses her talents both as an additional source of income (to buy the farm she still plans to have back home) and as a means of self-expression, which her husband callously misreads when he suggests a way of massproducing the wooden figures. Upon Cassie's death, Gerty slips into the madness of rage and despair; she also begins maniacally carving a large female figure bowed in grief—a figure to whom she is unable to give a face. In that action, her spiritual and imaginative hunger, denied by the material conditions of the life she must lead, is graphically epitomized: Fonda has never so effectively depicted the desperate realities crushing the best energies of working-class women, and in that regard, the film remains a milestone in her efforts to merge her feminist and moviemaking priorities.

Yet there are very clear reasons why this story, for all its stark honesty about women's lives, also suited Fonda's passion for affirmative—and, one must add, ultimately recuperative—treatments of feminist issues, so that *The Dollmaker* is not so completely removed from her more unsatisfying films as might be presumed. Gerty is, finally, an epic heroine, a modern filmic Earth Mother who recalls such noble female matriarchs as Ma Joad: the appeal of doing her own feminist version of *The Grapes of Wrath* must have been irresistible to Henry Fonda's daughter. The family's survival is the overriding value of Gerty's life, and her daily existence is predicated on the kinds of self-sacrifice needed to ensure that outcome. She is rewarded for her tenacity and compensated for the ravaging of her spirit at the end of the film, when she is allowed to recover both family and homestead, as Clovis decides to return the Nevels' brood to Kentucky. The ruptures that have been exposed in Gerty's wifely acquiescence are dismissed by Clovis's remark, "You've won, old woman," and the affectionate grins they exchange. His bullying authoritarianism, with its disregard for her strongly held opinions; her collapse into madness in retaliation against the forces attempting to compel her mute docility; her willful pursuit of aesthetic nourishment in the face of Clovis's obvious insensitivity—all of these telling breaks in the assumed harmony of her married life focus viewer attention on the incompatibilities within conventional notions of female existence. Yet, by the end, Gerty's right values have been accorded their due, saving her from having to break irreparably with the pattern of her life; her righteousness has been validated by the depth of her suffering rather than by active intervention on her part to redirect things. Once again the woman's film has achieved its contradictory impulses by allowing masochistic identification to offer assurances of female victory in the face of the more powerful agents arrayed against essentially powerless women. The turn of the screw in that dynamic is Gerty's own enormous strength of character: she faces the increasing agonies inflicted upon her with a courage of heroic proportions, and so the masochistic dimension of her endurance is masked. These plot movements are, of course, inherent in Arnouw's original material, but one can see the appeal they would have for Fonda, given the progression of her own life toward a reaffirmation of familial solidarity and her determination to make "films that strengthen people."

For all their limitations, however, *Julia* and *The Dollmaker* provide the standard of Fonda's highest achievements as a feminist in Holly-

wood and they become their own subtle indictment of the slick insubs-
tantiality typifying other IPC vehicles, all of which preclude any
serious feminist reeducation of their audiences by the very nature of
their female characterizations (it should also be noted that *Julia* was
not an IPC production in the first place). When Fonda has worked in
genres outside the woman's film, she has marginalized or trivialized
her feminism even more than she did in *Coming Home,* gaining in
exchange considerable commercial success with essentially unthreatening Hollywood forms. Admittedly, each of the films produced
by IPC since 1978 depicts a woman who yearns to be taken more
seriously as a person or professional. Kimberly Wells in *The China
Syndrome* chafes against the witless reportage she is regularly assigned; Lee Winters in *Rollover* fumes at the sexist barriers thwarting
her entry into the corporate hierarchy; Judy Bernly strives to regain a
foothold in a discriminatory working world in *9 to 5;* and Chelsea
Thayer struggles to win her father's long-denied respect in *On Golden
Pond.* Yet because none of these women provides much evidence that
she deserves to be taken very seriously, Fonda compromises the feminist complaints she ostensibly sets out to validate.

Kimberly, for example, projects the quintessentially plastic media
personality. Unable to assert her own will or talent in order to escape
her stereotyped function as the "human interest" anchorwoman at the
television station, she must be prodded into serious investigative reporting of the highly newsworthy situation at the nuclear power plant
by her more aggressive cameraman, played by Michael Douglas. Like
other Fonda protagonists, Kimberly does attain greater insight into the
political corruption around her and makes a risky decision to expose it,
and she does not have to fall in love with either of the male leads in the
film to reach that decision. Nonetheless, Kimberly fails to demonstrate
the kind of moral courage that would make her problems in pursuing
the story as compelling as those of Jack Goddell, the plant engineer
whose willingness to confront the hypocrisies of his employers makes
him the martyred hero of the drama. Rather than orchestrate events
herself, Kimberly reacts to the directives and actions of the men
around her, who are really calling the shots and pointing out to her the
implications of their discoveries. She is in many ways Sally Hyde
redux: a well-meaning, rather simple woman, bewilderingly caught up
in events outside her initial conception of the world. She tentatively
attempts to assimilate all this new information within her still fundamentally establishment identity. Her voice ends the film, but she is
actually eulogizing the murdered Goddell as she chokes back tears:
once more a woman serves as admiring chorus for the man who has

risked everything for his ideals. She, after all, gets a monumental story that saves her with her bosses and will no doubt bring her the reportorial responsibility she so craves.

If Kimberly Wells fails to become a satisfactory feminist heroine, Lee Winters of *Rollover* offers an even greater disappointment. Lee appears more interested in being a glamorous clotheshorse than a credible corporate executive. Her access to the power circles of high finance results from her widowhood rather than from any personal victories within the business arena; before her marriage to a wealthy tycoon, she was, appropriately, a movie star. Fonda insists that she is "fascinated by the struggles of women inside the corporate structure,"[64] but in this film, her struggles amount to little more than an alignment with men who can initiate her to the money games at which she proves decidedly inept. The film's romantic liaison between Fonda and Kris Kristofferson, yet another calculated star coupling, further weakens the plot, since one questions the likelihood that even an ex–movie star would jeopardize her coveted financial power for an ill-conceived love affair. The limitations of this film hurt it at the box office as well as with critics: it remains the major financial failure among IPC productions to date.

In contrast, *9 to 5* (1980) has been one of the company's most notable successes, ostensibly because of its satiric feminist assault on sexism in the workplace. Its bite, however, was for many critics a decidedly benign one, buffered by the dismissible hyperbole of its zany comic format. Fonda's prerelease rhetoric about the film, honed at numerous public rallies on behalf of American office workers, implied that she was producing a hard-hitting attack upon conditions under which women work in the office ghetto, and some aspects of the finished film justify this publicity. Fonda again depicts women who overcome their conditioned antagonisms toward one another in order to develop supportive friendships among themselves. She also escapes the familiar Hollywood plot contrivances of love affairs, so that the primary interactions among the women take precedence in the film. Moreover, one should not ignore Fonda's selflessness in selecting the least interesting role in the film for herself: obviously she decided to give the screen over to the distinctly different comic skills of Lily Tomlin and Dolly Parton.

While the marginalization of women's issues that has marred other IPC productions does not occur here, the film nonetheless recalls the safe satire of *Fun with Dick and Jane* or *Electric Horseman*. The comedy itself relies upon female viewers recognizing the similarities between their own working conditions and those depicted in the film, but the caricatured exaggeration of Dabney Coleman's villain, Parton's naively sexy secretary, and Tomlin's radicalized office manager protect the audience from having to confront too painfully the implications of such situations. The comedy, in effect, particularizes sexism within its own avowedly absurd parameters, allowing viewers guilty of the same offenses to distance themselves smugly from making comparisons that might cut too close to the bone. No systematic analysis of the insidious, often invisible, operation of sexism against working women is attempted, even suggestively. The miseries of the three protagonists are directly relatable to one openly malicious male: eliminate or tame him, the film tells us, and a renaissance in working conditions will occur. It is thus unsurprising that the heroines are permitted very few real opportunities to redefine the nature of their working lives. First, they can only express their frustrations through elaborate but impotent fantasies of retribution, always targeting the boss alone. When they are finally empowered to act upon their grievances (but only because of an unintentional and grisly mistake on Tomlin's part, as she seemingly poisons Coleman with rat poison), their behavior becomes even more outrageous and slapstick than even their daydreams, and the film abandons realistic redress altogether. The film ends with the monster male caged and the women in charge, making the office a utopia that is as much a violation of rationality as what preceded it: those expecting penetrating commentary on the problems of the contemporary workplace will get none here. Again Fonda offered her by-now-familiar justification for the compromises that sour this weakly politicized film:

> Art shouldn't be a mirror to life; art should recreate life in such a way that it elevates, teaches and allows you to go beyond your present consciousness. And I think laughter is the greatest way of all. You can go much further through farce.[65]

One wonders where *9 to 5* was expected to take its audience: is its comedy the galvanizing force Fonda claims it to be, or simply a relaxing and mind-lulling purgative?

IPC's most successful picture to date, *On Golden Pond* (1981), demonstrates quite candidly the difficulty feminist critics face in expecting Fonda to articulate in any consistent or penetrating manner the neglected contours of female desire. On every level the film celebrates the Hollywood system and its reductive notions of female self-realization. Fonda made it as a gift to and reconciliation with her father, casting him opposite Hollywood's most durable female iconoclast, Katharine Hepburn. Fonda's own role possesses feminist dimensions because Chelsea's relationship with Norman dramatizes the second-class status often accorded daughters by fathers who wished for sons. Chelsea does succeed in winning her father's respect by performing a difficult diving maneuver, but in doing so she reverts to tomboyish competitiveness with an adolescent boy, even though she is a woman in her forties. She still feels compelled to adhere to male standards of personal achievement—standards whose primacy is reinforced when the boy achieves an intimacy with Norman that he has never permitted his daughter. When Fonda asserts her womanhood in the movie, she does so by means of the very fetishizing she had ostensibly renounced following her break with Vadim: bikini-clad, she gains the audience's ogling admiration for her exquisitely sculpted body as she preens by the lake. Not a few commentators have remarked on the obvious connection between her exhibitionist testimonial to sexiness past forty and her recently published exercise manual. In crushing the Hollywood myth that older women must renounce their sexuality if they are to continue to make movies, she deprives that act of its potentially feminist import by reaffirming rather than challenging the preeminence of the voyeuristic male gaze.

In contrast to the sentimental holiday Fonda offered viewers in *On Golden Pond*, her recent release, *Agnes of God* (1985), is a more serious film. IPC did not produce that film, for reasons not hard to fathom. While *Agnes* seems to extend Fonda's proven interest in scripts about the dynamic interplay among women with its trio of female leads, the story is far more abstract, even allegorical, than any of the simpler, more familiar dramas to which IPC gives its imprimatur. Fonda herself appears curiously ill at ease and at times frantic as Martha Livingston, the psychiatrist whose goal is to release the simple-minded novice Sister Agnes (Meg Tilly) from what Martha perceives as the sinister isolation and superstition of the cloistered convent, where she has apparently murdered her newborn infant. Martha's struggles with Mother Miriam (Anne Bancroft) for the young nun's soul draw upon deeper reservoirs in both women of guilt and anger about religion, motherhood, and personal moral responsibility, and the central mystery at the heart of the script posits faith against reason as irreconcilable paths toward understanding human existence.

Agnes proved to be a disappointment at the box office, perhaps a telling indicator that Fonda's loyal supporters felt she had violated her commercial dictum to provide comfortably recognizable women who undergo moderate growth and change as the result of crisis, in the meantime offering reassurance about the basic camaraderie that women enjoy with one another. Here the three protagonists are locked in a grueling battle of wills over the interpretation of the grisly events that have set the drama in motion: moments of compassionate sisterhood are soon followed by shrill condemnations of betrayal. More important, the film's Gothic conceptualization of the female stands in glaring contradiction to feminist efforts to demystify notions concerning women's nature. John Pielmeier's original play and the script adapted from it seem obsessed with the very notions about female sexuality that, through the rational investigation of the doctor, they ostensibly refute. The female body becomes the locus of sinister violation; blood spills over the credits, fills the wastebasket where the dead child is found, and covers Agnes's white habit as the marks of the stigmata suddenly burst forth from her flesh. Her terror of menstruation, her preoccupation with physical self-mortification in penance for her "sins," and her absolute refusal to entertain scientific facts about conception and pregnancy all provide further testimony to the antithesis she perceives between the truly pure of heart and the pollution generated by her femaleness. The story's setting in a cloister heightens the atmosphere of Gothic medievalism and misogyny, in contrast to the much more progressive character of contemporary female religious life in reality. Finally, the film abounds with failed or horrific mothers and repeatedly equates the failure of motherhood with a woman's profound antipathy to her own procreativity. Martha has had an abortion and must now deal with a senile mother who perversely insists on her preference for her other daughter, a nun rather than a divorcee; Mother Miriam entered religious life after the debacle of a bad marriage and disastrous parenting, and seems to be renewing her failure of vision by having missed the nightmarish sequence of events unfolding in her own convent to her own niece; Agnes herself is the product of an illegitimate pregnancy and an abusive, insane mother, who inculcated her own self-loathing within her child by mutilating her genitals. Not surprisingly, then, her pregnancy and motherhood are abominations to which Agnes cannot permit the barest legitimacy of fact. Sexual relations themselves are subsumed within equally sinister alternatives: Agnes was the victim either of an exploitative and cowardly male or of a raping God. Miriam has abandoned a sexual life altogether, and Martha skittishly continues to date. In none of the women's lives is sexuality allowed even remotely to suggest the complexities of female desire.[66] *Agnes of God* thus offers the perplexing combination of strong female roles devoted to exploring and validating reactionary notions of female identity and experience. Its impact is the antithesis of the woman's film, where Fonda's feminist impulses have been most fruitfully realized to date; instead of affirming the power, dignity, and honest reality of women's lives, *Agnes* presents so abstract and ominous a depiction of women that one leaves the theater enveloped in the pernicious mythology of the female as "Other," inscrutable and terrible in her destructive rage, even to herself.

The complex evolution of Jane Fonda's film career has made her one of the most extensively reported upon media figures of her generation. The various stages of her feminist odyssey have allowed her to view herself consistently as a symbol for the modern American woman. During the past decade she has brought to the screen women who mirror the changes in the social fabric wrought by the women's movement and who sometimes even escape those givens of Hollywood moviemaking, love and marriage. To the degree that Fonda approaches each film venture with a zealous determination to give women fuller and fairer dramatic representation, she deserves the respect of feminist critics. Yet the nature of commercial film entertainment, to which her larger devotion to Hayden and to CED commits her, prevents IPC from addressing the complex questions inherent in any feminist analysis of women's experience. As a bona fide child of the Hollywood system, she also works most congenially in those filmmaking forms and within the industry system that comprise the dominant cinema, whose hegemony in delimiting the treatment of women in film is the primary target of feminist theorists. Fonda's hybrid status as feminist "star" is itself a successful exploitation of an industry staple, as well as an expression of the cultural approval she has won for seeming to ford the treacherous challenges with which feminism threatens bourgeois comfort: she reassures the public that her career, her activism, and her family can exist in satisfying equilibrium, and she provides evidence of an integrated public personality that has weathered the strains of women's liberation with style and success. Fonda has attained a popular importance, however, which obscures her intellectual and political shortcomings as a legitimate feminist advocate standing at the cutting edge of reform.

The more insidious consequences of Fonda's excessively high profile as a feminist leader in Hollywood involve the public misapprehension that her personal success testifies to the gains made by women as a whole within the industry. Such has not been the case, and Fonda has done little to correct the inequities facing women within the industry. In 1969, Pauline Kael prophesied that Fonda "stands a good chance of personifying American tensions and dominating our movies in the seventies as Bette Davis did in the thirties."[67] She has done just that in the past decade, by dramatizing our cultural ambivalence about feminism through her vacillating public image and her inconsistent film roles—not through any willingness to address the theoretical implications of imagining a cinema that gives voice to women's vision and experience. Her prominent role as Hollywood's feminist conscience is in the very least a disturbing index as to how successfully the dominant industry can coopt challenges by tapping an essentially unthreatening spokesperson—herself an insider—to embody its skin-deep "revolution" in sensibility. Fonda misleads herself and her public when she professes to be anything more.

Notes

1. Annette Kuhn, *Women's Pictures: Feminism and Cinema* (Boston: Routledge & Kegan Paul, 1982), 21.

2. In 1979, for example, Fonda was voted one of America's most admired women by readers of *Good Housekeeping* (quoted by Gail Sheehy, "Hers: Women and Leadership: Jane Fonda," *New York Times*, 10 January 1980).

3. *Time*, 3 October 1977, 91.

4. Tracy Young, "Fonda Jane," *Film Comment* (March/April 1978): 57.

5. Richard Schickel, *Intimate Strangers: The Culture of Celebrity* (Garden City, New York: Doubleday & Company, 1985), 36.

6. "Four Successful Women Talk about What They Want and Can't Have," *Redbook,* February 1977, 166.

7. Alfred Aronwitz, "Henry Fonda's Daughter Zooms to Fame: Lady Jane," *The Saturday Evening Post,* 23 March 1963, 24.

8. Quoted by Stephen Farber and Marc Green in *Hollywood Dynasties* (New York: Fawcett Crest, 1984), 151.

9. Thomas Thompson, "Up and Away Goes Jane Fonda," *Life,* 29 March 1968, 70.

10. Joel Kotkin, "Fonda: 'I Am Not More Respectable,'" *New Times,* 20 March 1978, 59.

11. Martin Kasindorf, "Jane Fonda: A Person of Many Parts," *The New York Times Magazine,* 3 February 1974, 17.

12. "*Playboy* Interview: Jane Fonda and Tom Hayden," *Playboy,* April 1974, 85.

13. Thomas Kiernan, *Jane Fonda: Heroine for Our Time* (New York: Delilah Books, 1982), 109.

14. In *Brigitte Bardot and the Lolita Syndrome,* de Beauvoir celebrated Bardot's destruction of sexist myths about female sexual passivity, romantic emotionalism, and personality insecurity (1959; Arno Books, 1972).

15. Laura Mulvey, "Visual Pleasure and Narrative Cinema," in *Women and the Cinema: A Critical Anthology,* ed. Karyn Kay and Gerald Peary (New York: E. P. Dutton, 1979), 418, 422.

16. "*Playboy* Interview: Jane Fonda and Tom Hayden," 85.

17. Quoted by Kiernan, *Jane Fonda,* 132.

18. Quoted by Kiernan, *Jane Fonda,* 142, 179.

19. Clare Johnston, "Women's Cinema as Counter-Cinema," in *Sexual Stratagems: The World of Women in Film,* ed. Patricia Erens (New York: Horizon Press, 1979), 135.

20. Marjorie Rosen, *Popcorn Venus: Women, Movies and the American Dream* (New York: Coward, McCann and Geoghegan, 1973), 331–32.

21. Molly Haskell, *From Reverence to Rape: The Treatment of Women in the Movies* (New York: Holt, Rinehart and Winston, 1974), 321.

22. Thomas Kiernan, *Jane: An Intimate Biography of Jane Fonda* (New York: G. P. Putnam's Sons, 1973), 301.

23. Donald Katz, "Jane Fonda: A Hard Act to Follow," *Rolling Stone,* 9 March 1978, 41.

24. Aimee Lee Ball, "The Unofficial Jane Fonda," *Redbook,* January 1982, 30.

25. Betty Friedan, *The Feminine Mystique* (New York: W. W. Norton & Company, 1963), 261.

26. Celeste Fremon, "Jane Fonda," *Playgirl,* January 1982, 45.

27. Quoted by Gary Herman and David Downing, *Jane Fonda: All American Anti-Heroine* (New York: Quick Fox, 1980), 86.

28. Rex Reed, "Jane: 'Everybody Expected Me to Fall on My Face,'" *The New York Times,* 25 January 1970.

29. Jane Fonda, "I Want to Work with Women," *The New York Times,* 31 October 1971.

30. "Letter to Jane," *Women & Film,* 1973, pp. 45–46.

31. Diane Giddis, "The Divided Woman: Bree Daniels in *Klute,*" in *Women and the Cinema,* 25–26.

32. Quoted by Herman and Downing, *Jane Fonda,* 96.

33. Teresa de Lauretis, *Alice Doesn't: Feminism, Semiotics, Cinema* (Bloomington: Indiana University Press, 1984), 155.

34. Joan Mellen, *Women and Their Sexuality in the New Film* (New York: Horizon Press, 1973), 53–56.

35. "'I Prefer Films that Strengthen People': An Interview with Jane Fonda," *Cineaste* 6 (1975): 8.

36. "'I Prefer Films that Strengthen People'," 8.

37. Jack Kroll, "Hollywood's New Heroines," *Newsweek,* 10 October 1977, 82.

38. De Lauretis, *Alice Doesn't,* 155–56.

39. "'I Prefer Films that Strengthen People'," 3.

40. "'I Prefer Films that Strengthen People'," 4.

41. "'I Prefer Films that Strengthen People'," 5.

42. Farber and Green, *Hollywood Dynasties,* 162.

43. Jim Harwood, "St. Jane and the Hollywood Dragon," *Playboy,* July 1978, 170.

44. George Haddad Garcia, "My Side: Jane Fonda," *Working Woman,* September 1979, 96.

45. Kasindorf, "Jane Fonda," 28.

46. "Growing Fonda of Jane," *Time,* 3 October 1977, 90.

47. Kuhn, *Women's Pictures,* 61, 110.

48. Fremon, "Jane Fonda," 46.

49. Katz, "Jane Fonda," 43.

50. Farber and Green, *Hollywood Dynasties,* 160.

51. Kuhn, *Women's Pictures,* 135.

52. Andrea Walsh, *Women's Film and Female Experience* (New York: Praeger, 1984), 42.

53. Cited by E. Ann Kaplan, *Women & Film: Both Sides of the Camera* (New York: Methuen, 1983), 26.

54. Mary Ann Doane, "The 'Woman's Film': Possession and Address," in *Re-Vision: Essays in Feminist Film Criticism* (New York: The American Film Institute, 1984), 79.

55. Kuhn, *Women's Pictures,* 139–40.

56. Quoted by George Haddad Garcia, *The Films of Jane Fonda* (Secaucus, New Jersey: The Citadel Press, 1981), 67.

57. Molly Haskell, "Home from the Hell," *New York,* 27 February 1978, 69.

58. Lee Israel, "Women in Film: Saving an Endangered Species," *Ms.,* February 1975, 51–54.

59. Tania Modleski, "Time and Desire in the Woman's Film," *Cinema Journal* 23 (Spring 1984): 23.

60. Kuhn, *Women's Pictures,* 136–37.

61. Molly Haskell, "On Not Seeing the Trees for the Forest," *New York,* 10 October 1977, 61.

62. Pauline Kael, "A Woman for All Seasons?" *New Yorker,* 10 October 1977, 100–01.

63. Margaret Drabble, "Jane Fonda: Her Own Woman at Last?" *Ms.,* October 1977, 52.

64. George Haddad Garcia, "My Side," 96.

65. Kotkin, "Fonda," 58.

66. Many of these ideas grew from several very stimulating discussions with my friend and colleague, Dorothy Berkson.

67. Pauline Kael, "Gloria, the Girl Without Hope," in *Deeper into Movies* (Boston: Little, Brown and Company, 1973), 71.

11

Marguerite Duras's Cinematic Spaces

SUSAN H. LÉGER
Northern Illinois University

Marguerite Duras's achievement as a filmmaker has been marked by her refusal to become a professional of the cinema, with all that this implies in terms of prestige, influence, financial backing and even know-how. Although she has made some fifteen films, she has said that she knows very little about the technology of cinema and that she has no reason to want to learn any more: "I want to remain where I am, on the first grounds of cinema, in the primitive zones."[1] This wish, when one considers the highly complex technical apparatus of the cinema, is striking first for its apparent naïveté. We are reminded of little Ernesto, the hero of a story Duras has written for children, who after his first day at school returns home to announce to his mother that he does not want to go back because "at school they teach me things that I don't know."[2] Duras's refusal, like Ernesto's, underlines a certain fear, not so much of knowledge itself, but rather of what knowledge does, the ways in which it patterns our thinking processes, limits our creativity, and perhaps even more importantly here, determines the ways in which we *see*. Knowledge, in this case knowledge of the techniques of cinema, imposes boundaries on the filmmaker within which, or outside of which, she must work. Duras's refusal is, in effect, a refusal to be caught on either side of these rules, or standards, of filmmaking; inside, in the traditional narrative cinema, or outside, in an avant-garde that works against these rules, but which is just as determined by them as the films they oppose.

This same refusal makes Duras's own comments on her work particularly significant for us. Duras began making films, she has said, when she had finished writing books.[3] Although she has continued to publish texts (*Agatha, L'Homme assis dans le couloir, L'Homme atlantique, Savannah Bay,* and most recently, *La maladie de la mort*), none of these works has had the amplitude of her novels, published for the most part during the 1950s and 1960s, of which *L'Amour* (1971) was the last. Thus, for Duras, the making of films has, in a sense, replaced the writing of fiction. This shift from the novel to film was not made for any of the reasons we might term ordinary. Duras does not seem to have been interested in using the cinema, for example, to reach a larger audience or to turn her novels into films in the traditional sense.[4] Nor, of course, was she interested in learning anything about making movies. The reason she herself has given for this turn to cinema is typically understated and appealingly paradoxical. She began her "Notes on *India Song*" in a volume dedicated to her work in cinema in 1975 with the following statement:

> I make films to occupy my time. If I had the strength to do nothing, I would do nothing. It is because I do not have the strength to do nothing that I make films. For no other reason. That is the most truthful thing that I can say about my undertaking.[5]

A copy of this statement in Duras's handwriting appears as an epigraph to Michelle Porte's interviews with Duras, published two years later, underlining its importance not only obviously for Duras herself, but for those of us who attempt to deal with her cinema. We can but take her seriously and marvel at the calm insistence with which she apparently calls her work into question. In addition, it seems to me that if we are to understand Duras as an artist, as a woman who writes and makes films, as well as do justice to her work, we need to set about adjusting our critical focus so that the field of our response can somehow comprehend such a renunciation of artistic intent.

If we can equate in a general way filmmaking with writing, and if, as Edward Said suggests, "writing is the complex, orderly translation of innumerable forces into decipherable script,"[6] then it is with these "innumerable forces" that we must first concern ourselves in approaching Duras's films. It is undoubtedly somewhere in this pre-script region that can be located, for example, the cluster of forces that determine Duras's desire to do nothing, to remain silent. What will interest me here is not so much the content of the films themselves, as how these films came into existence, how they fit into her own work, and how they relate to the institution of cinema as a whole. Said suggests abandoning units of study like the novel or poem or, presumably, the film, and considering instead

> a set of contingent and worldly circumstances or conditions from which came the decision—selected from other courses of action—to write. The unit of study is determined by those circumstances that, for the writer in question, seem to have enabled, or generated, the *intention* to write.[7]

This change in focus, from the work itself to that which brings the work about, is in the present context a crucial one. It allows us to locate our analysis of Duras's films at the intersection between her own texts, including her comments on her cinema, and the institution of cinema itself. I have chosen as my units of study what I will call here Duras's cinematic spaces: cultural, filmic, and interior. All three are integral to an understanding of how Duras came to each film, as well as of the importance of her cinematic enterprise as a whole. My hope is that beginning to define these spaces will help us to see the commercial, technical, and literary aspects of her cinema in a new perspective, help us to discover new intersections between them. It is in this way that we can begin to determine the forms and effects of her cinematic writing, which in turn will perhaps provide insights into the possibility of a feminine cinematic writing.

The cinema seems to have an attraction for Duras that corresponds to a dissatisfaction with the written word, with the closure that the novel, and the language that constitutes it, impose on the text. Recently she wrote that she "can no longer . . . write a coherent story, work it out, take a subject as a pretext and develop it, in all its consequences, from the first to the last. That's over."[8] As this seems to have been over for more than a decade, storytelling, we can safely assume, is not a necessary requirement for the films that she makes.

Indeed, one could claim that Duras's cinematic aesthetic developed from this inability to tell stories in the traditional sense.

Duras is not, of course, the first writer, nor the first woman, to reject traditional narratives. Virginia Woolf, for example, some forty years earlier, had liberated herself from the constraints of the nineteenth-century novel and begun to search for new forms of expression. Woolf sensed that the cinematic image could be one of these forms. Writing in 1926, Woolf lamented the fact that filmmakers were not exploiting cinema's possibilities, and that they seemed content to reproduce everyday reality when they might do so much more. "Is there," asks Woolf, "some secret language which we feel and see, but never speak and, if so, could this be made visible to the eye? Is there any characteristic which thought possesses that can be rendered visible without the help of words?"[9]

This same question has been implicit in Duras's cinematographic project since its inception. That there might exist a nonspoken but visible language is without a doubt one of the hopes on which Duras has founded her cinema. Since Le ravissement de Lol. V. Stein, a novel published in 1964, Duras has been concerned with circumscribing the inexpressible, with uncovering the boundaries of a certain silence, a silence she has been defining during the course of her work.

In what has become the most famous passage in all of Duras's writing, Lol. V. Stein is searching for a way to relive a moment of abandonment. Had she succeeded in reaching the memory of this moment, "it would have been forever, for her head and body, their greatest pain and their greatest joy confused [confondus] even in their definition become unique but unnameable for lack of a word."[10] The impossibility of naming this confusion, this fusion of head and body, of pain and joy, constitutes Lol's desire and determines Lol's apparent placidity: "if Lol is silent in life it is because she believed, for a brief moment [l'espace d'un éclair], that this word might exist" (54). Lol is silent, not for lack of this word, but because she believed for an instant—the space of a lightning flash—that this word might exist. At the moment of believing, in the space of this belief, Lol finds her desire for silence. And it is in the space of this desire for silence that Duras's texts find their origin. The description of a moment of departure, of separation, provokes as well the images of L'Homme atlantique, Duras's most recent film. Having recognized the emptiness that follows this moment, the narrator has turned to the cinema: "I said to myself why not. Why not make a film. Writing would be too much from now on. Why not a film."[11]

Cultural Spaces

I don't know if I've found cinema. I've made
some movies. For the professionals, my cinema
does not exist.
                              —Marguerite Duras

One is tempted to counter Duras's "why not a film" with "why a
film?" If writing is henceforth to be "too much," why and in what ways
does cinema somehow escape that excessiveness? In what ways does
language itself participate in the excessiveness of writing?

Duras is among those women writers in France who have questioned or rejected "a language produced by a social order in whose
history they have played no part."[12] For Duras, a woman who writes,
who uses language, runs a certain risk, that of plagiarism. Duras sees
the relationship between women and language as problematic, and
believes that sexual difference cuts across writing: men "begin from a
theoretical platform that is already in place, already elaborated, the
writing of women is really translated from the unknown, like a new
way of communicating rather than an already formed language."[13]
Duras has also expressed this difference as one of location: "we don't
write at all in the same place as men. And when women don't write in
the place of desire [dans le lieu du désir], they don't write, they
plagiarize."[14] Women's writing, then, for Duras, is associated with a
language not yet formed, not molded; it is a new "way of communicating" that originates in "the place of desire," rather than from a "theoretical platform." Although Duras has never developed extensively
this notion of sexual difference in relation to language, she has expressed in many ways, as we shall see, her conviction of the existence
of this difference and its importance for her work. Language, to the
extent that it is not woman's, is undoubtedly at least partially responsible for what Duras calls the excessiveness of writing. Lol. V. Stein is
silent, having believed that her word, this definition of herself, might
have existed. Commentaries on this text have not insisted enough on
the implications of this word that is lacking. It is not simply a word that
is missing from the lexicon—poets tell us there are many of these—nor
is it a word that might somehow be invented. It is, instead, a word that
would *destroy* the meaning of all other words, a word "in which all
other words would have been buried."[15] Making room for it in the
dictionary would invalidate the rest of the language, necessitate the
rewriting of the definitions of all other words. Lol's strength, Lol's
silence, comes, in fact, from the force of her belief in the possible

existence of this word. If Duras herself does not have the strength to do nothing, to remain silent, she has attempted to come as close as possible to this silence in her cinema. We might suspect that it is for this reason that Duras "would like to go back to the beginning of cinema, use a very primitive grammar . . . very simply, almost primary: not to move, begin everything again."[16]

Is this possible? Does cinema somehow permit a new way of communicating, a possibly feminine one, that language only hampers? If written texts are grounded in a language that has always enjoyed a certain relationship to patriarchy and power, responsible for that "theoretical platform" Duras speaks of, cinema and its images have nevertheless not escaped entirely such determinations. On the contrary, cinema is in many ways just as inextricably tied to the cultural order, in perhaps even more obvious ways.

The first and probably most important of these links is an economic one—the making of a film requires considerable financial resources, a fact that has kept women from making any significant impact on the history and development of cinema. Laura Mulvey has pointed out that although some women did direct very early films, "the coming of the studio system, and, even more so, the economic reorganization with the introduction of sound which involved large-scale investment from banks and electronics industry," effectively marginalized women in the film industry.[17] Duras sees herself in opposition to those she calls the "quantitative filmmakers," those whose films are little more than a pretext for a colossal financial exchange and who consider the final judgment made on a movie to be equivalent to the number of spectators who pay to see it.[18]

These are, of course, the "professionals" of cinema, the professionals for whom Duras's cinema does not exist. For them, says Duras, "we are the malefactors who take 'their' money."[19] Those who make marginal cinema are, in a way, stealing from those who make mainstream cinema, and it is certain that what is being stolen is more than cash. Cinema, insofar as it is a discourse on the world, has become as well a point of view on the world, a point of view whose "codes . . . have been constructed by men (inventors, engineers, etc.)"[20] and thus cinema has been informed throughout its history by a certain ideology. In addition, cinema's "viewpoint" is a direct result of its adoption of a Renaissance pictorial perspective, and, as Stephen Heath has pointed out, "in this history it is men who are professionals of painting, the authoritative gaze."[21] Cinema is a certain way of seeing that is intricately bound up in the techniques that make this sight possible and the financial resources that allow its production. The exclusion of women from those powerful forces has necessarily contributed both to cinema's development and, more importantly, to the ways we think about cinema. As Laura Mulvey has demonstrated, the success of the cinematic image depends on the masculine point of view, what she calls the "determining male gaze."[22] That a woman does not necessarily "see" in the same way as a man and that she will thus produce, in spite of cinema's masculine bias, a cinema that is in some way different seems at once a necessary corollary of this truth and an unthinkable prospect. Thus the angry man on French television who declared that "giving money to Duras to make *Le Camion* will result in making spectators disgusted with the cinema for six months."[23] Such an opinion, based on criteria presumably aesthetic, follows a seemingly logical progression from financial considerations to Duras to a remarkably general disgust with the cinema, one movie affecting the way all other films are seen. If it is possible for one film by one filmmaker to affect so completely the perception we have of cinema as a whole, it is because spectators have become accustomed to having cinema express and coincide with their own positions in the world. Writing may indeed be a perilous undertaking for a woman, but it is equally true that "the cinema is all the more thoroughly and completely determined [by the ideology which produces it] because unlike other arts . . . its very manufacture mobilizes powerful economic forces in a way that the production of literature . . . does not."[24]

It would be fanciful to suggest that Duras's cinema, or any woman's films, can somehow, or simply, escape these cultural determinations. What we shall begin to examine here is how Duras's cinema operates in relation to these rules and the effects that they have had on her work. Duras's cinema shares with all marginal cinema the problem of having to work with very limited financial resources. She has never deplored this lack of funds; on the contrary, it has at least in part influenced and underlined the development of her cinematic aesthetic, being in many ways compatible with her desire to use a "primitive grammar" in making her films. A fourth of her total production is regularly constituted by films made partially or completely from her other films. *Son Nom de Venise* is made up of the sound track from *India Song* set against new images; *Césarée* and *Les Mains négatives* were made from the images trimmed from *Navire Night;* and *L'Homme atlantique* was put together from the outtakes of *Agatha*.

Le Camion became the film that it is—the story of a possible film or, more accurately, the possible story of a possible film—for material reasons. There was first of all the difficulty of filming inside the cabin of a truck in cold January weather. In addition, the two actresses

(Simone Signoret and Suzanne Flon) that Duras had considered to play the role of the woman in the film were both unavailable.[25] It is these two conditions, at least the first easily resolvable given enough financial resources, that were finally responsible for the film that *Le Camion* finally became. When Duras decided not to *make* the film but to *tell* it, she felt, she says, "liberated."[26] It was as if she had made a discovery. Indeed, it seems possible, paradoxically, to say that Duras's lack of financial resources has helped her to "find" the cinema, to find the possibilities of the cinema that Woolf foresaw for it in 1926. For Woolf, a shadow looming in the corner of the screen or a gardener seen through an open window pushing a lawn mower back and forth across the lawn were more important than the prominent figures on the screen. They were indications of cinema's possibly secret language. It is not the story itself that counts for Woolf, but the movement of the traces of the world outside inscribed in the workings of the cinema. When Duras liberated herself, or was obliged to liberate herself, from the filming of the fiction that we finally only glimpse in *Le Camion*, she was free to use the screen as an empty terrain on which to inscribe movement, on which to write. The large blue truck, as it traverses the barren landscape of the screen, caught in a fiction that escapes narration, acts both as a vehicle for and resists the scenario that Gérard Depardieu and Marguerite Duras are reading, sitting around a table in a darkened room. *Le Camion* is not, as Pauline Kael would have it, "a spiritual autobiography, a life's-journey, end-of-the-road movie."[27] It is not a film about Duras herself, about her life, at least not in the usual sense. *Le Camion* is about, if it is "about" anything, the disjunction between sound and image, the impossibility of narration, the gulf between fact and fiction. It is a film, in short, about the impossibility of making a film.

Laura Mulvey has seen one of the possibilities of filmmaking for women, one of its pleasures, in the "foregrounding of the process itself."[28] Avant-garde filmmakers in general have, of course, worked at making us aware that we are watching a film. A Godard or a Brakhage, for example, works at subverting traditional cinematic practices in various ways, seeking to disconcert, aggress, or jeer at the spectator, attempting to establish a position from which to speak that can rival established traditions. Duras, rather than attempting to disrupt or destroy the power of the image, explores the origins of this power, and works to reveal or dislocate these origins. If other avant-garde filmmakers have used, or played with, cultural references and political ideas, and have stood on that "theoretical platform" to better perform their acrobatics, Duras's cinema has made "tabula rasa of all cultural reference, all systems of thought, all religious subsistence."[29] And she works at it "with an imprudence of which only woman is undoubtedly capable of giving extreme examples," and with an energy "from which . . . could come an unprecedented and specifically feminine form of poetic imagination, the passion to know and the work of thought."[30]

Duras's refusal to learn more about the cinema is a refusal to be caught in the web of culture, a refusal to participate, thus a refusal to accept. When Duras tells us that if she had the strength to do nothing, she would do nothing, she is suggesting that silence and inactivity require more strength than does collaboration with the system: "inertia, refusals, passive refusal, the refusal to answer, in short, is a colossal strength, it is the strength of the child, for example, it is the strength of the woman."[31]

Filmic Spaces

> . . . I know that when I make a film, I write,
> it is writing. *India Song* is writing, it is
> displaced writing, displaced from my sheet of
> paper to the screen, but it is writing.
> —Marguerite Duras

Duras includes in the notion of writing both the composing of a text and the making of a film, suggesting that the two processes involve the same faculties, demand the same concentration of the artist. Nevertheless, as it is displaced from the sheet of paper to the cinema screen, writing loses the specificity proper to the printed page and is reinscribed in a cultural space that has its own history and its own codes. When the novel *Le Vice-consul* becomes the film *India Song*, there seems more than a change in location of the writing: the images of the film signify, find their meaning, according to a radically different set of criteria.

If from the beginning, cinema's "magic" has been able to fool us into taking for real what we see on the screen, it is largely because the screen itself becomes invisible, seems to be contiguous with the space around it. Offscreen space, in classical cinema, is either dismissed as inconsequential (to the story being told) or else reincorporated into the fiction of the film through various technical conventions. There is a "constant movement of reappropriation" of that which is not on the screen, a continuous drawing into the filmic space of that which is outside it.[32] Duras's screen, however, refuses such mastery of offscreen space. Her filmic space not only acknowledges an unapproachable and nonappropriable outside, but is constructed so that this space weighs on the film, shapes it, determines in fact what we see and how we understand it.

When Duras decided that no actress would play the woman in *Le Camion,* she understood that it was in this way that the entire film could in fact be constructed around her. Although the woman is never seen, she is described by Duras, or rather by the narrator whom Duras plays. The woman of *Le Camion* is "small. Thin. Gray. Banal. She possesses the nobility of banality. She is invisible." She is one of Duras's "lost" women, women who can no longer be contained within the confines of the world as we know it, a woman who escapes definition. The woman of *Le Camion* is invisible in the sense that she looks just like everyone else, she is Everywoman, that part of Everywoman who wanders, tells stories, finds it impossible to "order [her] ideas, follow one idea without noticing another on its way." It is because of this invisibleness that she does not, cannot, become the object of the camera, the subject of a fiction. Although it may at the outset have been motivated by material conditions, it is precisely the invisibility of this woman that links *Le Camion* to Duras's other films, notably her masterpiece, *India Song.* The beggarwoman in this earlier film plays a similar, nonvisible yet central role. We never see her, and though we hear her voice, cannot understand her. Yet it is this woman that determines the ultimate meaning of the film and influences, indeed permits, our description of the woman we do see on the screen.

In the novel, *Le Vice-consul,* the beggarwoman's story is being imagined, written by a character in the novel, Peter Morgan, one of the personnel at the French Embassy in Calcutta. She is the subject of the fiction he is writing. We know her story, learn her history, only through his eyes. When *Le Vice-consul* becomes *India Song,* the beggarwoman slips out of the fictional gridwork. Like *Le Camion,* "which would have been much more false if it had been acted inside the truck," *India Song* would have participated in a fundamental error if it had simply reproduced *Le Vice-consul,* if there had been an actress playing the beggarwoman. The beggarwoman is that part of India that cannot be narrated, that cannot be fictionalized. Duras has made it clear that there is an essential difference between the novel and the film: "The characters evoked in this story have been dislodged from the book entitled *Le Vice-consul* and projected into new narrative regions."[33] It is no accident that the limits of these narrative regions coincide with the limits of the screen, with that which can be seen. And in *India Song,* what we see on the screen is important first of all for what it is not: "All of the action of the film takes place 'off-screen.'"[34]

India Song, Sun Child Productions and Les Filmes Armorial
Courtesy of Museum of Modern Art/Film Stills Archive

The soundtrack of *India Song* begins with the voice of the beggar-woman, who is speaking and singing in an oriental language, thus incomprehensible to a western audience. The language is, in fact, Lao. The beggarwoman comes, as the Voices of the film will tell us, from Savannakhet, Laos. Like Anne-Marie Stretter, the woman that we do see in the film, the beggarwoman is a foreigner in Calcutta, where the events described in the film once took place. The beggarwoman is invisible, part of the unimaginable and indescribable suffering that Calcutta represents. Since she cannot be seen, we tend, as well, to discount her words. Marie-Claire Ropars-Wuilleumier has suggested, for example, that

> the musicality of the chanting becomes opaque in the presence of signs which require deciphering, while the signs themselves, their linguistic

code blocked out for the Occidental audience, lose their meaning value, becoming mere sounds, just like the music or the background noises.[35]

While the singing of the beggarwoman may indeed be in a certain sense equivalent to the music and background noises, there are nevertheless important differences. Her voice is, unmistakably, a human one, and a female one. Moreover, her calling and shouting indicate that she has lost her oriental composure, that she is, in fact, mad.[36] She speaks of the heat of Savannakhet and her desire to die and sings two songs, both about flowers. The first describes the lotus, the flower that, though it grows in the mud, is very beautiful, and surrounded by insects in the same way that a beautiful woman is surrounded by men. In a variation of a traditional Lao song, the beggarwoman then sings of the frangipani, this beautiful flower whose scent reminds her of what is in her heart. It is through the flower that she understands how the events of her life have come about. The frangipani is associated, in Southeast Asia, with both beauty and death. Duras thus inscribes, in the very beginning of her film, in Lao, the themes and images that will be central to the film: madness and death; the beautiful Anne-Marie Stretter surrounded by her lovers; and a certain knowledge that only Anne-Marie Stretter and the beggarwoman possess.

The other music of *India Song* is in sharp contrast to the singing of the beggarwoman. It is all instrumental and most of it is what we would call light, dance music: the Island Rumba, Tango Tango, Frangie (waltz), and the Charleston, for example, help us to identify the characters and space on the screen as belonging to a specific culture and moment of history. The music marks the screen space as western; the chanting of the beggarwoman marks the offscreen space as nonwestern, invisible, incomprehensible. The meaning of the film is established at the edge of this space, the text of the film identifying in fact the meeting point of two worlds. In speaking of *Le Vice-consul,* Duras commented that "the impenetrability of of the world of the India of the whites and that other world is denounced at every instant in the book."[37] Even more effectively than the novel, the film *India Song* demarks this space that separates the two worlds, a space that is made visible at every instant, in every image.

The four narrative voices, which are always off, seem to provoke the images of the film while at the same time becoming involved in their own fiction. Rather than explicating the film, however, they move closer and closer to the beggarwoman's nonsensical (for us) singing. They are never able to capture the story of Anne-Marie Stretter, it is constantly slipping away from them, continually being lost, refusing their attempts at history-making. The film operates on the edge of history, on the edge of the textual creation that becomes history. Duras refuses the fiction that is history, returns us to its origins to show it as an image-making, textual-producing process. The narration is a fiction, and the fiction itself "narrates" in a sense the Voices. Duras's use of offscreen voices does not cancel the difference between on/off; on the contrary,

> far from abolishing the distinction between *on* and *off,* the film activates it, preventing the attribution of stable functions to either: the *off* position of all voices—fictional or narrative—causes a contamination of the fiction and of the narration, giving the tension between *off* and *on* all its corrosive force, which prevents the definition of the interiority of the fiction and the exteriority of the narration in specific terms.[38]

Ropars-Wuilleumier's description of the soundtrack is equally true for the image track. By activating the distinction between what we see and what we do not see (traditional cinema ignores this distinction or effaces it), by making the impenetrability of the India of the Europeans and the India of the Indians visible, Duras in fact prevents a stable definition of either.

The two women of the film—Anne-Marie Stretter and the beggarwoman—are affected by the instability of the fictional territory. As the film progresses, it becomes more and more difficult for the Voices to distinguish one woman from the other, to tell the story of one without also telling the story of the other. When Voice two asks "Is she sleeping?" Voice one responds "Which one?"[39] Both Anne-Marie Stretter and the beggarwoman have made the same trip through Asia. The beggarwoman was born in Savannakhet, Laos, and for Anne-Marie Stretter, Savannakhet was the place of "her first marriage, the first post. . . ." They are both foreigners in Calcutta, and they both have been searching for a means of losing their way. By the end of the film, Anne-Marie Stretter, the beautiful, desirable, European woman, and the oriental, bald, and famished beggarwoman have become one. The effects of history on them are the same; their final descents into madness and death are parallel journeys.

Anne-Marie Stretter and the beggarwoman are both victims, of their particular stories, of the particular situation of the India of the 1930s. By showing them to be identical, by setting up the tension between onscreen and offscreen space, however, Duras refuses to make them victims of the camera as well. Their experience is never aestheticized or reappropriated by the camera. When Duras speaks of the "failure" of *India Song,* it is this failure, the failure of her film to recapture the story of Anne-Marie Stretter, the failure of her film-text to comprehend, explain, or encompass the separation of these two worlds.[40]

The significance of this "failure" cannot be appreciated without looking for a moment at the history of cinema. In an excellent essay, William Wees has analyzed the ways in which the development of pictorial perspective in the Quattrocento determined the relationship between how we see and how the camera operates.[41] Leonardo da Vinci was the first to see a parallel between the workings of the *camera obscura* and the functioning of the eye and the implications of this parallel for painting. The image on the wall, or screen, opposite the hole in the *camera obscura,* by being seemingly identical to the image formed by the eye, was thought to be the perfect example for the painter. It served as a model for reproducing three-dimensional space on a two-dimensional plane. Later, cameras, projectors, and their lenses were "made to embody the same rules of optics and geometry that are assumed to produce perspective in seeing as well as picture making."[42] Wees underlines the limitations of this point of view, in which the eye of the observer is not only an absolutely fixed point, but also assumed to be perceiving Truth:

> Producing a picture by these means was like catching images in a rigid net strung between the eye of the observer and the objects observed. No matter how complex or ambiguous those objects might be—in form, spatial relationships, emotional content—they were caught in the same geometrical net, and seen depicted within the same rigid framework. Anything unmeasurable, idiosyncratic or subjective was ruled out by this mechanical system of grids and immobilized points of view.[43]

It is important that we begin to see the development of this single point of view (which will become the ideal eye of the camera) as more than a technical innovation. Determining a space that we can suppose conformed to certain obligations and desires of Renaissance man, this point of view has an interesting parallel in the literature of the period. Joan Kelly, in her analysis of women in the Renaissance, has shown that it was during this period that a literature of self-reflection dominated exclusively by a male point of view developed.[44] In Dante's *Vita Nuova,* for example, "it is the inner life, *his* inner life, that Dante objectifies."[45] Woman, as physical presence and influential personality, essentially disappears in the literature of the Renaissance, Kelly argues, underlining the fact that real women were losing power and control over their own lives. Kelly sees this change as having come about as a result of the political and economic changes that brought into being the noble's new role as courtier. Castiglione's courtier, for example, was seeking a way of life that would replace lost economic and political power. Needing to regain at least a sense of his own worth, the courtier made an effort to remain detached: "in love, as in service, the courtier preserves independence by avoiding desire for real love, real power. He does not touch or allow himself to be touched by either."[46] Woman, rather than partner, became mediator. She inspired the lover, the poet, the painter, but she did not participate in shaping the society in which she lived. Kelly's conclusion tells us a great deal about the aspirations of Renaissance man:

> All the advances of Renaissance Italy, its proto-capitalist economy, its states, and its humanistic culture, worked to mold the noblewoman into an aesthetic object: decorous, chaste, and doubly dependent—on her husband as well as the prince.[47]

What seems certain is that woman's role, and man's image of her role, narrowed, and the narrower understanding of the feminine became institutionalized and accepted as the norm. It is not irrelevant in this context to return to Wees's critique of the cinematic image. Adopting the rules of Renaissance perspective, the cinematic machinery produces an image we consider "normal," in much the same way that Renaissance culture produced the image of the "woman" and normalized it. Wees's conclusion regarding the cinematic image as it developed from the Renaissance perspective could be applied, with remarkable accuracy, to the image of woman:

> . . . the "norms" for that image are relevant only to a very small part of what we actually see: approximately 2 degrees of the 200 degree angle which constitutes our total visual field. . . . Perspectivist norms deny the cinematic image much of what the eye actually sees. This has produced the odd situation in which a visually deprived image has been generally accepted as an accurate visualization of sight; for the measure of its accuracy is not what we actually see, but what the perspectivist tradition has produced as *pictures* of what we see. The situation has become so thoroughly institutionalized, however, that is oddness is seldom recognized and its effects rarely challenged.[48]

This way of seeing is a way of appropriating and controlling, and within this framework, woman is always seen, never the beholder, always the object, never the subject. In addition, this way of seeing, of capturing in a grid, of defining hierarchically, is essentially a masculine one. Stan Brakhage, for example, has described it as "that form of seeing we could call 'westward-hoing man,' which is to try to clutch a landscape or the heavens or whatever. That is a form of sight which is aggressive and which seeks to make any landscape a piece of real-estate."[49] At the same time, woman becomes an aesthetic object. Renaissance man was redefining himself while objectifying and aesthetisizing his world, including woman.

Avant-garde filmmakers have reacted in various ways to this aggressive, and finally false, way of seeing the world. No one but Duras, however, has been so intent on revealing the equivalence between representation and life, nonrepresentation and death. In her most recent film, *L'Homme atlantique,* she both plays with this equivalence and plays it out, stretches it to its most logical and devastating conclusions. The narrator discovers an absence: "You have left the camera field. You are absent. . . . *You are precisely no longer anywhere*" (my emphasis). Later she tells this man she loves, "do not try to understand this photographic phenomenon, life."

The "failure" of *India Song* is the failure to reappropriate the experience of India, the refusal to allow the cinema to function as it was meant to, to perform its unending normalization of all that it "sees." Duras has understood in some way that a woman who "writes" with a camera must question the image, dislocate its origins, radically alter the subject/object dichotomy. If woman has, at least since the Renaissance, been the "other scene" that has made possible "the seen," then the making of a woman's film, if it is to be feminine or feminist, must redefine sexual difference, radically altering the conditions of possibility for representation. In revealing, in *India Song,* woman as screen—the ultimate object and the final fiction—Duras begins as well a reevaluation of the filmic space. Her cinematic writing, like Lol. V. Stein's missing word, begins to destroy all the other "words" of the cinema.

Interior Spaces

A woman inhabits a place completely, the presence of a woman fills a place. A man passes through it, he doesn't really live there.

—Marguerite Duras

Interior spaces have been privileged in Duras's work at least since *Le ravissement de Lol. V. Stein.* Lol projects her loss of memory onto her living space. In arranging the furniture in her house, in demanding perfect order around her, Lol succeeds in emptying this space. When she speaks about her life since her marriage, "she in fact is telling the story of the emptying [dépeuplement] of a house with her arrival." This empty space becomes, paradoxically, even more important when Lol herself is not there. In this perfectly still and silent space is inscribed Lol's failure to find the word with which she could describe herself. If language excludes Lol, then the house reveals this exclusion: "Did not the house, in the afternoon, in her absence, become the empty stage on which was being played the soliloquy of an absolute passion whose meaning escaped?" Lol's house becomes the mark of an-other story, the one that cannot be narrated. The narrative we do read is told in a masculine voice, a voice that imposes and controls, reinscribing the abandonment in a space that determines its ultimate meaning for Lol herself and the novel.

On the screen, the interior spaces need no longer be subordinate to a narrating voice. In Duras's films, images of interior spaces essentially replace the narrative, take the place of, take the space of, the story. Very literally, in *Le Camion,* the room in which Depardieu and Duras are reading *is* the narrative space, the point of origin of the (possible) fiction. Pauline Kael objects to the fact that Duras, after luring us into the fiction with images of the blue truck moving through the desolate landscape, suddenly "yanks us back to the room . . . it's an emotional wrench, a classic rude awakening, to be sent back to Square One, the room."[50] While this continual returning to the room undoubtedly interrupts the film's fiction, it is nevertheless the single factor responsible for the continuity of the film. Not only is the room equivalent to the cabin of the truck, it is as well rigorously identical to the space of the screen on which the film is being projected. The reading is being done in a darkened room, closed to the outside and to the light of day. The room, like the screen and the cinema itself, is a space of enclosure. And this enclosure, common to all of Duras's films, constitutes perhaps the most significant and revealing aspect of her work, for it is through these interior spaces that Duras reaches "through" the cinema to what we have called its cultural and filmic dimensions and pulls them into new interpretive realms.

While Kael sees this repeated return to the room as disruptive and disturbing, the truth is that, when we look at Duras's cinema as a whole, the images of her enclosed spaces are for the most part soothing for the spectator. Jean-Pierre Oudart, for example, sees the images in *Son Nom de Venise dans Calcutta désert* as "a restful bed for the eye."[51] In this film, Duras moves her camera through a deserted mansion, caressing its rooms, its walls, its empty spaces. Like Lol

Le Camion, Cinema 9
Courtesy of Museum of Modern Art/Film Stills Archive

searching for her word, this word "which waits for you around the corner of language," the camera seems to be looking, slowly but nevertheless insistently, for something that it believes is there, somewhere. Oudart suggests that the rooms of this house and the surroundings constitute a sort of writing:

> The large building, the crumbling salons, the park, the statues: everything is matter for memory. A memory which would be enclosed in these scraps of fossilized writing: the architecture, the design on the wainscoting, the traces of time on the walls, the rows of trees, the stones.[52]

The camera thus records in its movement nothing but these fragments of an embedded writing, capturers of memory. The pieces, however, never come together, the story is never found, so that these fragments are in fact signs whose referents have been lost, whose meanings have been forever forgotten. The rooms become a text, but a text that, rather than telling a story, seems to prevent a story from being told. The Voices on the soundtrack, the same as those of *India Song,* are unable to recover the story of Anne-Marie Stretter. The bits and pieces of the story of this woman that were uncovered in *India Song* have vanished. We often find in Duras's work a movement, not toward clarifying and comprehending, but rather toward confusion (of Anne-Marie Stretter and the beggarwoman, for example) and toward knowing less and less. In searching, in fact, we manage only to move gradually toward ignorance. The narrator of *Le ravissement de Lol. V. Stein,* in trying to reconstruct Lol's life, finds he is moving further and further away from knowledge of her: "This was my first discovery about her: to know nothing about Lol was to know her already. One could, it seemed to me, know less and less about Lol. V. Stein" (94). In following Lol's footsteps through the text, through the language of the text, we move closer and closer only to the missing word, and Lol seems to disappear completely in the darkness of its absence.

All of Duras's interiors will be versions of Lol's house: a theater in which the drama being played refuses definition and marks its space as other than that of the fiction in progress. The loss connected to the interior space—the loss of memory, of a story, of the image—functions in a certain sense as an interior "story," a story that cannot be told, but whose space is marked out, delineated by the surface fiction. Luce Irigaray has made it clear in her work that what woman says and what she desires to say can never coincide. To roughly translate Irigaray: "If everything that woman says is in some way language, language cannot signify for all that everything that she says. The fact that what she says finds in language the conditions for the possibility of the meaning [of what she says] is another matter."[53] The meaning, then, of her story, inasmuch as it will be able to be read within the parameters of masculine signifying systems, has little or nothing to do with what woman desires to say. "Her text" will be, to a certain extent, like the "other side" of the language she is using, will find its "non-sense" in a region whose borders will be drawn by the fiction.

If, in *India Song* and *Son Nom de Venise,* the Voices seem to lose the image, if they have, at best, a tenuous control over the story they are trying to tell, it is because they are being pulled in other directions and responding to other desires. Unraveling the very story they are trying to tell, the Voices lead us further and further away from the story of Anne-Marie Stretter.

I am not suggesting here that the woman's text will contain a story that is somehow hidden from view, which might be found somewhere, by someone who possesses the necessary keys to her text. On the contrary, a woman's text, rather than concealing her story, never ceases revealing, along the paths of every sentence, what she cannot say, what it is not possible for her to put into language.

In *L'Homme atlantique,* Duras went even further than wandering voices and fading images. As Duras was putting this film together from the leftovers of *Agatha,* she found she did not have enough footage to make a complete film. Rather than do more filming, Duras filled the spaces in the film with sequences of nothing—with blackness—thus discovering, she says, "the full use of the text that I had written for this film."[54] She wrote in fact more and more text to set against this absence of images, until there were a full ten minutes of blackness—ten minutes during which she refuses to let the camera see. The making of *L'Homme atlantique* led Duras to the discovery of the importance of this blackness for her cinema as a whole: "I believe that blackness [le noir] is in all my films, buried, under the image. Through all of my films, I have only tried to reach the deep current of the film, once the permanence of the image is cleared away."[55]

This blackness under the image, a filmic equivalent of Lol's missing word, this "other side" of woman's language, is the aspect of Duras's films that deserves most of our attention here. It is through Duras's interior spaces, the location of sexual difference, that we have access to this blackness under the image. Through the fossilized writing inscribed in the images of *Son Nom de Venise,* for example, we find the outline of the "non-story" of Duras's film. It is by embedding this region of blackness in her film that Duras refuses the power of the image, the normalization of the camera's sight, which has taken its authority from the radical differentiation of the sexes. If we agree with Fredric Jameson that "sexism and the patriarchal are to be grasped as the sedimentation and the virulent survival of forms of alienation specific to the oldest mode of production of human history, with its division of labor between men and women,"[56] then we can begin to see Duras's fossilized writing as the inscription, the making visible, of the masculine parameters of the image.

It is in this context that we will look further at Duras's interiors, for they are the places of inscription of this writing that, in making itself visible, marks as well the place of woman in the film.

There is always, in Duras's films, a strong association between woman and this interior space. In *India Song,* as we have seen, there is a single space, the embassy, and two women (Anne-Marie Stretter and the beggarwoman) who come together in it and merge into one. In

Baxter, Vera Baxter, there is one woman and two disparate spaces that merge in her. There is, first, the luxurious villa that Vera Baxter has come to consider as a place for her family's summer vacation; and second, the ruins of what was once perhaps a chateau, fragments of walls whose roof disappeared long ago, leaving rooms open to the sky. It is here that lived perhaps the "first" Vera Baxter, who lived here near the Atlantic, as the film will suggest, in medieval times. The film thus is made up of images of rooms in which no one lives any more, juxtaposed to images of rooms in which no one lives yet. We first see Vera in the villa, and the film ends as she is leaving it. The time of the film and its space thus coincide almost exactly with Vera's presence in the villa.

The villa in *Baxter, Vera Baxter,* like the interiors of all of Duras's films, participates in two different stories. In the film's fiction, the villa is part of the deception planned by Jean Baxter, Vera's husband. He has already paid a million francs for the rental of the villa, a sum that matches the sum paid to Michel Cayre for the seduction of Vera. Although *Baxter, Vera Baxter* is in some ways very different from Duras's other films—and it is the only one about which she has expressed serious reservations—the "second story" of the film corresponds in many ways to the stories told by the interior spaces of her other films. Like Lol's house, which describes her exclusion in the fiction and inscribes this exclusion in the novel, the villa both surrounds and excludes Vera. Like the embassy in *India Song,* the villa in *Baxter, Vera Baxter* is a sort of tomb; a monument, in *India Song,* to the dead Anne-Marie Stretter; an execution chamber, in *Baxter, Vera Baxter,* for Vera Baxter: "It is in this place, funereal, that Vera Baxter has shut herself up," Duras tells us.[57] Speaking to her husband on the telephone, Vera Baxter looks around her, at the villa, and tells him: "I shut myself up here in order to kill myself, I think" (61). The furniture in the villa is covered by sheets, signaling its state of abandon, recalling shrouds and foreboding death. Like the fragments of writing in *Son Nom de Venise,* the interior of the villa contains the story that will never be told, which escapes the fiction of the film.

In perhaps the most comprehensive study ever done of spaces, Gaston Bachelard sees the house as a privileged space for the daydreamer and the poet, for it has "one of the greatest powers of integration for the thoughts, memories and dreams of mankind."[58] The connotations of interior spaces are many and include, in the examples given by Bachelard, intimacy, warmth, privacy, solitude, protection, secrecy, familiarity. For Bachelard, houses are decidedly maternal—he returns again and again to maternal metaphors to explain the attraction and powers of the enclosed space for the poet. Like the Renaissance poet and painter, Bachelard aestheticized the woman-house so that he can understand and explain why the poet "creates." While the qualities that Bachelard attributes to the house are not absent from Duras's spaces, Duras radically changes the way in which we experience these interior spaces. If in some cases we feel enclosed and even protected by her spaces, she manages as well to inject into them an element of the unknown and the beginning of a certain refusal.

Duras's enclosures seem, for example, paradoxically limitless. In *Baxter, Vera Baxter,* we first visit the villa with Vera and Monique Combès: "the rooms arrive one after the other. . . ."; then again later in the film, with the unnamed woman played by Delphine Seyrig, and this time we see "different rooms than those seen by Monique Combès, as if the house were interminable, without end." We suspect that new visitors to the villa would produce still more rooms as they draw different versions of the "truth" from Vera. From the outside, the villa seems "a dark fortress" and its shutters remain closed. All of Duras's dwellings—the Palais Rothschild in *India Song,* the hotel in *La Femme du Gange,* even Duras's own house in *Nathalie Granger*—give us the impression of being single, solid, impenetrable masses of stone from the outside and an interminable series of rooms on the inside, as if the house refused to be contained in its exterior limits.

Duras sees woman's experience, woman's "story," as being inextricably linked to the house, and she has gone so far as to say that "the house belongs to her in the same way that tools belong to the worker."[59] It is, after all, in the house, as Virginia Woolf reminds us in *A Room of One's Own,* that woman has been for "these millions of years."[60] For Duras, the space of the house is taken up by the woman, she lives in the house so completely that she finally becomes the house. When Isabelle Granger, in *Nathalie Granger,* "walks through the house, it is as if she were walking around herself, as if she were moving around her own body."[61]

This equivalence between the house and the woman is nowhere more brilliantly drawn than in *Nathalie Granger.* Filmed in 1972 in Duras's own home in a village in the Yvelines, *Nathalie Granger* is the story of a refusal, a refusal in which the house participates, for which the house is in a very real sense responsible. Nathalie Granger is a little girl who will no longer be allowed to attend the village school. She is, the school principal tells us, "violent." Although we learn first of Nathalie through the words of this figure of authority, we never see Nathalie as an uncontrollable child in the film. In fact, the only thing we know about Nathalie, Duras tells us, is the kiss she gives to her cat when no one is looking.[62] *Nathalie Granger* is a film about making a space for, making room for, the "violence" of a little girl. It is her mother, Isabelle, who, during the course of the film and the space of the house, comes to an understanding of the love she has for her child, of the violence of the love she has for her child, thus finding the strength to refuse to participate in the efforts to "control" Nathalie.

The most remarkable aspect of *Nathalie Granger* is the fact that Duras succeeds in showing us a child through the eyes of her mother. She succeeds, that is, in "depatriarchalizing" the relationship between mother and daughter, taking it out of the bounds of masculine values and patriarchal law. Irigaray has suggested that "the mother/daughter, daughter/mother relationship constitutes an extremely explosive kernel in our societies. To think about it, change it, is equivalent to shaking up the patriarchal order."[63] In this sense, *Nathalie Granger* is the most political and most feminist film that Duras has made.

Isabelle Granger cannot approach her child; instead, she walks through the house with the "deambulation of a prisoner. She . . . looks at this house, this cavern, hers" (27), and comes to her decision, the enormity of which we only fully understand at the end of the film when the house itself becomes frightening.

The house not only belongs to the woman for historical reasons. There is also

> . . . the fact that the woman is, in herself, a dwelling, the dwelling place of the child, that she has that feeling of protection, by her body, of this enclosing of the child by her own body, that fact is probably not foreign to the way in which she herself is inserted in the habitat, in her dwelling.[64]

Duras has asked elsewhere: "Why discourage women from the colossal swallowing up which is the essence of all motherhood, the mad love (for it is there, the love of a mother for her child), and the madness that maternity represents?"[65] Isabelle Granger is, in the space of the film *Nathalie Granger,* being swallowed up in the madness of motherhood as well as in the interior of her house, her dwelling. And it is through this interior, which helps Isabelle reject the "image" of Nathalie that has been given to her from the outside, that we move into a new cultural and filmic space. It is significant to recall here than Jean Bethke Elshtain, in a recent article in *Signs,* concludes her reflections on women and language with the assertion that one of the keys to a truly feminist thinking is a revalorization of the woman as mother:

> For women to affirm the protection of fragile and vulnerable human existence as the basis of a mode of political discourse and to create the terms for its flourishing as a worthy political activity, for women to stand firm against cries of "emotional" or "sentimental," even as they refuse to lapse into a sentimental rendering of the values of language that flow from "mothering," would signal a force of great reconstructive potential.[66]

Duras has often been criticized for writing books and making films whose heroines seem passive, resigned, and submissive. More sympathetic critics see the creation of these silent women as the outcome of the rejection of masculine language. While this is in many ways accurate, it does not take into account the potential for destruction of the image and of the film as a production of the cinema, which each of Duras's heroines comes to embody. Duras has proceeded in making her films with the sure sense that we cannot simply jump out of masculine discourse and think up a woman who would somehow exist outside of the patriarchy. As Irigaray, Catharine MacKinnon, and others have pointed out, there is no such possibility. If, as MacKinnon asserts, feminism's project is "to uncover and claim as valid the experience of women, the major content of which is the devaluation of women's experience,"[67] then Duras is a truly feminist filmmaker. Duras has attempted to explore the origins of the image, of the image of woman and of sexual difference, and to describe those origins and that difference from a radically different point of view. She does not create utopias; her great contribution to feminine language and feminist thinking has been precisely her refusal to ignore the realities of the patriarchy for women. MacKinnon's description of feminism is a very accurate account of Duras's cinema:

> Feminism claims the voice of women's silence, the sexuality of our eroticized desexualization, the fullness of "lack," the centrality of our marginality and exclusion, the public nature of privacy, the presence of our absence.[68]

If Duras has insisted on remaining a woman who makes films rather than on becoming a "professional" of the cinema, it is surely because she has felt the full effect of these paradoxes and their importance to women's cultural endeavors. Remaining in the "primitive zones" of a cinema whose history and parameters are masculine, Duras has succeeded in approaching a redefinition of this territory, moving us ever closer to a feminine cinematic language and a truly feminist cinema.

Notes

1. Marguerite Duras, in a filmed interview with Patrice Molinard for *Chroniques de France,* 137. At the time the interview was made, Duras was planning *Baxter, Vera Baxter,* a film made in 1976. All translations from the French, unless otherwise indicated, are mine.

2. Marguerite Duras, *"Ah! Ernesto!"* (Boissy-St. Léger: François Ruy-Vidal and Harlin Quist, 1971). Pages unnumbered.

3. Marguerite Duras and Michelle Porte, *Les Lieux de Marguerite Duras* (Paris: Editions de Minuit, 1977), 11. Hereafter referred to as *Les Lieux.*

4. Duras has indicated that she has the same number of spectators for her films (between fifteen- and forty-thousand) as readers of *Le ravissement de Lol. V. Stein.* In *Les yeux verts,* a special issue of *Cahiers du Cinéma* on Marguerite Duras, 312/313 (June 1980): 12. Hereafter referred to as *Les yeux verts.*

5. "Notes sur *India Song,*" in Marguerite Duras, et al., *Marguerite Duras* (Paris: Editions Albatros, 1975), 12. Hereafter referred to as *Marguerite Duras.* I am considering this statement in the present context in one sense as a personal statement made by Duras, but more importantly, as a text—that is, a system made possible by and participating in a cultural network, having all the significance that Michel Foucault, for example, would give it: "Foucault's thesis is that individual statements, or the chances that individual authors *can* make statements, are not really likely. Over and above every opportunity for saying something, there stands a regularizing collectivity that Foucault has called a discourse, itself governed by the archive." Edward Said, *The World, the Text, and the Critic* (Cambridge: Harvard University Press, 1983), 186. I will be asking, throughout my paper, not so much why Duras said this as how it was possible for Duras to make such a statement.

6. Edward Said, *The World,* 129.

7. Said, *The World,* 130.

8. Duras, *Les Yeux verts,* 5.

9. Virginia Woolf, "The Movies and Reality," in *Film and/as Literature,* ed. John Harrington (Englewood Cliffs, New Jersey: Prentice Hall, 1977), 266.

10. Marguerite Duras, *Le ravissement de Lol V. Stein* (Paris: Gallimard, 1964), 53–54. All further references to this novel are taken from this edition.

11. Marguerite Duras, *L'Homme atlantique* (Paris: Editions de Minuit, 1982), 21.

12. Linda Gillman, "The Looking-Glass through Alice," *Women & Literature* NS 1/ *Gender and Literary Voice,* ed. Janet Todd (New York: Holmes and Meier, 1980), 12.

13. Marguerite Duras, in "An Interview with Marguerite Duras," by Susan Husserl-Kapit, *Signs: Journal of Women in Culture and Society,* 1 (1975): 425.

14. Duras and Porte, *Les Lieux,* 102.

15. Duras, *Le ravissement de Lol. V. Stein,* 54.

16. Duras and Porte, *Les Lieux,* 94.

17. Laura Mulvey, "Feminism, Film and the *Avant-Garde*," in *Women Writing and Writing About Women*, ed. Mary Jacobus (New York: Barnes and Noble, 1979) 180.

18. Duras, *Les yeux verts*, 25.

19. Duras, *Les yeux verts*, 24. The money that Duras is speaking of here is not immediately that of the spectators but that of the advance given by the French government for the production of a film.

20. Stephen Heath, *Questions of Cinema* (Bloomington: Indiana University Press, 1982), 224.

21. Heath, *Questions*, 34.

22. Laura Mulvey, "Visual Pleasure and Narrative Cinema," *Screen*, 16, 3 (1975): 11.

23. Recounted by Duras in *Les yeux verts*, 24. It should be noted that Duras had not, in fact, received an advance for *Le Camion*.

24. Jean-Louis Comolli and Jean Narboni, "Cinema/Ideology/Criticism," in *Screen Reader 1: Cinema/Ideology/Politics*, ed. John Ellis (London: The Society for Education in Film and Television, 1977), 4.

25. Duras describes the production of *Le Camion* in her interview with Michelle Porte in *Le Camion, suivi de Entretien avec Michelle Porte* (Paris: Editions de Minuit, 1977), 83–136.

26. Duras and Porte, *Le Camion*, 86.

27. Pauline Kael, *When the Lights Go Down* (New York: Holt Rinehart and Winston, 1980), 292.

28. Mulvey, "Feminism, Film and the *Avant-Garde*," 189.

29. Dionys Mascolo, "Naissance de la tragédie," in *Marguerite Duras*, 113.

30. Mascolo, "Naissance," 111.

31. Marguerite Duras and Xavière Gauthier, *Les Parleuses* (Paris: Editions de Minuit, 1974) 109–10.

32. Heath, *Questions*, 45.

33. Marguerite Duras, *India Song* (Paris: Gallimard, 1973), 9.

34. Mascolo, "Naissance," 114.

35. Marie-Claire Ropars-Wuilleumier, "The Disembodied Voice: *India Song*," *Yale French Studies*, 60 (1980): 249.

36. I would like to thank Professor John Hartmann of Northern Illinois University and Houmphanh Sati for their translation of the two songs and background information about them.

37. Duras and Gauthier, *Les Parleuses*, 177.

38. Ropars-Wuilleumier, "The Disembodied Voice," 252.

39. Duras, *India Song*, 39.

40. Duras, *Marguerite Duras*, 20.

41. William C. Wees, "The Cinematic Image as a Visualization of Sight," *Wide Angle: A Film Quarterly of Theory, Criticism, and Practice*, 4, 3 (1980): 28–37.

42. Wees, "The Cinematic Image," 34.

43. Wees, "The Cinematic Image," 32.

44. Joan Kelly-Gadol, "Did Women have a Renaissance," in *Becoming Visi-*

ble: Women in European History, ed. Renate Bridenthal and Claudia Koonz (Boston: Houghton Mifflin, 1977), 137–64.

45. Kelly-Gadol, "Did Women," 153.

46. Kelly-Gadol, "Did Women," 158.

47. Kelly-Gadol, "Did Women," 161.

48. Wees, "The Cinematic Image," 34.

49. Quoted by Wees, "The Cinematic Image," 32.

50. Kael, *When the Lights Go Down,* 293.

51. Jean-Pierre Oudart, "Sur *Son Nom de Venise dans Calcutta désert,*" *Cahiers du Cinéma,* 268–69 (July-August 1976): 76.

52. Oudart, "Sur *Son Nom,*" 75.

53. Luce Irigaray, *Ce Sexe qui n'en est pas un* (Paris: Editions de Minuit, 1977), 110. "Et, si tout ce qu'elle dit est de quelque manière du langage, il ne le signifie pas pour autant. Qu'il en tire les conditions de possibilité de son sens est une autre affaire."

54. Marguerite Duras, "Le noir Atlantique," *Des femmes en mouvements,* 57 (September 1981): 30.

55. Duras, "Le noir Atlantique," 31.

56. Fredric Jameson, *The Political Unconscious: Narrative as a Socially Symbolic Act* (Ithaca, New York: Cornell University Press, 1981), 99–100.

57. Marguerite Duras, *Vera Baxter ou les plages de l'Atlantique* (Paris: Editions Albatros, 1980), 23.

58. Gaston Bachelard, *The Poetics of Space,* trans. Maria Jolas (New York: The Orion Press, 1964), 6.

59. Duras and Porte, *Les Lieux,* 21.

60. Virginia Woolf, *A Room of One's Own* (New York: Harcourt, Brace and World, 1929), 91.

61. Duras and Porte, *Les Lieux,* 20.

62. Marguerite Duras, *Nathalie Granger, suivi de La Femme du Gange* (Paris: Gallimard, 1973), 86.

63. Luce Irigaray, *Le corps-à-corps avec la mère* (Ottawa: Editions de la pleine lune, 1981), 86.

64. Duras and Porte, *Les Lieux,* 22–23.

65. Duras interview with Husserl-Kapit, 433.

66. Jean Bethke Elshtain, "Feminist Discourse and Its Discontents: Language, Power, and Meaning," *Signs: Journal of Women in Culture and Society* 7 (1982): 621.

67. Catharine A. MacKinnon, "Feminism, Marxism, Method and the State: Toward Feminist Jurisprudence," *Signs: Journal of Women in Culture and Society* 8 (1983): 638.

68. MacKinnon, "Feminism, Marxism," 639.

Discourses of Terrorism, Feminism, and the Family in von Trotta's *Marianne and Juliane*

E. ANN KAPLAN
State University of New York at Stony Brook

Made in 1980, Margarethe von Trotta's *Die bleierne Zeit / Marianne and Juliane* (1981) has become the focus of intense debate among feminists, at least in Germany and America. In dealing with terrorism, feminism, and the family, the film touched upon issues already of deep concern to women. The controversy that the film has aroused has

This essay first appeared in *Persistence of Vision* 1, no. 2 (Fall 1985).

important ramifications, which a close examination of its discourses, in the contexts of its production, may help to illuminate.

Part of the reaction to the film in Germany had to do with von Trotta's position in the German film scene. Somewhat older than the current generation of explicitly feminist German women filmmakers, von Trotta (like many first-generation female feature-filmmakers) cannot avoid being marked as a woman who has made it because of her relations with an established, successful male director—her husband Volker Schlöndorff. As one of the first German male directors to break into the American art cinema market, Schlöndorff set the trend for those to follow, helping to create what has been called an *American* phenomenon, namely "The New German Cinema."[1] Von Trotta (who worked with Schlöndorff as actress and scriptwriter) thus learned her cinematic practice in that context, which set her apart from the women coming up alone later on, under quite different personal and political conditions. Taking far more risks with their cinematic enunciation, these women have been unable to penetrate the American market.[2]

Von Trotta's professional break with Schlöndorff in 1977, when she made her first feature, *Das zweite Erwachen der Christa Klages / The Second Awakening of Christa Klages,* did not end her positioning as complicit with what had now become a successful male cinematic establishment that shaped its styles for the American market. *Klages* and its successor, *Schwestern oder Die Balance des Glücks / Sisters or the Balance of Happiness* (1979), got attention in the U.S. but neither was exactly a blockbuster. It was with *Marianne and Juliane* that von Trotta finally evoked interest and was generally viewed, in the critics' discourse, as "an exciting new director."

The discrepancy between responses to von Trotta in America and Germany is as interesting as these cross-national discrepancies always are.[3] While American feminists found resonances with their own lives in von Trotta's film, German feminists criticized the film in the context of specific, ongoing political debates. Both groups may be said to have misread the film for different reasons. American women, responding within the tradition of feminist individualism, focused on the relationship between the sisters. (Presumably aware that this focus would capture women's interest over here, the distribution company changed the German title, "Leaden Times," to the sisters' individual names. "Leaden Times" [taken from a Hölderlin poem] foregrounds the historical period, while the American title foregrounds the sisters over history and encourages a reading of the film as "merely" about women's issues.) This results in oversimplifying the film's complex arguments and ignoring the intricate interconnections that the film exposes within history—past and present, national and personal—and that are built into its discourses.

German women, meanwhile, tended to dismiss the film as simply reproducing dominant establishment images of the terrorist. In a review in *Frauen und Film*, Charlotte Delorme accuses von Trotta of first misusing the lives of the historical Gudrun and Christiane Ensslin, who inspired the film; and second, of duplicating the banal clichés about terrorism propagated by Gilian Becker and by reactionary family psychologists like Helm Stierlin.[4] While it is true that *Marianne and Juliane* is indeed based on the historical Ensslins, and embodies images of terrorists not unlike those presented by Gilian Becker (though the film only alludes once to a possible connection between Nazism and terrorism), to pull these references out of their context in the film is to distort von Trotta's text.

Since the immediate political context is embedded in the film's discourse and shapes von Trotta's project, let me say a few words about it. Von Trotta's film looks back to 1977, the year when the terrorist activity of the past period reached its climax in the capture and killing of industrialist Hans Schleyer and the hijacking of a Lufthansa plane, events that shocked the nation and the world. These events signaled the final desperate attempts by the *Rote Armee Faktion* to obtain release of their jailed leaders, who included Baader, Meinhof, and Gudrun Ensslin. The ensuing increased repression by the state in itself created the climate for more terrorism in a familiar circular pattern.[5]

But while the establishment was mobilizing its forces against terrorism and constructing the terrorist as alien Other, the left was split over its relationship to allies who had become terrorists. If leftists found the logic of terrorism unassailable, they could not condone its inhumane implications. Put thus in conflict, leftists felt impotent. They could not go forward, if forward meant terrorism; but they could not go back, since terrorist logic confirmed what many leftists had learned—i.e., that less drastic strategies failed to produce meaningful change.

On the political level, it is around this debate, embodied in the sisters, that the narrative of *Marianne and Juliane* revolves. But before dealing with the film's political discourses, it is important to discuss briefly von Trotta's general cinematic strategies, since these have bearing on what the film is able to show and on feminist responses to it.

Feminists are divided about what constitutes a "feminist" film. Making women's relationships and political struggles the center of a film narrative is seen by some as in itself "revolutionary," while others have argued that to be feminist a film has to interrogate the very notion of the "feminine" as patriarchy has constructed it. The first group, often called "essentialist," assumes the category "woman," and proceeds to focus on women's specific needs (e.g., day care, abortion, equal pay, divorce, etc.); the second rather looks at the cinematic mechanisms through which the "feminine" is produced on the screen and the relation of these mechanisms to woman as producer of desire in culture generally.

Von Trotta is clearly working in the first "essentialist" mode; her film does not raise questions about female representations as such, nor are her cinematic strategies self-reflexive. For comparison, think of the films by Helke Sander or Ulrike Ottinger, which question and subvert established cinematic strategies as part of their questioning of the established order. Sander's *Die allseitig reduzierte Persönlichkeit— REDUPERS / The All-Round Reduced Personality—REDUPERS* (1977), for instance, deconstructs established notions of representation through the device of a narrative about women photographers, while Ottinger's extraordinary figures take us into a world not unlike Bakhtin's carnivalesque, forcing us to reevaluate our established notions, to see/experience *otherwise*.

This failure to radicalize her cinematic discourse opens von Trotta to the danger of having failed to communicate her radical message. While contemporary film theory may have been too quick in ruling out *all* realism, realist strategies used uncritically remain a problem. In their most blatant form, realist texts, as Colin MacCabe noted some time ago, establish "a hierarchy amongst the discourses which compose the text . . . defined in terms of an empirical notion of truth." Not regarded as material, the metalanguage is then seen as a transparent "window on the world." In such texts, the narrative discourse is seen as "allowing reality to appear," and "denies its own status as articulation."[6]

Underlying this use of representation is the key notion of the unified self, which characterizes presemiological thought. Realist feminist film directors often assume that there is a basic "essential" truth about woman that patriarchal society has kept hidden. Frequently assumed to be a more humane, moral mode of being, this repressed "feminine" is considered potentially beneficial to society, could it only be brought to light.

Antirealist feminism on the other hand seeks to understand the processes through which female subjectivity is constituted in patriarchal society. This cannot be done, however, using realist strategies uncritically, since these strategies are deeply enmeshed with essentialist philosophy, and can only duplicate the patriarchal feminine.[7]

Now, while von Trotta falls prey to some of these dangers, I want to argue that her film does attempt to set up some distance between images and spectator—that the film does not merely aim to be a transparent window on the world. Von Trotta has a radical message that she wants to communicate and she is dealing with issues of real concern to the left. She is not content to reiterate fashionable left or feminist sentiments but rather seeks to address genuine problems regarding family and the politics of terrorism that leftists need to consider.

What I want to argue is that even within her realist strategies, von Trotta uses devices that raise questions about the construction of the feminine, the family, and terrorism. The film arguably *attempts* (this is not to say "succeeds") to create a certain distance between the viewer and some of its discourses; that is, it attempts to locate certain elements as discourses rather than as transparent reflections of the "real world," as in standard realist cinema.

One of the devices that distance the viewer from the film's discourse is the way in which Juliane's narrative voice, speaking the film as it were, is foregrounded. While flashback narration is a staple of classical Hollywood cinema, von Trotta's use differs in focusing on the speaker's processes of change, particularly in relation to the public discourses of terrorism, feminism, and the family. Juliane does not narrate a single, closed, and finished past event; rather, she narrates her processes of change as they are still going on. The events set far back in her childhood (which are "completed" events) occur as flashbacks within the larger flashback, which is of a recent past. By showing Juliane undergoing a process of change, von Trotta makes room for the influence of historical positioning, for the effect on Juliane of her place in history, past and present.

The date of the film's present, and of the time-span of the main flashback, is established in the opening shot when the camera moves from Juliane's point-of-view shot (looking out of the window) to pan her bookshelves with files dated from 1968 to 1980. In its unrealistic, dark lighting and nonrealist use of sound—echoing footsteps and the atonal music used throughout the film—the scene sets up an uncanny space—a space of difficulty, of questioning rather than harmony. After Juliane's main flashback (within which the seven childhood flashbacks occur, dating from 1945 to 1955), the film returns to its present at the moment when Juliane has discovered that Marianne could not have hanged herself after all—that her death was murder. (We know it is 1980 because of the phone call to the newspaper editor.) Jan's burning and other events involving Marianne thus take place in the film's present, shortly after the present of the opening shot. It is the photo (released by the authorities on Marianne's death) that we saw in this shot in Juliane's room which Jan tears up in the last shot, when he demands to be told everything about his mother.

The film falls into two parts, divided by Marianne's death. In the first half, von Trotta deals with the discourses of terrorism and feminism as these function to separate the sisters, while in the second, she focuses on the discourse of the family, only present earlier as a subtext in the childhood flashbacks.

In the first part of the film, Juliane presents Marianne as the irresponsible terrorist of the capitalist imagination. For the capitalist constructs the terrorist in opposition to himself—a construction that terrorists in part are forced to embody in adopting the oppositional stance. Thus, if the capitalist respects property, the terrorist scorns it; if the capitalist hoards money, the terrorist lives by stealing; if the capitalist honors the family, the terrorist abandons it; if the capitalist lives for the future, the terrorist lives only in the present; if the capitalist fears death, the terrorist welcomes it.

This particular symbiosis explains the fascination of the terrorist for the capitalist and vice versa. Each group fetishizes the other, creating signifiers (images, representations, words) that further lock each into the polarized positions fostered by linguistic binarism.[8] It is this process that von Trotta exposes in first letting us see Juliane's use of the establishment view of terrorism in representing her sister, and then Juliane's realization of her sister's humanity, as she increasingly empathizes with Marianne.

The first section of the film sets up the political differences between the sisters as Juliane sees them. Critical of the path Marianne has taken, Juliane refuses to look after Marianne's son, Jan. She resents Marianne for always wanting the opposite of what Juliane has, reading Marianne's move to terrorism from the "perfect" bourgeois life as a reaction against Juliane's move from the counterculture into the mainstream (at least to the extent of living comfortably with her architect boyfriend).

Juliane's resentment of Marianne for this negative symbiosis is partly responsible for Juliane's use of dominant terrorist imagery in her representation of Marianne in the first part of the film. This imagery is most obvious in the scene in which Marianne breaks abruptly into Juliane and Wolfgang's apartment in the early morning hours. Marianne and her friends are presented through establishment codes for terrorists in both dress (leather jackets, scruffy jeans, bedraggled hair) and their arrogance, machismo, and hostile behavior. Interestingly, Marianne's gender is undifferentiated from that of her comrade, suggesting erasure of the feminine in terrorism; this is a masculine discourse, in contrast to the explicitly feminine one of Juliane and her feminist friends. The camera frames the terrorists in a long shot, setting them up as objects of Juliane and Wolfgang's observation—a stance that mimics the way that terrorists are made objects of spectacle for the establishment gaze. The disrespect for property and privacy, dismissed by terrorists as "bourgeois" notions, is enforced by Marianne's abrupt search through Juliane's clothes. Finding nothing useable (are they too "feminine"—in the patriarchal mode—for her?), she impatiently throws them down on the floor.

Scenes showing Juliane demonstrating against abortion laws and working for the feminist journal she helps to edit establish her politics of reformism, which contrast with Marianne's terrorist tactics. The high-angle long shot used in Juliane's memory-reconstruction of one demonstration, taken together with her still, rhetorical speech, falling flat on the few women gathered around, suggests Juliane's distance from that earlier self, a questioning of the validity of that kind of political work.

Juliane continues to construct Marianne according to establishment terrorist codes in the jail scenes later on, when Marianne is presented as angry, rebellious, and scornful. But then the focus shifts to changes within Juliane and her relationship to Marianne as a result of these jail visits.

To begin with, Juliane's own secure life, conventionally divided between domesticity with Wolfgang and her public political work, begins to be threatened by Marianne's presence. Juliane cannot help but see herself as she is seen by Marianne; although she stoutly defends her reformist politics as strategically better than Marianne's terrorism, the arguments seem to influence her.

Secondly, Juliane gets a taste of what Marianne is up against through the way she herself is treated in jail. She also sees that the way Marianne is treated justifies some of Marianne's political stances. The jailers form a kind of silent, sinister, and ever-watchful spectator-chorus as they sit taking notes while the sisters talk. The wardens have a surreal aspect, like figures in a dream, and the constant cut-ins to their impassive faces remind the spectator of their oppressive presence, as it was experienced by Juliane.

Finally, Juliane's increasing involvement with Marianne intrudes on her relationship with Wolfgang. The couple quarrel about the time

Marianne and Juliane, New Yorker Films
Courtesy of Museum of Modern Art/Film Stills Archive

Juliane spends attending to Marianne's needs and visiting her in jail. Ultimately reaffirming their bond, the couple decide to take a vacation, and it is, significantly, while they are away that Marianne dies, precipitating the crisis in Juliane that splits the film in two.

What differentiates the second from the first part of the film is Juliane's changed relationship to the discourses of feminism and terrorism through which she had constructed her world in the first part of the film. The change is important in exposing certain superficial aspects of feminist and leftist thinking, but it is problematic in apparently having recourse to a discourse of the family as alone enabling a deeper level of apprehending the world. It is this problematic use of the discourse of the family that I want to explore in discussing the second half of the film.

Marianne's death crystallizes a process, already started, in which the discourse of the family begins to displace those of feminism and terrorism in Juliane's consciousness. The discourse of the family, inserted quite early, is nevertheless in the first half of the film contained totally within the flashbacks, which function on the periphery of the narrative. Their reason for being is unclear at this point, but their frequency and number create a kind of subtext, which takes on meaning only in the second half of the film.[9]

Significantly, after Marianne's death the childhood flashback scenes disappear altogether. Often triggered earlier on by the visits to Marianne in the jail, suggesting the reevocation of important unconscious and previously repressed material, the flashbacks cease to be necessary once Juliane confronts her relationship to her sister directly. Shortly after the last flashback, occurring during Juliane's last visit to Marianne in the old jail, Juliane identifies with Marianne in a remarkable scene recalling Bergman's *Persona*. As Juliane sits facing Marianne in the newfangled prison, which puts glass and microphones between them, we have a shot of Juliane's image fused with that of Marianne. The combined face stares silently at the camera and back at Juliane, signaling that the two have temporarily found a space beyond the public political discourses that hitherto divided them. The wordless, purely visual linking suggests a mystical bonding transcending the patriarchal symbolic, now seen as inadequate for embodying the sisters' new way of relating.

The difficulty here lies in properly understanding the political and feminist implications of this new space. To begin with, it is by no means clear that the fusing is intended only positively. For the image could equally well imply a kind of demonic possession of Juliane by Marianne, something that events in the rest of the film might support. But whichever way we read the bonding, it does seem that von Trotta is attempting to move to a deeper analysis of female/female relationships through inserting the discourse of the family. This discourse may itself be interpreted as leading in either subversive or reactionary directions.

To read the new space as subversive would mean that von Trotta intended first to posit a pre-Oedipal, prelinguistic realm, not unlike Kristeva's "semiotic," where female/female bondings, repressed in patriarchy, can be rediscovered; and second, to argue that such a space can dislocate/disrupt traditional familial relationships, structured around the law of the father.

Certain parts of the film would support such a reading; for instance, some scenes in the first half subtly critique the patriarchal family through exposing the pompous authoritarianism of the sisters' father; there is also a brief reference to the way Nazism exploited the ideal mother to monstrous ends in a series of shots showing some of Juliane's research for an article. Other scenes early on show an illicit, subversive, and silent bonding between Juliane and her mother (viz., the family dinner scene, where the mother silently supports Juliane in her rebellions against the father; or the dance hall scene, where again, we see the mother's delight in her daughter's rebellion against the artificial male/female interactions that take place, ritually, at dances).

Then, in the second half of the film, it is possible to show how the new bonding between Marianne and Juliane is subversive in its taking precedence over Juliane's heterosexual relationship to Wolfgang and even over her reformist work. And finally, the bonding with Marianne is subversive of established codes in permitting Juliane to see the falsity of the establishment discourse about terrorism.

On the other hand, it is possible to see the film as supporting the family as a basic institution. In this view, the film posits the family as the only structure in capitalism able to provide security and identity. Furthermore, one can read the film's ending as coming round full circle in Juliane's positing of herself as the authority, replacing her father as head of the Protestant family with its puritan ethic. Juliane's agreeing to tell Jan all about Marianne, together with Jan's ripping up of his mother's photo, would seem to leave Juliane as sole master of the discourse, having eliminated all the others.[10]

In this reading, the film apparently supports establishment notions about the error of both reformists and terrorists in abandoning the family. Not having anything to replace the family with, radicals ended up alienated and restless. The film thus shows the reconstitution of the family as positive, since it is through the family memories that Juliane recreates her links with Marianne and that Marianne comes to appreciate Juliane. Juliane is left in charge of the "family" (literally Jan, figuratively Marianne, keeping her alive through memory) and back in the private sphere.

I want to argue that the film's actual position lies somewhere in between these two extremes. If von Trotta indeed retreats from what might have been a more radical position about the family, the film is not quite as circular as might at first appear. For Juliane's new "family" significantly comprises not herself, a husband, and a child, but two people (one alive, one dead) who symbolize victimization. Through these victims, Juliane is linked to the historical discourse around oppression that has functioned as a second subtext throughout the film.

This subtext is embodied in the images of violence to the human body, on the part of a repressive state, that recur throughout the film and that refer to different historical contexts. In all cases, Juliane is passive spectator of these violent images. There are first the images of the bloodied body of Christ in the painting outside the family door; there are images of Nazi camp victims, projected as a film (Resnais' *Nuit et Brouillard / Night and Fog* [1955]) within the film to Marianne and Juliane as teenagers; there are the images in another documentary film that the sisters watch as young adults—this time the victims are Vietnamese villagers. All of these experiences are seen to contribute to the sisters' oppositional politics.

But for Juliane there are two more damaged bodies that she has to confront and that provide links back to the earlier (more distanced) representations (i.e., in art or film). There is first the image of Marianne's own bruised, battered body, her face beyond recognition in the coffin, that causes Juliane's trauma and subsequent dedicated research into the causes of Marianne's death. And there is the sight of Jan's burnt body in the hospital, last victim of a violence that, like that done to his mother, is inflicted by people who share the dominant discourse about terrorism.

Taking in Jan, then, symbolizes Juliane's shouldering of the cause of innocent victims that had so motivated Marianne's terrorism. This is not to say that she will participate in terrorist actions—far from it. Her last interchange with Jan, who asks to be told everything about his mother, suggests rather that the mode will be one of interrogation, investigation, understanding. Nothing else is promised.

This reading of the film stresses the historical discourse within which the sisters' actions are placed, rather than merely focusing on the relationship between the women, or on the discourse of the family, which does move into the center in the second half of the film. The history of the children's oppression within the family is echoed by the (suggested) history of oppression at the level of the state; and, in adopting Jan, Juliane arguably expresses her identification with the oppressed. She is thus seen to move into a space that is more ambiguous and open-ended than that within which she was placed at the film's start.

Thus, while it clearly falls within the essentialist mode, von Trotta's film is not limited to the individualist frame. Her choice of remaining within realism, however, does cause problems in that it prevents a clear and unambiguous expression of her radical and exploratory positions. She obviously tries to do much more with realist strategies than any of the so-called women's films made out of Hollywood in the past ten years or more, at least showing awareness of how public discourses shape her heroine's ways of seeing. But her text leaves itself open to various, contradictory readings, as either progressive or reactionary, because she is unable to position herself clearly within realist devices. There is a danger that the positions of her narrator, Juliane, will be taken as the positions of the film, rather than as a way of exposing *how discourses shape and position people.*

My effort here has been to illuminate what von Trotta was attempting within her chosen form, while at the same time, hopefully, showing that we should not automatically label realism reactionary. Each realist film needs careful analysis to see how far its strategies are able to critique patriarchal and capitalist positions, and how far they are simply and unreflectively complicit.

Notes

1. Cf. Eric Rentschler, "American Friends and the new German Cinema," *New German Critique* 24–25 (Fall/Winter, 1981–82): 7–35.

2. For example, Helma Sanders-Brahms (*Deutschland, bleiche Mutter/Germany, Pale Mother* [1979]); Helke Sander (*Die allseitig reduzierte Persönlichkeit-REDUPERS/The All-Round Reduced Personality-REDUPERS* [1977]); Jutte Bruckner (*Hungerjahre / Hunger Years* [1980]); Ulrike Ottinger (*Bildnis einer Trinkerin / Ticket of No Return* [1975]), to name only a few filmmakers and films.

3. For a good recent example, the 1950s' adulation by the French of American Hollywood films that were at the time scorned by intellectuals in the United States.

4. Charlotte Delorme, "Zum Film, *Die bleierne Zeit* von Margarethe von Trotta," *Frauen und Film* 31 (1981): 52–55. Cf., Gilian Becker, *Hitler's Children* (Philadelphia and New York: Lippincott, 1977) and Helm Stierlin, *Delegation und Familie* (Frankfurt: Zurkamp, 1981).

5. The RAF (*Rote Armee Faktion*) was one of the leading terrorist groups in Germany between 1970 and 1977. For discourses in the popular media about the group, see Tatjana Botzat, Elisabeth Kiderlen, and Frank Wolff, *Ein deutscher Herbst: Zustände-Dokumente, Berichte, Kommentare* (Frankfurt/M.: Verlag Neue Kritik, 1978).

6. Colin MacCabe, "Realism and the Cinema: Notes on Some Brechtian Theses," *Screen*, 15.2 (Summer, 1974): 8–9.

7. Cf. E. Ann Kaplan, *Women and Film: Both Sides of the Camera* (London and New York: Methuen, 1983), chapters 10 and 11 especially; also, Mary Ann Doane, "Woman's Stake: Filming the Female Body," *October* 17 (Summer, 1981): 23–36.

8. The outpouring of books on terrorism in the 1970s reflects the anxiety of the establishment to take measures against terrorists. The very titles indicate what concerns governments: *Terrorism: Threat, Reality, Response; Political Terrorism and Business; Threat and Response; Managing Terrorism: Strategies for the Corporate Executive; The Struggle Against Terrorism; The War Against Terrorism; Political Terrorism: Theory, Tactics, Counter-Measures.* More generally reflective are the books by Yonah Alexander (e.g., *Interna-*

tional Terrorism). Few books are interested in understanding or exploring things from the terrorists' point of view; the authors simply assume terrorists are the enemy that has to be squashed.

9. These flashbacks actually take up more scenes than one might realize, for they are quite short. From scene 29 to scene 67, fifteen scenes in all are flashbacks. Of the seven memory units, there is one from 1945, two from 1947, three from 1955, and one from 1968. For more details regarding the script, see Hans Jurgen Weber and Ingeborg Weber, eds., *Die bleierne Zeit: ein Film von Margarethe von Trotta* (Frankfurt am Main: Fischer Taschenbuch, 1981).

10. Miriam Hansen has, for one, suggested this sort of reading of the film.

Select Bibliography

Berger, John. *Ways of Seeing*. New York: Penguin Books, 1977.

Bruno, Michael. *Venus in Hollywood: The Continental Enchantress from Garbo to Loren*. New York: Lyle Stuart Inc., 1970.

Doane, Mary Ann, Patricia Mellencamp, and Linda Williams, eds. *Re-Vision: Essays in Feminist Film Criticism*. Los Angeles: American Film Institute, 1984.

Dyer, Richard, *The Stars*. London: British Film Institute, 1979.

Erens, Patricia, ed. *Sexual Strategies: The World of Women in Film*. New York: Horizon Press, 1979.

French, Brandon. *On the Verge of Revolt: Women in American Films of the Fifties*. New York: Ungar, 1978.

Haskell, Molly. *From Reverence to Rape: The Treatment of Women in the Movies*. New York: Holt, Rinehart and Winston, 1974.

Heath, Stephen. "Difference," *Screen* 19 (Autumn 1978).

——. *Questions of Cinema*. Bloomington: Indiana University Press, 1981.

Johnston, Claire, ed., *Notes on Women's Cinema*. London: Society for Education in Film and Television, 1973.

——, ed. *The Work of Dorothy Arzner*. London: British Film Institute, 1975.

——. "Feminist Politics and Film History," *Screen* 16, 3 (Autumn, 1975).

Kael, Pauline. *Deeper into Movies*. Boston: Little, Brown & Co., 1976.

Kaplan, E. Ann. *Women in Film Noir*. London: British Film Institute, 1980.

——. *Women & Film: Both Sides of the Camera*. New York: Methuen and Co., 1983.

Kay, Karyn and Gerald Peary. *Women and the Cinema*. New York: E. P. Dutton, 1977.

Klein, Michael and Gillian Parker, eds. *The English Novel in the Movies*. New York: Ungar, 1981.

Kuhn, Annette. "Women's Cinema and Feminist Film Critics," *Screen* 16, 3 (Autumn 1975).

——. *Women's Pictures: Feminism and Cinema*. London: Routledge and Kegan Paul, 1982.

——. "Real Women," In *Feminist Criticism and Social Change*, edited by J. Newton and D. Rosenfelt. London: Methuen, 1985.

LeSage, Julia. "The Human Subject—You, He, or Me? (Or, the Case of the Missing Penis)," *Jump Cut* 4 (Nov.–Dec. 1974); reprinted with comments in *Screen* 16, 2 (Summer 1975).

271

Mayne, Judith, "The woman at the keyhole: women's cinema and feminist criticism," *New German Critique* 23 (1981): 27–43.

Mellen, Joan. *Women and Their Sexuality in the New Film.* New York: Horizon Press, 1973.

Morin, Edgar. *The Stars.* translated by R. Howard. New York: Grove Press, 1960.

Mulvey, Laura. "Visual Pleasure and Narrative Cinema," *Screen* 16, 3 (Autumn 1975).

Rosen, Michael. *Popcorn Venus: Women, Movies and the American Dream.* New York: Coward, McCann and Geoghegan, 1973.

Smith, Sharon. *Women Who Make Movies.* New York: Hopkinson and Blake, 1975.

Wollen, Peter. *Signs and Meaning in the Cinema.* Bloomington: Indiana University Press, 1969.

Wollen, Peter. "The field of language in film," *October* 17 (1981): 53–60.

Index